BREAD FOR THE DAY

DAILY BIBLE READINGS AND PRAYERS

2014

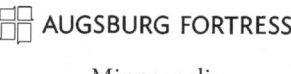
AUGSBURG FORTRESS

Minneapolis

BREAD FOR THE DAY 2014
Daily Bible Readings and Prayers

Editors: Dennis Bushkofsky, Suzanne Burke
Cover design: Laurie Ingram
Interior design: Jessica Hillstrom
Cover art: Nicholas Wilton
Interior art: Claudia McGehee, Tanja Butler

Contributors to the weekday prayers: Karen Bates-Olson, Pasco, Washington (January); Javier (Jay) Alanis, Austin, Texas (February); Scott A. Moore, Erfurt, Germany (March); Robin McCullough-Bade, Baton Rouge, Louisiana (April); Barb Larsen, Princeton, Minnesota (May); Nancy Raabe, Bexley, Ohio (June); Terry MacArthur, Geneva, Switzerland (July); Benjamin Larzelere III, Santa Fe, New Mexico (August); Jim Drury, Price, Utah (September); Shelley Cunningham, Rochester, Minnesota (October); David L. Miller, Naperville, Illinois (November); Kristin Berkey-Abbott, Hollywood, Florida (December)

ACKNOWLEDGMENTS
Scripture quotations are from the New Revised Standard Version Bible © 1989 Division of Christian Education of the National Council of the Churches of Christ in the United States of America. Used by permission.

Hymn suggestions and prayers of the day for Sundays and festivals are from *Evangelical Lutheran Worship,* copyright © 2006 Evangelical Lutheran Church in America.

Materials prepared by the Consultation on Common Texts (CCT), published in *Revised Common Lectionary: 20th Anniversary Annotated Edition* © 2012 and *Revised Common Lectionary Daily Readings* © 2005. Used by permission.

Materials prepared by the English Language Liturgical Consultation (ELLC), published in *Praying Together* © 1988: "Blessed are you, Lord" and "My soul proclaims the greatness of the Lord." Used by permission.

ISBN 978-1-4514-2565-9

Manufactured in the U.S.A.

CONTENTS

FOREWORD

Beloved of God,

For generations, the living word has sustained God's people. In times of prosperity and turmoil, joy and sorrow, the church has found hope and consolation in scripture.

The Evangelical Lutheran Church in America has embraced the initiative called Book of Faith. In it we have committed ourselves to deepening our fluency in the first language of faith, holy scripture. *Bread for the Day* is a wonderful resource for your daily encounter with the word. You will be nourished, encouraged, and sustained, as have the saints before you.

As the Conference of Bishops, we invite you to join us, and this whole church, in persistent attentiveness to the word. Your faith will be deepened, your witness empowered, and your church enriched. God bless your journey in faith.

Conference of Bishops
Evangelical Lutheran Church in America

For more about Book of Faith, visit www.bookoffaith.org.

Introduction

Daily prayer is an essential practice for those who seek to hear God's voice and cultivate an inner life. Whether you pray alone or with others, with brevity or sustained meditation, the rhythm of daily prayer reveals the life-sustaining communion to which God invites all human beings. Such prayer is a serene power silently at work, drawing us into the ancient yet vital sources of faith, hope, and love.

The guiding principle of the selection of daily readings in *Bread for the Day* is their relationship to the Sunday readings as presented in the Revised Common Lectionary (a system of readings in widespread use across denominations). The readings are chosen so that the days leading up to Sunday (Thursday through Saturday) prepare for the Sunday readings. The days flowing out from Sunday (Monday through Wednesday) reflect upon the Sunday readings.

How this book is organized

- Each day's page is dated and named in relationship to the church's year. Lesser festivals are listed along with the date as part of the day heading. Commemorations are listed just below in smaller type. Notes on those commemorated can be found on pages 410–418.
- Several verses of one of the appointed scripture texts are printed. The full text citation is provided for those who would like to reflect on the entire text. In addition, two or three additional reading citations with short descriptions are provided.
- Two psalms are appointed for each week; one psalm for Monday through Wednesday and a second psalm for Thursday through Saturday. In this way the days leading up to Sunday or flowing out from Sunday have a distinct

relationship with one another in addition to their relationship with the Sunday readings.

- Following the printed scripture text is a hymn suggestion from *Evangelical Lutheran Worship* and a prayer that incorporates a theme present in one or more of the readings.
- Household prayers and blessings appropriate to the changing seasons are placed throughout the book. Simplified forms of morning and evening prayer, waking prayers, and bedtime prayers, including prayers with children, can be found on pages 424–431.

How to use this book

- Use the weekday readings to prepare for and reflect on the Sunday readings.
- Use the questions printed on page 432 to guide your reflection on the scripture texts.
- Use the resources for household prayer placed throughout the book. See the Contents on pages 3–4 for a complete list.
- Use the page at the beginning of each month to record prayer requests.
- In addition to being used to guide individual prayer, this book may also be used to guide family prayer, prayer in congregational or other settings during the week, prayer with those who are sick or homebound, or with other groups.

Even though Christians gather on the Lord's day, Sunday, for public worship, much of our time is spent in the home. We first learn the words, gestures, and songs of faith in the home. We discover our essential identity as a community of faith and mark significant transitions of life in the home. To surround and infuse the daily rhythm of sleeping and waking, working, resting, and eating with the words and gestures of Christian prayer is to discover the ancient truth of the gospel: the ordinary and the human can reveal the mystery of God and divine grace.

Like planets around the sun, our daily prayer draws us to the Sunday assembly where we gather for the word and the breaking of the bread in the changing seasons of the year. From the Sunday assembly, our daily prayer flows into the week.

Nathan / job interviews

Bonita / thyroid surgery?

Adrian / get well - bad flu

Becky, Stefan - harmony

Gil / kidney health

Natty / grades, college entrance

Gabby / improved attitude

Bonnie / improved kidney labs

Jesno / improved health

Gloria / improved confusion

Tommie / improved C.I.L.L.

Blessing for the New Year

O God,
you have been our help in ages past,
our hope for years to come.
As we welcome this new year,
bless us with peace.
Fill our days with the light of Christ
and lead us on the path of life
until we see you in our heavenly home.
You live and reign forever and ever.
Amen.

Wednesday, January 1, 2014

Name of Jesus

Philippians 2:5-11
God takes on human form

Therefore God also highly exalted him
    and gave him the name
    that is above every name,
so that at the name of Jesus
    every knee should bend,
    in heaven and on earth and under the earth,
and every tongue should confess
    that Jesus Christ is Lord,
    to the glory of God the Father. (Phil. 2:9-11)

Psalm
Psalm 8
How exalted is your name

Additional Readings
Numbers 6:22-27
The Aaronic blessing

Luke 2:15-21
The child is named Jesus

Hymn: All Hail the Power of Jesus' Name! ELW 634

Eternal Father, you gave your incarnate Son the holy name of Jesus to be a sign of our salvation. Plant in every heart the love of the Savior of the world, Jesus Christ our Lord, who lives and reigns with you and the Holy Spirit, one God, now and forever.

Thursday, January 2, 2014

Week of Christmas 1

Johann Konrad Wilhelm Loehe, renewer of the church, died 1872

Psalm 72
Prayers for the king

Give the king your justice, O God,
   and your righteousness to a king's son.
May he judge your people with righteousness,
   and your poor with justice.
May the mountains yield prosperity for the people,
   and the hills, in righteousness.
May he defend the cause of the poor of the people,
   give deliverance to the needy,
   and crush the oppressor. (Ps. 72:1-4)

Additional Readings
Genesis 12:1-7
Abram and Sarai

Hebrews 11:1-12
Abraham's faith

Hymn: The God of Abraham Praise, ELW 831

Gracious God, as you called Abraham and Sarah to live by faith, not by sight, so you call us forward in faithfulness. Grant us courage to follow your call, trusting in your mercy.

Friday, January 3, 2014

Week of Christmas 1

Genesis 28:10-22

Jacob's ladder

Jacob left Beer-sheba and went toward Haran. He came to a certain place and stayed there for the night, because the sun had set. Taking one of the stones of the place, he put it under his head and lay down in that place. And he dreamed that there was a ladder set up on the earth, the top of it reaching to heaven; and the angels of God were ascending and descending on it. . . . Then Jacob woke from his sleep and said, "Surely the LORD is in this place—and I did not know it!" And he was afraid, and said, "How awesome is this place! This is none other than the house of God, and this is the gate of heaven."

So Jacob rose early in the morning, and he took the stone that he had put under his head and set it up for a pillar and poured oil on the top of it. (Gen. 28:10-12, 16-18)

Psalm

Psalm 72

Prayers for the king

Additional Reading

Hebrews 11:13-22

Abraham, Isaac, and Jacob act on faith

Hymn: The First Noel, ELW 300

Holy God, as the angels descended in Jacob's dream, so they filled the sky over Bethlehem, announcing the birth of the Savior. Still our hearts to listen to their song and ever join in sharing its joy.

Saturday, January 4, 2014

Week of Christmas 1

Exodus 3:1-5

The burning bush

Moses was keeping the flock of his father-in-law Jethro, the priest of Midian; he led his flock beyond the wilderness, and came to Horeb, the mountain of God. There the angel of the LORD appeared to him in a flame of fire out of a bush; he looked, and the bush was blazing, yet it was not consumed. Then Moses said, "I must turn aside and look at this great sight, and see why the bush is not burned up." When the LORD saw that he had turned aside to see, God called to him out of the bush, "Moses, Moses!" And he said, "Here I am." Then he said, "Come no closer! Remove the sandals from your feet, for the place on which you are standing is holy ground." (Exod. 3:1-5)

Psalm

Psalm 72

Prayers for the king

Additional Reading

Hebrews 11:23-31

Moses acts on faith

Hymn: Your Little Ones, Dear Lord, ELW 286

As Moses heard you when you spoke from the bush, dear Lord, so help us hear you speak. Cause us to know that as we draw near to you we stand on holy ground.

Sunday, January 5, 2014

Second Sunday of Christmas

John 1:[1-9] 10-18
God with us

And the Word became flesh and lived among us, and we have seen his glory, the glory as of a father's only son, full of grace and truth. (John testified to him and cried out, "This was he of whom I said, 'He who comes after me ranks ahead of me because he was before me.'" From his fullness we have all received, grace upon grace. The law indeed was given through Moses; grace and truth came through Jesus Christ. No one has ever seen God. It is God the only Son, who is close to the Father's heart, who has made him known. (John 1:14-18)

Psalm

Psalm 147:12-20
Praising God in Zion

Additional Readings

Jeremiah 31:7-14
Joy as God's scattered flock gathers

Ephesians 1:3-14
The will of God made known in Christ

Hymn: Hark! The Herald Angels Sing, ELW 270

Almighty God, you have filled all the earth with the light of your incarnate Word. By your grace empower us to reflect your light in all that we do, through Jesus Christ, our Savior and Lord, who lives and reigns with you and the Holy Spirit, one God, now and forever.

Blessing of the Home at Epiphany

Matthew writes that when the magi saw the shining star stop overhead, they were filled with joy. "On entering the house, they saw the child with Mary his mother" (Matt. 2:10-11). In the home, Christ is met in family and friends, in visitors and strangers. In the home, faith is shared, nurtured, and put into action. In the home, Christ is welcome.

Twelfth Night (January 5) or another day during the twelve days of Christmas or the time after Epiphany offers an occasion for gathering with friends and family members for a blessing of the home, using the following as a model. Someone may lead the greeting and blessing, while another person may read the scripture passage. Following an eastern European tradition, a visual blessing may be inscribed with white chalk above the main door; for example, 20 + CMB + 14. The numbers change with each new year. The three letters stand for either the ancient Latin blessing *Christe mansionem benedica,* which means "Christ, bless this house," or the legendary names of the magi (Caspar, Melchior, and Balthasar).

Gathering
Peace to this *house/dwelling/room* and to all who enter here.
A reading from Proverbs: By wisdom a house is built,
and through understanding it is established;
through knowledge its rooms are filled
with rare and beautiful treasures. *(Prov. 24:3-4)*

Reading
As we prepare to ask God's blessing on this household,
let us listen to the words of scripture.
A reading from John: In the beginning was the Word,
and the Word was with God, and the Word was God.
He was in the beginning with God.
All things came into being through him,
and without him not one thing came into being.

What has come into being in him was life,
and the life was the light of all people.
The Word became flesh and lived among us, and we have seen his glory,
the glory as of a father's only son, full of grace and truth.
From his fullness we have all received, grace upon grace.
(John 1:1-4, 14, 16)

Inscription

This inscription may be made with chalk above the entrance:

20 + C M B + 14
The magi of old, known as

C Caspar,

M Melchior, and

B Balthasar,

followed the star of God's Son who came to dwell among us

20 two thousand

14 and fourteen years ago.

+ Christ, bless this house,

+ and remain with us throughout the new year.

Prayer of Blessing

O God,
you revealed your Son to all people by the shining light of a star.
We pray that you bless this home and all who live here
with your gracious presence.
May your love be our inspiration, your wisdom our guide,
your truth our light, and your peace our benediction;
through Christ our Lord. **Amen.**

Then everyone may walk from room to room, blessing the house with incense or by sprinkling with water, perhaps using a branch from the Christmas tree.

Monday, January 6, 2014

Epiphany of Our Lord

Matthew 2:1-12
Christ revealed to the nations

Then Herod secretly called for the wise men and learned from them the exact time when the star had appeared. Then he sent them to Bethlehem, saying, "Go and search diligently for the child; and when you have found him, bring me word so that I may also go and pay him homage." When they had heard the king, they set out; and there, ahead of them, went the star that they had seen at its rising, until it stopped over the place where the child was. When they saw that the star had stopped, they were overwhelmed with joy. On entering the house, they saw the child with Mary his mother; and they knelt down and paid him homage. Then, opening their treasure chests, they offered him gifts of gold, frankincense, and myrrh. (Matt. 2:7-11)

Psalm
Psalm 72:1-7, 10-14
All shall bow down

Additional Readings
Isaiah 60:1-6
Nations come to the light

Ephesians 3:1-12
The gospel's promise for all

Hymn: Bright and Glorious Is the Sky, ELW 301

O God, on this day you revealed your Son to the nations by the leading of a star. Lead us now by faith to know your presence in our lives, and bring us at last to the full vision of your glory, through your Son, Jesus Christ our Lord, who lives and reigns with you and the Holy Spirit, one God, now and forever.

On the Epiphany of Our Lord (January 6), the household joins the church throughout the world in celebrating the manifestation, the "epiphany," of Christ to the world. The festival of Christmas is thus set within the context of outreach to the larger community; it possesses an outward movement. The festival of the Epiphany asks the Christian household: How might our faith in Christ the Light be shared with friends and family, with our neighbors, with the poor and needy in our land, with those who live in other nations?

Table Prayer for Epiphany and the Time after Epiphany (January 6–March 4)

Generous God,
you have made yourself known in Jesus, the light of the world.
As this food and drink give us refreshment,
so strengthen us by your Spirit,
that as your baptized sons and daughters
we may share your light with all the world.
Grant this through Christ our Lord.
Amen.

Tuesday, January 7, 2014

Time after Epiphany

1 Kings 10:1-13

Gifts to Solomon from Sheba

When the queen of Sheba heard of the fame of Solomon (fame due to the name of the LORD), she came to test him with hard questions. She came to Jerusalem with a very great retinue, with camels bearing spices, and very much gold, and precious stones; and when she came to Solomon, she told him all that was on her mind. Solomon answered all her questions; there was nothing hidden from the king that he could not explain to her. When the queen of Sheba had observed all the wisdom of Solomon, the house that he had built, the food of his table, the seating of his officials, and the attendance of his servants, their clothing, his valets, and his burnt offerings that he offered at the house of the LORD, there was no more spirit in her. (1 Kings 10:1-5)

Psalm	Additional Reading
Psalm 72	Ephesians 3:14-21
Prayers for the king	*Knowing the love of Christ*

Hymn: Brightest and Best of the Stars, ELW 303

Gracious God, as the Queen of Sheba, we can be overwhelmed by your gifts of grace. Give us courage both to receive those gifts and to share them gladly. We pray in Jesus' name.

Wednesday, January 8, 2014

Time after Epiphany

Ephesians 4:7, 11-16
Gifts according to Christ

The gifts he gave were that some would be apostles, some prophets, some evangelists, some pastors and teachers, to equip the saints for the work of ministry, for building up the body of Christ, until all of us come to the unity of the faith and of the knowledge of the Son of God, to maturity, to the measure of the full stature of Christ. (Eph. 4:11-13)

Psalm
Psalm 72
Prayers for the king

Additional Reading
1 Kings 10:14-25
Solomon's splendor

Hymn: As with Gladness Men of Old, ELW 302

We would grow up into your full stature as you bid, Lord Jesus: into the faith, knowledge, and maturity that are in you. Grace us with the gifts and mercy to do so.

Thursday, January 9, 2014

Time after Epiphany

Psalm 29
The voice of God upon the waters

Ascribe to the LORD, O heavenly beings,
  ascribe to the LORD glory and strength.
Ascribe to the LORD the glory of his name;
  worship the LORD in holy splendor.

The voice of the LORD is over the waters;
  the God of glory thunders,
  the LORD, over mighty waters.
The voice of the LORD is powerful;
  the voice of the LORD is full of majesty.

The voice of the LORD breaks the cedars;
  the LORD breaks the cedars of Lebanon. (Ps. 29:1-5)

Additional Readings

1 Samuel 3:1-9
Samuel, a boy, says "Here I am"

Acts 9:1-9
Saul on the road to Damascus

Hymn: Before You, Lord, We Bow, ELW 893

We worship and praise you, O God, for your mighty voice that calls to us from the deep, powerfully testifying to your will for our salvation. Move us to hear and obey.

Friday, January 10, 2014

Time after Epiphany

Acts 9:10-19a
Ananias receives Saul into the church

The Lord said to him, "Get up and go to the street called Straight, and at the house of Judas look for a man of Tarsus named Saul. At this moment he is praying, and he has seen in a vision a man named Ananias come in and lay his hands on him so that he might regain his sight." But Ananias answered, "Lord, I have heard from many about this man, how much evil he has done to your saints in Jerusalem; and here he has authority from the chief priests to bind all who invoke your name." But the Lord said to him, "Go, for he is an instrument whom I have chosen to bring my name before Gentiles and kings and before the people of Israel." (Acts 9:11-15)

Psalm
Psalm 29
The voice of God upon the waters

Additional Reading
1 Samuel 3:10—4:1a
Samuel receives the word of God at Shiloh

Hymn: Amazing Grace, How Sweet the Sound, ELW 779

As you called Ananias to see Saul with new eyes, O God, so call us to so see our neighbors. Help us to anticipate that you work through them, even as you work through us.

Saturday, January 11, 2014

Time after Epiphany

1 Samuel 7:3-17
Samuel guides Israel to peace

Then Samuel took a stone and set it up between Mizpah and Jeshanah, and named it Ebenezer; for he said, "Thus far the LORD has helped us." So the Philistines were subdued and did not again enter the territory of Israel; the hand of the LORD was against the Philistines all the days of Samuel. The towns that the Philistines had taken from Israel were restored to Israel, from Ekron to Gath; and Israel recovered their territory from the hand of the Philistines. There was peace also between Israel and the Amorites. (1 Sam. 7:12-14)

Psalm
Psalm 29
The voice of God upon the waters

Additional Reading
Acts 9:19b-31
Barnabas introduces Saul/Paul in Jerusalem

Hymn: Come, Thou Fount of Every Blessing, ELW 807

You have helped us, O Lord, in countless ways, and your mercies come upon us new every morning. Move us, as Samuel, to acknowledge your care and give thanks for your goodness. We pray in Jesus' name.

Sunday, January 12, 2014

Baptism of Our Lord

Matthew 3:13-17

Christ revealed as God's servant

Then Jesus came from Galilee to John at the Jordan, to be baptized by him. John would have prevented him, saying, "I need to be baptized by you, and do you come to me?" But Jesus answered him, "Let it be so now; for it is proper for us in this way to fulfill all righteousness." Then he consented. And when Jesus had been baptized, just as he came up from the water, suddenly the heavens were opened to him and he saw the Spirit of God descending like a dove and alighting on him. And a voice from heaven said, "This is my Son, the Beloved, with whom I am well pleased." (Matt. 3:13-17)

Psalm

Psalm 29

The voice of God upon the waters

Additional Readings

Isaiah 42:1-9

The servant of God brings justice

Acts 10:34-43

Jesus' ministry after his baptism

Hymn: When Jesus Came to Jordan, ELW 305

O God our Father, at the baptism of Jesus you proclaimed him your beloved Son and anointed him with the Holy Spirit. Make all who are baptized into Christ faithful to their calling to be your daughters and sons, and empower us all with your Spirit, through Jesus Christ, our Savior and Lord, who lives and reigns with you and the Holy Spirit, one God, now and forever.

Monday, January 13, 2014

Time after Epiphany

Psalm 89:5-37
God anoints David to be a son

Then you spoke in a vision to your faithful one, and said:
    "I have set the crown on one who is mighty,
    I have exalted one chosen from the people.
I have found my servant David;
    with my holy oil I have anointed him;
my hand shall always remain with him;
    my arm also shall strengthen him.
The enemy shall not outwit him,
    the wicked shall not humble him.
I will crush his foes before him
    and strike down those who hate him." (Ps. 89:19-23)

Additional Readings
Genesis 35:1-15
God calls and blesses Jacob

Acts 10:44-48
Through Peter, God calls Gentiles to be baptized

Hymn: Blessed Be the God of Israel, ELW 250

You have chosen us in baptism, O God, to live according to your will and to share the word of your love. Give us joy in your call and strength for living it out.

Tuesday, January 14, 2014

Time after Epiphany

Jeremiah 1:4-10
God calls Jeremiah

Now the word of the LORD came to me saying,
  "Before I formed you in the womb I knew you,
  and before you were born I consecrated you;
  I appointed you a prophet to the nations."
Then I said, "Ah, Lord GOD! Truly I do not know how to speak, for I
am only a boy." But the LORD said to me,
  "Do not say, 'I am only a boy';
  for you shall go to all to whom I send you,
  and you shall speak whatever I command you.
  Do not be afraid of them,
  for I am with you to deliver you,

  says the LORD." (Jer. 1:4-8)

Psalm	Additional Reading
Psalm 89:5-37	**Acts 8:4-13**
God anoints David to be a son	*Philip preaches and baptizes*

Hymn: Lord, Speak to Us, That We May Speak, ELW 676

Lord, we bear a sense of unworthiness about your gracious call to appoint us as witnesses to your love, grace, and mercy. Reign in our fears and help us to follow you.

Wednesday, January 15, 2014

Time after Epiphany

Martin Luther King Jr., renewer of society, martyr, died 1968

Isaiah 51:1-16
Through water God's people cross over

Awake, awake, put on strength,
   O arm of the Lord!
Awake, as in days of old,
   the generations of long ago!
Was it not you who cut Rahab in pieces,
   who pierced the dragon?
Was it not you who dried up the sea,
   the waters of the great deep;
who made the depths of the sea a way
   for the redeemed to cross over?
So the ransomed of the Lord shall return,
   and come to Zion with singing;
everlasting joy shall be upon their heads;
   they shall obtain joy and gladness,
   and sorrow and sighing shall flee away. (Isa. 51:9-11)

Psalm
Psalm 89:5-37
God anoints David to be a son

Additional Reading
Matthew 12:15-21
The words of Isaiah applied to Jesus

Hymn: Come, We That Love the Lord, ELW 625

Gracious God, give us everlasting joy. Return us to you singing your praises for all you have done for us. Cause us to work to advance your kingdom in all that we do.

Thursday, January 16, 2014

Time after Epiphany

Psalm 40:1-11
Doing the will of God

I waited patiently for the LORD;
  he inclined to me and heard my cry.
He drew me up from the desolate pit,
  out of the miry bog,
and set my feet upon a rock,
  making my steps secure.
He put a new song in my mouth,
  a song of praise to our God.
Many will see and fear,
  and put their trust in the LORD.

Happy are those who make
  the LORD their trust,
who do not turn to the proud,
  to those who go astray after false gods.
You have multiplied, O LORD my God,
  your wondrous deeds and your thoughts toward us;
  none can compare with you.
Were I to proclaim and tell of them,
  they would be more than can be counted. (Ps. 40:1-5)

Additional Readings

Isaiah 22:15-25
God replaces disobedient leaders

Galatians 1:6-12
Paul's calling through a revelation of Christ

Hymn: Out of the Depths I Cry to You, ELW 600

Your works of mercy cannot be counted, O Lord, and they come to us new every morning. Keep us aware of your mighty hand and continue to hold us in your gracious love.

Friday, January 17, 2014

Time after Epiphany

Antony of Egypt, renewer of the church, died around 356
Pachomius, renewer of the church, died 346

Acts 1:1-5
The promise of the Holy Spirit

In the first book, Theophilus, I wrote about all that Jesus did and taught from the beginning until the day when he was taken up to heaven, after giving instructions through the Holy Spirit to the apostles whom he had chosen. After his suffering he presented himself alive to them by many convincing proofs, appearing to them during forty days and speaking about the kingdom of God. While staying with them, he ordered them not to leave Jerusalem, but to wait there for the promise of the Father. "This," he said, "is what you have heard from me; for John baptized with water, but you will be baptized with the Holy Spirit not many days from now." (Acts 1:1-5)

Psalm
Psalm 40:1-11
Doing the will of God

Additional Reading
Genesis 27:30-38
Isaac and Esau discover Jacob's deceit

Hymn: This Is the Spirit's Entry Now, ELW 448

You have sent the Holy Spirit upon your church, O God. Renew us by that gift and send us out through it to proclaim the name of Jesus in word and in deed.

Saturday, January 18, 2014

Confession of Peter

Week of Prayer for Christian Unity begins

Matthew 16:13-19

Peter confesses: You are the Messiah

[Jesus] said to them, "But who do you say that I am?" Simon Peter answered, "You are the Messiah, the Son of the living God." And Jesus answered him, "Blessed are you, Simon son of Jonah! For flesh and blood has not revealed this to you, but my Father in heaven. And I tell you, you are Peter, and on this rock I will build my church, and the gates of Hades will not prevail against it. I will give you the keys of the kingdom of heaven, and whatever you bind on earth will be bound in heaven, and whatever you loose on earth will be loosed in heaven." (Matt. 16:15-19)

Psalm

Psalm 18:1-6, 16-19

My God, my rock, worthy of praise

Additional Readings

Acts 4:8-13

Salvation is in no one other than Jesus

1 Corinthians 10:1-5

Drinking from the spiritual rock of Christ

Hymn: Built on a Rock, ELW 652

Almighty God, you inspired Simon Peter to confess Jesus as the Messiah and Son of the living God. Keep your church firm on the rock of this faith, so that in unity and peace it may proclaim one truth and follow one Lord, your Son, Jesus Christ our Savior, who lives and reigns with you and the Holy Spirit, one God, now and forever.

Sunday, January 19, 2014

Second Sunday after Epiphany

Henry, Bishop of Uppsala, martyr, died 1156

John 1:29-42
Christ revealed as the Lamb of God

The next day [John] saw Jesus coming toward him and declared, "Here is the Lamb of God who takes away the sin of the world! This is he of whom I said, 'After me comes a man who ranks ahead of me because he was before me.' I myself did not know him; but I came baptizing with water for this reason, that he might be revealed to Israel." And John testified, "I saw the Spirit descending from heaven like a dove, and it remained on him. I myself did not know him, but the one who sent me to baptize with water said to me, 'He on whom you see the Spirit descend and remain is the one who baptizes with the Holy Spirit.' And I myself have seen and have testified that this is the Son of God." (John 1:29-34)

Psalm
Psalm 40:1-11
Doing the will of God

Additional Readings
Isaiah 49:1-7
The servant brings light to the nations

1 Corinthians 1:1-9
Paul's greeting to the church at Corinth

Hymn: Lamb of God, ELW 336

Holy God, our strength and our redeemer, by your Spirit hold us forever, that through your grace we may worship you and faithfully serve you, follow you and joyfully find you, through Jesus Christ, our Savior and Lord.

Monday, January 20, 2014

Time after Epiphany

Psalm 40:6-17
Not sacrifice, but divine mercy

Sacrifice and offering you do not desire,
    but you have given me an open ear.
Burnt offering and sin offering
    you have not required.
Then I said, "Here I am;
    in the scroll of the book it is written of me.
I delight to do your will, O my God;
    your law is within my heart." (Ps. 40:6-8)

Additional Readings
Exodus 12:1-13, 21-28
The passover lamb

Acts 8:26-40
Philip teaches about the lamb

Hymn: Lord of Glory, You Have Bought Us, ELW 707

*Here we are, good Lord. Use us for your purposes. Fill our hearts with
your love. Release us to share our time and our talents willingly for the
sake of your kingdom.*

Tuesday, January 21, 2014

Time after Epiphany

Agnes, martyr, died around 304

Hebrews 10:1-4

Animal sacrifices cannot take away sins

Since the law has only a shadow of the good things to come and not the true form of these realities, it can never, by the same sacrifices that are continually offered year after year, make perfect those who approach. Otherwise, would they not have ceased being offered, since the worshipers, cleansed once for all, would no longer have any consciousness of sin? But in these sacrifices there is a reminder of sin year after year. For it is impossible for the blood of bulls and goats to take away sins. (Heb. 10:1-4)

Psalm

Psalm 40:6-17

Not sacrifice, but divine mercy

Additional Reading

Isaiah 53:1-12

The one like a lamb

Hymn: Rock of Ages, Cleft for Me, ELW 623

Dear God, your Son Jesus' death has saved us from the power of sin. Thank you for your sacrifice for the world. Thank you for your love for us. Help us to live in that love always.

Wednesday, January 22, 2014

Time after Epiphany

Isaiah 48:12-21

God saves the people through water

Thus says the LORD,
    your Redeemer, the Holy One of Israel:
I am the LORD your God,
    who teaches you for your own good,
    who leads you in the way you should go.
O that you had paid attention to my commandments!
    Then your prosperity would have been like a river,
    and your success like the waves of the sea;
your offspring would have been like the sand,
    and your descendants like its grains;
their name would never be cut off
    or destroyed from before me.
Go out from Babylon, flee from Chaldea,
    declare this with a shout of joy, proclaim it,
send it forth to the end of the earth;
    say, "The LORD has redeemed his servant Jacob!" (Isa. 48:17-20)

Psalm
Psalm 40:6-17
Not sacrifice, but divine mercy

Additional Reading
Matthew 9:14-17
Christ, the bridegroom, the new wine

Hymn: When Peace like a River, ELW 785

You teach us for our good, gracious God. Help us to keep that in mind. Your will is to make us new and to bring us into your kingdom with unbridled joy. Keep us ever mindful of your ways.

Thursday, January 23, 2014

Time after Epiphany

Psalm 27:1-6
God is light and salvation

The LORD is my light and my salvation;
   whom shall I fear?
The LORD is the stronghold of my life;
   of whom shall I be afraid?

When evildoers assail me
   to devour my flesh—
my adversaries and foes—
   they shall stumble and fall.

Though an army encamp against me,
   my heart shall not fear;
though war rise up against me,
   yet I will be confident. (Ps. 27:1-3)

Additional Readings
1 Samuel 1:1-20
The birth of Samuel

Galatians 1:11-24
The divine origin of Paul's gospel

Hymn: If God My Lord Be for Me, ELW 788

You are our light and our salvation, O God. With you before us, we have nothing to fear; neither sin, nor death, nor the power of the devil. Keep us in you and help us to live boldly through you.

Friday, January 24, 2014

Time after Epiphany

Galatians 2:1-10

Paul's authority in the growing church

Then after fourteen years I went up again to Jerusalem with Barnabas, taking Titus along with me. I went up in response to a revelation. Then I laid before them (though only in a private meeting with the acknowledged leaders) the gospel that I proclaim among the Gentiles, in order to make sure that I was not running, or had not run, in vain. But even Titus, who was with me, was not compelled to be circumcised, though he was a Greek. But because of false believers secretly brought in, who slipped in to spy on the freedom we have in Christ Jesus, so that they might enslave us—we did not submit to them even for a moment, so that the truth of the gospel might always remain with you. (Gal. 2:1-5)

Psalm
Psalm 27:1-6
God is light and salvation

Additional Reading
1 Samuel 9:27—10:8
Saul anointed by Samuel as king

Hymn: God, Whose Almighty Word, ELW 673

Gracious God, you have given us the gospel. We need do nothing to earn your love, for it is given to us in your Son. Bring that freedom to bear among us and let nothing stop or hinder its path.

Saturday, January 25, 2014

Conversion of Paul

Week of Prayer for Christian Unity ends

Galatians 1:11-24

Paul receives a revelation of Christ

You have heard, no doubt, of my earlier life in Judaism. I was violently persecuting the church of God and was trying to destroy it. I advanced in Judaism beyond many among my people of the same age, for I was far more zealous for the traditions of my ancestors. But when God, who had set me apart before I was born and called me through his grace, was pleased to reveal his Son to me, so that I might proclaim him among the Gentiles, I did not confer with any human being, nor did I go up to Jerusalem to those who were already apostles before me, but I went away at once into Arabia, and afterwards I returned to Damascus. (Gal. 1:13-17)

Psalm

Psalm 67

Let all the peoples praise you, O God

Additional Readings

Acts 9:1-22

Saul is converted to Christ

Luke 21:10-19

The end times will require endurance

Hymn: By All Your Saints, ELW 420 (stanza 8)

O God, by the preaching of your apostle Paul you have caused the light of the gospel to shine throughout the world. Grant that we may follow his example and be witnesses to the truth of your Son, Jesus Christ, our Savior and Lord, who lives and reigns with you and the Holy Spirit, one God, now and forever.

Sunday, January 26, 2014

Third Sunday after Epiphany

Timothy, Titus, and Silas, missionaries

Matthew 4:12-23

Christ revealed as a prophet

Now when Jesus heard that John had been arrested, he withdrew to Galilee. He left Nazareth and made his home in Capernaum by the sea, in the territory of Zebulun and Naphtali, so that what had been spoken through the prophet Isaiah might be fulfilled:
"Land of Zebulun, land of Naphtali,
   on the road by the sea, across the Jordan, Galilee of the Gentiles—
the people who sat in darkness
   have seen a great light,
and for those who sat in the region and shadow of death
   light has dawned." (Matt. 4:12-16)

Psalm

Psalm 27:1, 4-9
God is light and salvation

Additional Readings

Isaiah 9:1-4
Light shines for those in darkness

1 Corinthians 1:10-18
An appeal for unity in the gospel

Hymn: Light Shone in Darkness, ELW 307

Lord God, your lovingkindness always goes before us and follows after us. Summon us into your light, and direct our steps in the ways of goodness that come through the cross of your Son, Jesus Christ, our Savior and Lord.

Monday, January 27, 2014

Time after Epiphany

Lydia, Dorcas, and Phoebe, witnesses to the faith

Psalm 27:7-14
Take courage in God

Teach me your way, O LORD,
　　and lead me on a level path
　　because of my enemies.
Do not give me up to the will of my adversaries,
　　for false witnesses have risen against me,
　　and they are breathing out violence.

I believe that I shall see the goodness of the LORD
　　in the land of the living.
Wait for the LORD;
　　be strong, and let your heart take courage;
　　wait for the LORD! (Ps. 27:11-14)

Additional Readings
Judges 6:11-24
God calls Gideon to lead the people

Ephesians 5:6-14
Live as children of the light

Hymn: Lead Me, Guide Me, ELW 768

Gracious God, give us courage. Give us courage to live your ways, to believe in your goodness, and to wait upon your hand. Give us such courage especially when we sense that all other supports have failed.

Tuesday, January 28, 2014

Time after Epiphany

Thomas Aquinas, teacher, died 1274

Philippians 2:12-18
The call to shine like stars

Do all things without murmuring and arguing, so that you may be blameless and innocent, children of God without blemish in the midst of a crooked and perverse generation, in which you shine like stars in the world. It is by your holding fast to the word of life that I can boast on the day of Christ that I did not run in vain or labor in vain. But even if I am being poured out as a libation over the sacrifice and the offering of your faith, I am glad and rejoice with all of you— and in the same way you also must be glad and rejoice with me. (Phil. 2:14-18)

Psalm	**Additional Reading**
Psalm 27:7-14	Judges 7:12-22
Take courage in God	*God leads Gideon to victory*

Hymn: Rejoice in God's Saints, ELW 418

We confess to murmuring and to argument, gracious God. Cause us to repent. Move us to shine like stars for the sake of your kingdom. Let joy be our way and cause us to delight in your pathways.

Wednesday, January 29, 2014

Time after Epiphany

Luke 1:67-79
Christ, the light dawning

Then his father Zechariah was filled with the Holy Spirit and spoke this prophecy: . . .
    "And you, child, will be called the prophet of the Most High;
      for you will go before the Lord to prepare his ways,
    to give knowledge of salvation to his people
      by the forgiveness of their sins.
    By the tender mercy of our God,
      the dawn from on high will break upon us,
    to give light to those who sit in darkness and in the shadow of death,
      to guide our feet into the way of peace." (Luke 1:67, 76-79)

Psalm
Psalm 27:7-14
Take courage in God

Additional Reading
Genesis 49:1-2, 8-13, 21-26
Judah, Zebulun, Naphtali, and Joseph blessed

Hymn: Blessed Be the God of Israel, ELW 552

Guide our feet into peace, O God, and give light to we who sit in darkness and in the shadow of death. You have promised all this and more in your Son. Bring us into your ways in him.

Thursday, January 30, 2014

Time after Epiphany

Psalm 15

Abiding on God's holy hill

O Lord, who may abide in your tent?
　　Who may dwell on your holy hill?

Those who walk blamelessly, and do what is right,
　　and speak the truth from their heart;
who do not slander with their tongue,
　　and do no evil to their friends,
　　nor take up a reproach against their neighbors;
in whose eyes the wicked are despised,
　　but who honor those who fear the Lord;
who stand by their oath even to their hurt;
who do not lend money at interest,
　　and do not take a bribe against the innocent.

Those who do these things shall never be moved. (Ps. 15:1-5)

Additional Readings

Deuteronomy 16:18-20
Pursue only justice

1 Peter 3:8-12
Repay evil with a blessing

Hymn: God of Grace and God of Glory, ELW 705

O Lord, only the blameless can abide in your tent; only the good can dwell on your hill. Thank you that you take us as we are in your Son, and that through his cross you invite us to dwell with you.

Friday, January 31, 2014

Time after Epiphany

1 Timothy 5:17-24

Good works are conspicuous

In the presence of God and of Christ Jesus and of the elect angels, I warn you to keep these instructions without prejudice, doing nothing on the basis of partiality. Do not ordain anyone hastily, and do not participate in the sins of others; keep yourself pure.

No longer drink only water, but take a little wine for the sake of your stomach and your frequent ailments.

The sins of some people are conspicuous and precede them to judgment, while the sins of others follow them there. (1 Tim. 5:21-24)

Psalm
Psalm 15
Abiding on God's holy hill

Additional Reading
Deuteronomy 24:17—25:4
Do not deprive others of justice

Hymn: To Be Your Presence, ELW 546

O God, you call us into good, holy, and just living. When we fail, forgive us. Renew our hearts and our lives, that we may constantly bear witness to your kingdom through all we say and do.

- Becky, Stefan marriage & finance ~~chg. Stefan's, heart~~
- Gil's kidney/dialysis health
- my own kidney, liver function
- Tim's financial situation
- Gloria's worsening alzheimers
- Gil R's Parkinsons Disease
- Bonita's thyroid problem
- Lisa's concerns for Nathan
- Gabby's issues in college, in N.Y.

Saturday, February 1, 2014

Time after Epiphany

Micah 3:1-4

Should you not know justice?

And I said:
Listen, you heads of Jacob
  and rulers of the house of Israel!
Should you not know justice?—
  you who hate the good and love the evil,
who tear the skin off my people,
  and the flesh off their bones;
who eat the flesh of my people,
  flay their skin off them,
break their bones in pieces,
  and chop them up like meat in a kettle,
  like flesh in a caldron.

Then they will cry to the LORD,
  but he will not answer them;
he will hide his face from them at that time,
  because they have acted wickedly. (Micah 3:1-4)

Psalm
Psalm 15
Abiding on God's holy hill

Additional Reading
John 13:31-35
The new commandment

Hymn: There's a Wideness in God's Mercy, ELW 587/588

Holy One, you act on behalf of the righteous. Make us partners with your Son in the work of doing your justice in the world, that we may lead others in the way of truth.

Sunday, February 2, 2014

Fourth Sunday after Epiphany

Presentation of Our Lord (transferred to February 3)

Matthew 5:1-12

The teaching of Christ: Beatitudes

When Jesus saw the crowds, he went up the mountain; and after he sat down, his disciples came to him. Then he began to speak, and taught them, saying: . . .

"Blessed are those who are persecuted for righteousness' sake, for theirs is the kingdom of heaven.

"Blessed are you when people revile you and persecute you and utter all kinds of evil against you falsely on my account. Rejoice and be glad, for your reward is great in heaven, for in the same way they persecuted the prophets who were before you." (Matt. 5:1-2, 10-12)

Psalm

Psalm 15
Abiding on God's holy hill

Additional Readings

Micah 6:1-8
The offering of justice, kindness, humility

1 Corinthians 1:18-31
Christ crucified, the wisdom and power of God

Hymn: When the Poor Ones, ELW 725

Holy God, you confound the world's wisdom in giving your kingdom to the lowly and the pure in heart. Give us such a hunger and thirst for justice, and perseverance in striving for peace, that in our words and deeds the world may see the life of your Son, Jesus Christ, our Savior and Lord.

Monday, February 3, 2014

Presentation of Our Lord (*transferred*)

Ansgar, Bishop of Hamburg, missionary to Denmark and Sweden, died 865

Luke 2:22-40
The child is brought to the temple

Simeon took [the child Jesus] in his arms and praised God, saying,
"Master, now you are dismissing your servant in peace,
according to your word;
for my eyes have seen your salvation,
which you have prepared in the presence of all peoples,
a light for revelation to the Gentiles
and for glory to your people Israel." (Luke 2:28-32)

Psalm
Psalm 84
How dear to me is your dwelling, O God

Additional Readings
Malachi 3:1-4
My messenger, a refiner and purifier

Hebrews 2:14-18
Jesus shares human flesh and sufferings

Hymn: In Peace and Joy I Now Depart, ELW 440

Almighty and ever-living God, your only-begotten Son was presented this day in the temple. May we be presented to you with clean and pure hearts by the same Jesus Christ, our great high priest, who lives and reigns with you and the Holy Spirit, one God, now and forever.

Tuesday, February 4, 2014

Time after Epiphany

Psalm 37:1-17
God will bless the righteous

The wicked draw the sword and bend their bows
    to bring down the poor and needy,
    to kill those who walk uprightly;
their sword shall enter their own heart,
    and their bows shall be broken.

Better is a little that the righteous person has
    than the abundance of many wicked.
For the arms of the wicked shall be broken,
    but the LORD upholds the righteous. (Ps. 37:14-17)

Additional Readings

Ruth 2:1-16
Ruth, one of the hungry

James 5:1-6
A warning to the ungenerous

Hymn: Where Charity and Love Prevail, ELW 359

Righteous God, you have loved and defended the needy and upright in all times of trouble. Allow us to be stewards of your goodness that we may share with others from the bounty of your love.

Wednesday, February 5, 2014

Time after Epiphany

The Martyrs of Japan, died 1597

Ruth 3:1-13; 4:13-22

Ruth, one of the blessed

So Boaz took Ruth and she became his wife. When they came together, the LORD made her conceive, and she bore a son. Then the women said to Naomi, "Blessed be the LORD, who has not left you this day without next-of-kin; and may his name be renowned in Israel! He shall be to you a restorer of life and a nourisher of your old age; for your daughter-in-law who loves you, who is more to you than seven sons, has borne him." Then Naomi took the child and laid him in her bosom, and became his nurse. The women of the neighborhood gave him a name, saying, "A son has been born to Naomi." They named him Obed; he became the father of Jesse, the father of David. (Ruth 4:13-17)

Psalm

Psalm 37:1-17

God will bless the righteous

Additional Reading

Luke 6:17-26

The beatitudes in Luke's gospel

Hymn: Borning Cry, ELW 732

Loving God, you reveal yourself in acts of blessing that are beyond our understanding. Remind us daily of baptism, that we have already been declared your children and anointed to be a blessing to others.

Thursday, February 6, 2014

Time after Epiphany

Psalm 112:1-9 [10]
Light shines in the darkness

Praise the LORD!
  Happy are those who fear the LORD,
  who greatly delight in his commandments.
Their descendants will be mighty in the land;
  the generation of the upright will be blessed.
Wealth and riches are in their houses,
  and their righteousness endures forever.
They rise in the darkness as a light for the upright;
  they are gracious, merciful, and righteous. (Ps. 112:1-4)

Additional Readings
Deuteronomy 4:1-14
The discipline of faith

1 John 5:1-5
God's children obey God's commandments

Hymn: My Lord of Light, ELW 832

Living flame of love, you are the light of all generations who follow after your will. Help us to fear and love you in ways that delight your heart, so that others may see your goodness reflected in our lives.

Friday, February 7, 2014

Time after Epiphany

James 3:13-18
A gentle life born of wisdom

Who is wise and understanding among you? Show by your good life that your works are done with gentleness born of wisdom. But if you have bitter envy and selfish ambition in your hearts, do not be boastful and false to the truth. Such wisdom does not come down from above, but is earthly, unspiritual, devilish. For where there is envy and selfish ambition, there will also be disorder and wickedness of every kind. But the wisdom from above is first pure, then peaceable, gentle, willing to yield, full of mercy and good fruits, without a trace of partiality or hypocrisy. And a harvest of righteousness is sown in peace for those who make peace. (James 3:13-18)

Psalm
Psalm 112:1-9 [10]
Light shines in the darkness

Additional Reading
Isaiah 29:1-12
Hunger that goes unsatisfied

Hymn: Salvation unto Us Has Come, ELW 590

Gentle Father, you have been the wisdom of the ages. Create in us wise hearts and minds that everything we do in your name may reflect your grace and peace.

Saturday, February 8, 2014

Time after Epiphany

Isaiah 29:13-16
Hearts far from God

The Lord said:
Because these people draw near with their mouths
   and honor me with their lips,
   while their hearts are far from me,
and their worship of me is a human commandment learned by rote;
so I will again do
   amazing things with this people,
   shocking and amazing.
The wisdom of their wise shall perish,
   and the discernment of the discerning shall be hidden.
(Isa. 29:13-14)

Psalm
Psalm 112:1-9 [10]
Light shines in the darkness

Additional Reading
Mark 7:1-8
The hypocrisy of lip service

Hymn: Glorious Things of You Are Spoken, ELW 647

Ever-living God, your wisdom and love are eternal. Help us to love you with all of our hearts, so that falsehood and evil may have no place in our lives.

Sunday, February 9, 2014

Fifth Sunday after Epiphany

Matthew 5:13-20

The teaching of Christ: salt and light

"You are the salt of the earth; but if salt has lost its taste, how can its saltiness be restored? It is no longer good for anything, but is thrown out and trampled under foot.

"You are the light of the world. A city built on a hill cannot be hid. No one after lighting a lamp puts it under the bushel basket, but on the lampstand, and it gives light to all in the house. In the same way, let your light shine before others, so that they may see your good works and give glory to your Father in heaven." (Matt. 5:13-16)

Psalm	Additional Readings	
Psalm 112:1-9 [10]	Isaiah 58:1-9a [9b-12]	1 Corinthians 2:1-12 [13-16]
Light shines in the darkness	*The fast that God chooses*	*God's wisdom revealed through the Spirit*

Hymn: Gather Us In, ELW 532

Lord God, with endless mercy you receive the prayers of all who call upon you. By your Spirit show us the things we ought to do, and give us the grace and power to do them, through Jesus Christ, our Savior and Lord.

Monday, February 10, 2014

Time after Epiphany

Psalm 119:105-112

The law is light

Accept my offerings of praise, O LORD,
  and teach me your ordinances.
I hold my life in my hand continually,
  but I do not forget your law.
The wicked have laid a snare for me,
  but I do not stray from your precepts.
Your decrees are my heritage forever;
  they are the joy of my heart.
I incline my heart to perform your statutes
  forever, to the end. (Ps. 119:108-112)

Additional Readings

2 Kings 22:3-20
Huldah urges Josiah to keep the law

Romans 11:2-10
A remnant remains faithful

Hymn: Oh, That the Lord Would Guide My Ways, ELW 772

Lord God, you have revealed your law so we might live in ways that honor your name. Give us steadfast hearts and minds that your truth might be a sure and constant guide for peace with others.

Tuesday, February 11, 2014

Time after Epiphany

2 Corinthians 4:1-12
Christ, the light

Therefore, since it is by God's mercy that we are engaged in this ministry, we do not lose heart. We have renounced the shameful things that one hides; we refuse to practice cunning or to falsify God's word; but by the open statement of the truth we commend ourselves to the conscience of everyone in the sight of God. And even if our gospel is veiled, it is veiled to those who are perishing. In their case the god of this world has blinded the minds of the unbelievers, to keep them from seeing the light of the gospel of the glory of Christ, who is the image of God. For we do not proclaim ourselves; we proclaim Jesus Christ as Lord and ourselves as your slaves for Jesus' sake. For it is the God who said, "Let light shine out of darkness," who has shone in our hearts to give the light of the knowledge of the glory of God in the face of Jesus Christ. (2 Cor. 4:1-6)

Psalm
Psalm 119:105-112
The law is light

Additional Reading
2 Kings 23:1-8, 21-25
King Josiah keeps the law

Hymn: Christ, Be Our Light, ELW 715

Light of the nations, you have revealed your mercy through the life of your Son, Jesus. Cause his light to shine upon us continually that others might see his living truth in our lives and give praise.

Wednesday, February 12, 2014

Time after Epiphany

John 8:12-30

Christ the light of the world

Again Jesus spoke to them, saying, "I am the light of the world. Whoever follows me will never walk in darkness but will have the light of life." Then the Pharisees said to him, "You are testifying on your own behalf; your testimony is not valid." Jesus answered, "Even if I testify on my own behalf, my testimony is valid because I know where I have come from and where I am going, but you do not know where I come from or where I am going." (John 8:12-14)

Psalm

Psalm 119:105-112

The law is light

Additional Reading

Proverbs 6:6-23

The law is a lamp

Hymn: Drawn to the Light, ELW 593

Abba Father, you have desired that no one should perish but that all should come to the light of your grace. Allow us to give testimony of your love and mercy in ways that reflect your care for the world.

Thursday, February 13, 2014

Time after Epiphany

Psalm 119:1-8

Happy are those who walk in the law

Happy are those whose way is blameless,
   who walk in the law of the LORD.
Happy are those who keep his decrees,
   who seek him with their whole heart,
who also do no wrong,
   but walk in his ways. (Ps. 119:1-3)

Additional Readings

Genesis 26:1-5
God blesses Isaac

James 1:12-16
God tempts no one

Hymn: O God beyond All Praising, ELW 880

Blessed One, you are the delight of all generations who have known your name and sought you with all of their strength. Create in us clean hearts that we might please and honor you.

Friday, February 14, 2014

Time after Epiphany

Cyril, monk, died 869; Methodius, bishop, died 885; missionaries to the Slavs

1 John 2:7-17
Old and new commandments

Beloved, I am writing you no new commandment, but an old commandment that you have had from the beginning; the old commandment is the word that you have heard. Yet I am writing you a new commandment that is true in him and in you, because the darkness is passing away and the true light is already shining. Whoever says, "I am in the light," while hating a brother or sister, is still in the darkness. Whoever loves a brother or sister lives in the light, and in such a person there is no cause for stumbling. But whoever hates another believer is in the darkness, walks in the darkness, and does not know the way to go, because the darkness has brought on blindness. (1 John 2:7-11)

Psalm
Psalm 119:1-8
Happy are those who walk in the law

Additional Reading
Leviticus 26:34-46
God's covenant remembered

Hymn: The Right Hand of God, ELW 889

God of love, you are the source of all that is good and beautiful in creation. May your love have first place in our hearts that we might live in the light of your goodness and reveal your love to the world.

Saturday, February 15, 2014

Time after Epiphany

Deuteronomy 30:1-9a
God's fidelity assured

When all these things have happened to you, the blessings and the curses that I have set before you, if you call them to mind among all the nations where the Lord your God has driven you, and return to the Lord your God, and you and your children obey him with all your heart and with all your soul, just as I am commanding you today, then the Lord your God will restore your fortunes and have compassion on you, gathering you again from all the peoples among whom the Lord your God has scattered you. Even if you are exiled to the ends of the world, from there the Lord your God will gather you, and from there he will bring you back. The Lord your God will bring you into the land that your ancestors possessed, and you will possess it; he will make you more prosperous and numerous than your ancestors. (Deut. 30:1-5)

Psalm
Psalm 119:1-8
Happy are those who walk in the law

Additional Reading
Matthew 15:1-9
God's commandments and religious tradition

Hymn: Day by Day, ELW 790

Faithful God, you have not forgotten your people who have been exiled throughout the nations. Return us to that memory of when we first heard your name so that in remembrance we might give thanks and live again for you.

Sunday, February 16, 2014

Sixth Sunday after Epiphany

Matthew 5:21-37

The teaching of Christ: forgiveness

"You have heard that it was said to those of ancient times, 'You shall not murder'; and 'whoever murders shall be liable to judgment.' But I say to you that if you are angry with a brother or sister, you will be liable to judgment; and if you insult a brother or sister, you will be liable to the council; and if you say, 'You fool,' you will be liable to the hell of fire. So when you are offering your gift at the altar, if you remember that your brother or sister has something against you, leave your gift there before the altar and go; first be reconciled to your brother or sister, and then come and offer your gift. Come to terms quickly with your accuser while you are on the way to court with him, or your accuser may hand you over to the judge, and the judge to the guard, and you will be thrown into prison. Truly I tell you, you will never get out until you have paid the last penny." (Matt. 5:21-26)

Psalm

Psalm 119:1-8

Happy are those who walk in the law

Additional Readings

Deuteronomy 30:15-20

Choose life

1 Corinthians 3:1-9

God gives the growth

Hymn: God, When Human Bonds Are Broken, ELW 603

O God, the strength of all who hope in you, because we are weak mortals we accomplish nothing good without you. Help us to see and understand the things we ought to do, and give us grace and power to do them, through Jesus Christ, our Savior and Lord.

Monday, February 17, 2014

Time after Epiphany

Psalm 119:9-16
I delight in the law

Blessed are you, O LORD;
   teach me your statutes.
With my lips I declare
   all the ordinances of your mouth.
I delight in the way of your decrees
   as much as in all riches.
I will meditate on your precepts,
   and fix my eyes on your ways.
I will delight in your statutes;
   I will not forget your word. (Ps. 119:12-16)

Additional Readings

Exodus 20:1-21
The ten commandments

James 1:2-8
Facing trials

Hymn: All Depends on Our Possessing, ELW 589

Eternal One, you are the source of all life, for your law reveals your goodness and truth. Let our worship seek after your word that our lips might declare your praise.

Tuesday, February 18, 2014

Time after Epiphany

Martin Luther, renewer of the church, died 1546

James 2:1-13

The law, judgment, and mercy

You do well if you really fulfill the royal law according to the scripture, "You shall love your neighbor as yourself." But if you show partiality, you commit sin and are convicted by the law as transgressors. For whoever keeps the whole law but fails in one point has become accountable for all of it. For the one who said, "You shall not commit adultery," also said, "You shall not murder." Now if you do not commit adultery but if you murder, you have become a transgressor of the law. So speak and so act as those who are to be judged by the law of liberty. For judgment will be without mercy to anyone who has shown no mercy; mercy triumphs over judgment. (James 2:8-13)

Psalm

Psalm 119:9-16

I delight in the law

Additional Reading

Deuteronomy 23:21—24:4, 10-15

Israel's communal laws

Hymn: Our Father, God in Heaven Above, ELW 746/747

Merciful God, you gave us the law that we might turn to you and live. May your Spirit be the source of our guidance so that we might live in ways that honor our neighbors.

Wednesday, February 19, 2014

Time after Epiphany

Proverbs 2:1-15

The way of wisdom

My child, if you accept my words
   and treasure up my commandments within you,
making your ear attentive to wisdom
   and inclining your heart to understanding;
if you indeed cry out for insight,
   and raise your voice for understanding;
if you seek it like silver,
   and search for it as for hidden treasures—
then you will understand the fear of the LORD
   and find the knowledge of God. (Prov. 2:1-5)

Psalm

Psalm 119:9-16

I delight in the law

Additional Reading

Matthew 19:1-12

Jesus teaches about divorce

Hymn: Be Thou My Vision, ELW 793

Father God, you are wise beyond our understanding, for you gave us the law to be a light of knowledge and truth. Help us to guard your commandments in our hearts so that we might know your wisdom and love as revealed in Jesus.

Thursday, February 20, 2014

Time after Epiphany

Psalm 119:33-40
Walking in the path of the law

Teach me, O LORD, the way of your statutes,
  and I will observe it to the end.
Give me understanding, that I may keep your law
  and observe it with my whole heart.
Lead me in the path of your commandments,
  for I delight in it.
Turn my heart to your decrees,
  and not to selfish gain. (Ps. 119:33-36)

Additional Readings
Exodus 22:21-27   1 Corinthians 10:23—11:1
Compassion for neighbors   *Do not seek your own advantage*

Hymn: If You But Trust in God to Guide You, ELW 769

Holy God of compassion, you reveal your love for the world by creating a way to live that brings fullness of life. Let the light of love, revealed in your word, help us to lead others to you.

Friday, February 21, 2014

Time after Epiphany

Galatians 5:2-6

Faith working through love

Listen! I, Paul, am telling you that if you let yourselves be circumcised, Christ will be of no benefit to you. Once again I testify to every man who lets himself be circumcised that he is obliged to obey the entire law. You who want to be justified by the law have cut yourselves off from Christ; you have fallen away from grace. For through the Spirit, by faith, we eagerly wait for the hope of righteousness. For in Christ Jesus neither circumcision nor uncircumcision counts for anything; the only thing that counts is faith working through love. (Gal. 5:2-6)

Psalm
Psalm 119:33-40
Walking in the path of the law

Additional Reading
Leviticus 6:1-7
Sin against a neighbor

Hymn: O Christ, Your Heart, Compassionate, ELW 722

God of grace, belief in your Son, Jesus, is the way of salvation. Help us not to justify ourselves by the law but to keep faith in your Son who justified us through his death on the cross.

Saturday, February 22, 2014

Time after Epiphany

Matthew 7:1-12

The golden rule

"Ask, and it will be given you; search, and you will find; knock, and the door will be opened for you. For everyone who asks receives, and everyone who searches finds, and for everyone who knocks, the door will be opened. Is there anyone among you who, if your child asks for bread, will give a stone? Or if the child asks for a fish, will give a snake? If you then, who are evil, know how to give good gifts to your children, how much more will your Father in heaven give good things to those who ask him!

"In everything do to others as you would have them do to you; for this is the law and the prophets." (Matt. 7:7-12)

Psalm	Additional Reading
Psalm 119:33-40	Leviticus 24:10-23
Walking in the path of the law	*An eye for an eye*

Hymn: O Master, Let Me Walk with You, ELW 818

Generous God, you gave us the bread of life in your Son, Jesus, so that we might live for others. Nourish us with your word that we might eat of this bread and live.

Sunday, February 23, 2014

Seventh Sunday after Epiphany

Polycarp, Bishop of Smyrna, martyr, died 156

Matthew 5:38-48

The teaching of Christ: love

"You have heard that it was said, 'You shall love your neighbor and hate your enemy.' But I say to you, Love your enemies and pray for those who persecute you, so that you may be children of your Father in heaven; for he makes his sun rise on the evil and on the good, and sends rain on the righteous and on the unrighteous. For if you love those who love you, what reward do you have? Do not even the tax collectors do the same? And if you greet only your brothers and sisters, what more are you doing than others? Do not even the Gentiles do the same? Be perfect, therefore, as your heavenly Father is perfect." (Matt. 5:43-48)

Psalm

Psalm 119:33-40

Walking in the path of the law

Additional Readings

Leviticus 19:1-2, 9-18

Acts of mercy and justice

1 Corinthians 3:10-11, 16-23

Allegiance to Christ, not human leaders

Hymn: Lord of All Nations, Grant Me Grace, ELW 716

Holy God of compassion, you invite us into your way of forgiveness and peace. Lead us to love our enemies, and transform our words and deeds to be like his through whom we pray, Jesus Christ, our Savior and Lord.

Monday, February 24, 2014

Time after Epiphany

Psalm 119:57-64
Keeping the law in spite of the wicked

When I think of your ways,
  I turn my feet to your decrees;
I hurry and do not delay
  to keep your commandments.
Though the cords of the wicked ensnare me,
  I do not forget your law.
At midnight I rise to praise you,
  because of your righteous ordinances.
I am a companion of all who fear you,
  of those who keep your precepts.
The earth, O Lord, is full of your steadfast love;
  teach me your statutes. (Ps. 119:59-64)

Additional Readings
Proverbs 25:11-22
Caring for the enemy

Romans 12:9-21
Caring for the enemy

Hymn: Let the Whole Creation Cry, ELW 876

God of creation, you provided a way through the world's lost condition by the saving love of Jesus. Help us to seek him, for your word is the truth that sets people free.

Tuesday, February 25, 2014

Time after Epiphany

Elizabeth Fedde, deaconess, died 1921

Hebrews 12:14-16

Pursue peace with everyone

Pursue peace with everyone, and the holiness without which no one will see the Lord. See to it that no one fails to obtain the grace of God; that no root of bitterness springs up and causes trouble, and through it many become defiled. See to it that no one becomes like Esau, an immoral and godless person, who sold his birthright for a single meal. (Heb. 12:14-16)

Psalm
Psalm 119:57-64
Keeping the law in spite of the wicked

Additional Reading
Genesis 31:1-3, 17-50
Laban and Jacob reconcile

Hymn: Oh, Praise the Gracious Power, ELW 651

God of peace, you are the source of all desires that are true and holy. Help us not to lose sight of your life-giving word that we might be a source of new life for the world.

Wednesday, February 26, 2014

Time after Epiphany

Luke 18:18-30
The rich young ruler

A certain ruler asked him, "Good Teacher, what must I do to inherit eternal life?" Jesus said to him, "Why do you call me good? No one is good but God alone. You know the commandments: 'You shall not commit adultery; You shall not murder; You shall not steal; You shall not bear false witness; Honor your father and mother.'" He replied, "I have kept all these since my youth." When Jesus heard this, he said to him, "There is still one thing lacking. Sell all that you own and distribute the money to the poor, and you will have treasure in heaven; then come, follow me." (Luke 18:18-22)

Psalm
Psalm 119:57-64
Keeping the law in spite of the wicked

Additional Reading
Proverbs 3:27-35
Regard for neighbors

Hymn: Let Streams of Living Justice, ELW 710

Father, you desired that we might live when we were baptized and made your children. Help us not to count the cost of following you so that the world might find hope through the faith you have instilled in us.

Thursday, February 27, 2014

Time after Epiphany

Psalm 2
The one begotten of God

I will tell of the decree of the LORD:
    He said to me, "You are my son;
        today I have begotten you.
    Ask of me, and I will make the nations your heritage,
        and the ends of the earth your possession.
    You shall break them with a rod of iron,
        and dash them in pieces like a potter's vessel."
    Now therefore, O kings, be wise;
        be warned, O rulers of the earth.
    Serve the LORD with fear,
        with trembling kiss his feet,
    or he will be angry, and you will perish in the way;
        for his wrath is quickly kindled. (Ps. 2:7-12)

Additional Readings
Exodus 6:2-9
God promises deliverance through Moses

Hebrews 8:1-7
Christ, the mediator

Hymn: O God of Love, O King of Peace, ELW 749

Merciful God, we are governed in a world that lacks your justice and mercy. Allow us to be harbingers of your truth and light that your reign may spread throughout the world.

Friday, February 28, 2014

Time after Epiphany

Hebrews 11:23-28
The faith of Moses

By faith Moses was hidden by his parents for three months after his birth, because they saw that the child was beautiful; and they were not afraid of the king's edict. By faith Moses, when he was grown up, refused to be called a son of Pharaoh's daughter, choosing rather to share ill-treatment with the people of God than to enjoy the fleeting pleasures of sin. He considered abuse suffered for the Christ to be greater wealth than the treasures of Egypt, for he was looking ahead to the reward. By faith he left Egypt, unafraid of the king's anger; for he persevered as though he saw him who is invisible. By faith he kept the Passover and the sprinkling of blood, so that the destroyer of the firstborn would not touch the firstborn of Israel. (Heb. 11:23-28)

Psalm
Psalm 2
The one begotten of God

Additional Reading
Exodus 19:9b-25
Israel consecrated at Sinai

Hymn: We've Come This Far by Faith, ELW 633

God of our faith, you sent servants such as Moses into the world to be liberators of your people. Help us lead others to freedom in Christ by the word of our testimony and the witness of our lives.

PRAYER LIST FOR MARCH

_____

_____

_____

_____

_____

_____

_____

_____

_____

_____

_____

Saturday, March 1, 2014

Time after Epiphany

George Herbert, hymnwriter, died 1633

Mark 9:9-13
The coming of Elijah

As they were coming down the mountain, he ordered them to tell no one about what they had seen, until after the Son of Man had risen from the dead. So they kept the matter to themselves, questioning what this rising from the dead could mean. Then they asked him, "Why do the scribes say that Elijah must come first?" He said to them, "Elijah is indeed coming first to restore all things. How then is it written about the Son of Man, that he is to go through many sufferings and be treated with contempt? But I tell you that Elijah has come, and they did to him whatever they pleased, as it is written about him." (Mark 9:9-13)

Psalm
Psalm 2
The one begotten of God

Additional Reading
1 Kings 21:20-29
Elijah pronounces God's sentence

Hymn: How Good, Lord, to Be Here! ELW 315

God on high, you have called prophets throughout the ages to prepare a way for your people. Send us prophetic voices like Elijah. Open our ears and our hearts so that we may be led to your Son.

Sunday, March 2, 2014

Transfiguration of Our Lord

John Wesley, died 1791; Charles Wesley, died 1788; renewers of the church

Matthew 17:1-9

Christ revealed as God's beloved Son

Six days later, Jesus took with him Peter and James and his brother John and led them up a high mountain, by themselves. And he was transfigured before them, and his face shone like the sun, and his clothes became dazzling white. Suddenly there appeared to them Moses and Elijah, talking with him. Then Peter said to Jesus, "Lord, it is good for us to be here; if you wish, I will make three dwellings here, one for you, one for Moses, and one for Elijah." While he was still speaking, suddenly a bright cloud overshadowed them, and from the cloud a voice said, "This is my Son, the Beloved; with him I am well pleased; listen to him!" (Matt. 17:1-5)

Psalm

Psalm 2
The one begotten of God

Additional Readings

Exodus 24:12-18
Moses enters the cloud of God's glory

2 Peter 1:16-21
Shining with the glory of God

Hymn: Jesus on the Mountain Peak, ELW 317

O God, in the transfiguration of your Son you confirmed the mysteries of the faith by the witness of Moses and Elijah, and in the voice from the bright cloud declaring Jesus your beloved Son, you foreshadowed our adoption as your children. Make us heirs with Christ of your glory, and bring us to enjoy its fullness, through Jesus Christ, our Savior and Lord, who lives and reigns with you and the Holy Spirit, one God, now and forever.

Monday, March 3, 2014

Time after Epiphany

Psalm 78:17-20, 52-55
Israel led to God's holy mountain

Then he led out his people like sheep,
    and guided them in the wilderness like a flock.
He led them in safety, so that they were not afraid;
    but the sea overwhelmed their enemies.
And he brought them to his holy hill,
    to the mountain that his right hand had won.
He drove out nations before them;
    he apportioned them for a possession
    and settled the tribes of Israel in their tents. (Ps. 78:52-55)

Additional Readings
Exodus 33:7-23   Acts 7:30-34
Moses asks to see God's glory   *Moses on holy ground*

Hymn: All People That on Earth Do Dwell, ELW 883

*God our loving shepherd, you have been near us when we were lost
and you have led us safely along the way. Lead us now to the times and
places where we can find a home in you.*

Tuesday, March 4, 2014

Time after Epiphany

Romans 11:1-6
A remnant chosen by grace

I ask, then, has God rejected his people? By no means! I myself am an Israelite, a descendant of Abraham, a member of the tribe of Benjamin. God has not rejected his people whom he foreknew. Do you not know what the scripture says of Elijah, how he pleads with God against Israel? "Lord, they have killed your prophets, they have demolished your altars; I alone am left, and they are seeking my life." But what is the divine reply to him? "I have kept for myself seven thousand who have not bowed the knee to Baal." So too at the present time there is a remnant, chosen by grace. (Rom. 11:1-5)

Psalm
Psalm 78:17-20, 52-55
Israel led to God's holy mountain

Additional Reading
1 Kings 19:9-18
Elijah hears God

Hymn: Through the Night of Doubt and Sorrow, ELW 327

God of Abraham, you stand by those whom you have chosen. Grant us confidence in your graceful presence in our lives. Draw us to others in the faith that we may bear witness together of your love for the world.

LENT

Lent is a forty-day journey to Easter. Christians keep company with Noah and his family, who were in the ark for forty days; with the Hebrews, who journeyed through the desert for forty years; and with Moses, Elijah, and Jesus, who fasted for forty days before they embarked on the tasks God had prepared for them.

During Lent Christians journey with those who are making final preparations for baptism at Easter. Together, Christians struggle with the meaning of their baptismal promises: Do you reject evil? Do you believe in God the Father, the Son, and the Holy Spirit? Do you believe in the church, the forgiveness of sins, the resurrection of the dead?

The disciples of the Lord Jesus are called to contend against everything that leads them away from love of God and neighbor. Fasting, prayer, and works of love—the disciplines of Lent—help the household rejoice in the gifts of baptism: God's forgiveness and mercy.

Lent = fasting prayer works of love

Blessing for the Lenten Season

Use this blessing to begin your prayer time during the season of Lent.

God of mercy,
as we move through the journey of this season
incite us to truthful reflection, faithful action,
and quiet release of all that is false and fleeting.
Deliver us from every evil and protect us from all anxiety
as we wait in joyful hope for the great feast of Easter,
the passover of the Lord Jesus from death to life with you.
Amen.

Table Prayer for the Season of Lent

Blessed are you, O Lord our God, maker of all things.
Through your goodness you have blessed us
with the gifts of this table.
Turn our hearts toward you
and toward all those in need.
May our Lenten journey bring us to the rebirth of Easter,
through Christ our Lord.
Amen.

Table Prayer for Ash Wednesday (March 5)

Now, O Lord, is the day of salvation;
now, O Lord, you have given us life.
On this day of dust hear our praise
for all the life you grant us,
and hear our plea for all the world,
that you may have pity on the people
and gather them all into life,
through Christ our Lord.
Amen.

Wednesday, March 5, 2014

Ash Wednesday

Matthew 6:1-6, 16-21
The practice of faith

[Jesus said,] "Do not store up for yourselves treasures on earth, where moth and rust consume and where thieves break in and steal; but store up for yourselves treasures in heaven, where neither moth nor rust consumes and where thieves do not break in and steal. For where your treasure is, there your heart will be also." (Matt. 6:19-21)

Psalm
Psalm 51:1-17
Plea for mercy

Additional Readings
Joel 2:1-2, 12-17
Return to God

2 Corinthians
5:20b—6:10
Now is the day of salvation

Hymn: The Glory of These Forty Days, ELW 320

Almighty and ever-living God, you hate nothing you have made, and you forgive the sins of all who are penitent. Create in us new and honest hearts, so that, truly repenting of our sins, we may receive from you, the God of all mercy, full pardon and forgiveness through your Son, Jesus Christ, our Savior and Lord, who lives and reigns with you and the Holy Spirit, one God, now and forever.

Thursday, March 6, 2014

Week before Lent 1

Psalm 51
Create in me a clean heart

Have mercy on me, O God,
  according to your steadfast love;
according to your abundant mercy
  blot out my transgressions.
Wash me thoroughly from my iniquity,
  and cleanse me from my sin.

For I know my transgressions,
  and my sin is ever before me.
Against you, you alone, have I sinned,
  and done what is evil in your sight,
so that you are justified in your sentence
  and blameless when you pass judgment.
Indeed, I was born guilty,
  a sinner when my mother conceived me. (Ps. 51:1-5)

Additional Readings
Jonah 3:1-10
Nineveh hears Jonah's preaching and repents

Romans 1:1-7
Appointed to preach the good news of Christ

Hymn: Lord, Teach Us How to Pray Aright, ELW 745

Pure and loving God, we feel unworthy in your presence. It is in you, Lord, that we find our worth. Cleanse us from all sin. Guide us on your path of righteousness and heal us with your love.

Friday, March 7, 2014

Week before Lent I

Perpetua and Felicity and companions, martyrs at Carthage, died 202

Jonah 4:1-11
God mercifully reproves Jonah

But this was very displeasing to Jonah, and he became angry. He prayed to the LORD and said, "O LORD! Is not this what I said while I was still in my own country? That is why I fled to Tarshish at the beginning; for I knew that you are a gracious God and merciful, slow to anger, and abounding in steadfast love, and ready to relent from punishing. And now, O LORD, please take my life from me, for it is better for me to die than to live." And the LORD said, "Is it right for you to be angry?" Then Jonah went out of the city and sat down east of the city, and made a booth for himself there. He sat under it in the shade, waiting to see what would become of the city. (Jonah 4:1-5)

Psalm
Psalm 51
Create in me a clean heart

Additional Reading
Romans 1:8-17
Live by faith

Hymn: God, Whose Giving Knows No Ending, ELW 678

O Lord! You are often so patient with us in your righteousness. Shower upon us your steadfast love and lift us up again and again to be more like you: a source of patient love for the world around us.

Saturday, March 8, 2014

Week before Lent 1

Isaiah 58:1-12

The fast that God chooses

Is not this the fast that I choose:
   to loose the bonds of injustice,
   to undo the thongs of the yoke,
to let the oppressed go free,
   and to break every yoke?
Is it not to share your bread with the hungry,
   and bring the homeless poor into your house;
when you see the naked, to cover them,
   and not to hide yourself from your own kin?
Then your light shall break forth like the dawn,
   and your healing shall spring up quickly;
your vindicator shall go before you,
   the glory of the LORD shall be your rear guard.
Then you shall call, and the LORD will answer;
   you shall cry for help, and he will say, Here I am. (Isa. 58:6-9a)

Psalm

Psalm 51
Create in me a clean heart

Additional Reading

Matthew 18:1-7
The humble one is the greatest

Hymn: To Be Your Presence, ELW 546

Lord God, you hear us when we cry out to you. Open our ears to hear your will. Use our hearts and our hands to free those in chains of any kind, that we might act justly, feed the hungry, and clothe those in need.

Sunday, March 9, 2014

First Sunday in Lent

Matthew 4:1-11
The temptation of Jesus

Then Jesus was led up by the Spirit into the wilderness to be tempted by the devil. He fasted forty days and forty nights, and afterwards he was famished. The tempter came and said to him, "If you are the Son of God, command these stones to become loaves of bread." But he answered, "It is written,

'One does not live by bread alone,
    but by every word that comes from the mouth of God.'"
(Matt. 4:1-4)

Psalm
Psalm 32
Mercy embraces us

Additional Readings
Genesis 2:15-17;
3:1-7
Eating of the tree of knowledge

Romans 5:12-19
Death came, life comes

Hymn: O Lord, throughout These Forty Days, ELW 319

Lord God, our strength, the struggle between good and evil rages within and around us, and the devil and all the forces that defy you tempt us with empty promises. Keep us steadfast in your word, and when we fall, raise us again and restore us through your Son, Jesus Christ, our Savior and Lord, who lives and reigns with you and the Holy Spirit, one God, now and forever.

Monday, March 10, 2014

Week of Lent 1

Harriet Tubman, died 1913; Sojourner Truth, died 1883; renewers of society

Psalm 32
Mercy embraces us

Happy are those whose transgression is forgiven,
  whose sin is covered.
Happy are those to whom the LORD imputes no iniquity,
  and in whose spirit there is no deceit.

While I kept silence, my body wasted away
  through my groaning all day long.
For day and night your hand was heavy upon me;
  my strength was dried up as by the heat of summer.

Then I acknowledged my sin to you,
  and I did not hide my iniquity;
I said, "I will confess my transgressions to the LORD,"
  and you forgave the guilt of my sin. (Ps. 32:1-5)

Additional Readings
1 Kings 19:1-8   Hebrews 2:10-18
An angel feeds Elijah in the wilderness   *Christ goes before us in suffering*

Hymn: God, My Lord, My Strength, ELW 795

Merciful God, you have forgiven the sins of our ancestors time and time again. You want us to be at peace in you. Give us the courage to come to you with our sin so we may be forgiven and freed from our guilt.

Tuesday, March 11, 2014

Week of Lent 1

Hebrews 4:14—5:10
Christ was tempted as we are

Since, then, we have a great high priest who has passed through the heavens, Jesus, the Son of God, let us hold fast to our confession. For we do not have a high priest who is unable to sympathize with our weaknesses, but we have one who in every respect has been tested as we are, yet without sin. Let us therefore approach the throne of grace with boldness, so that we may receive mercy and find grace to help in time of need. (Heb. 4:14-16)

Psalm
Psalm 32
Mercy embraces us

Additional Reading
Genesis 4:1-16
God protects Cain

Hymn: Lord Jesus, Think on Me, ELW 599

God of grace, you reached out to us when you sent us your Son. Through Jesus you know what it is like to be human. Draw us to him so that we may know you and your divine love.

Wednesday, March 12, 2014

Week of Lent 1

Gregory the Great, Bishop of Rome, died 604

Matthew 18:10-14

Not one of these little ones should be lost

[Jesus said,] "Take care that you do not despise one of these little ones; for, I tell you, in heaven their angels continually see the face of my Father in heaven. What do you think? If a shepherd has a hundred sheep, and one of them has gone astray, does he not leave the ninety-nine on the mountains and go in search of the one that went astray? And if he finds it, truly I tell you, he rejoices over it more than over the ninety-nine that never went astray. So it is not the will of your Father in heaven that one of these little ones should be lost." (Matt. 18:10-14)

Psalm

Psalm 32

Mercy embraces us

Additional Reading

Exodus 34:1-9, 27-28

God's revelation of mercy

Hymn: Have No Fear, Little Flock, ELW 764

O God our shepherd, you know and love even the littlest of us. Find us when we stray and bring us back into your fold where we may feel the joy of your love for us.

Thursday, March 13, 2014

Week of Lent 1

Psalm 121
The Lord watches over you

The LORD is your keeper;
> the LORD is your shade at your right hand.
The sun shall not strike you by day,
> nor the moon by night.

The LORD will keep you from all evil;
> he will keep your life.
The LORD will keep
> your going out and your coming in
> from this time on and forevermore. (Ps. 121:5-8)

Additional Readings
Isaiah 51:1-3
Look to Abraham and Sarah

2 Timothy 1:3-7
Faith handed down from faithful mothers

Hymn: Sing Praise to God, the Highest Good, ELW 871

O Lord, you watch and protect us day and night. Keep us always under your watchful eye and guide our steps that we may walk in your ways our whole lives long.

Friday, March 14, 2014

Week of Lent 1

Micah 7:18-20

God's faithfulness

Who is a God like you, pardoning iniquity
   and passing over the transgression
   of the remnant of your possession?
He does not retain his anger forever,
   because he delights in showing clemency.
He will again have compassion upon us;
   he will tread our iniquities under foot.
You will cast all our sins
   into the depths of the sea.
You will show faithfulness to Jacob
   and unswerving loyalty to Abraham,
as you have sworn to our ancestors
   from the days of old. (Micah 7:18-20)

Psalm

Psalm 121

The Lord watches over you

Additional Reading

Romans 3:21-31

Paul relates law and faith

Hymn: Abide, O Dearest Jesus, ELW 539

God of promise, you use your strength to conquer sin and to exercise forgiveness. Turn to us in our sin and show us the face of your compassion.

Saturday, March 15, 2014

Week of Lent 1

Isaiah 51:4-8

God's word means justice for all

Listen to me, my people,
　　and give heed to me, my nation;
for a teaching will go out from me,
　　and my justice for a light to the peoples.
I will bring near my deliverance swiftly,
　　my salvation has gone out
　　and my arms will rule the peoples;
the coastlands wait for me,
　　and for my arm they hope.
Lift up your eyes to the heavens,
　　and look at the earth beneath;
for the heavens will vanish like smoke,
　　the earth will wear out like a garment,
　　and those who live on it will die like gnats;
but my salvation will be forever,
　　and my deliverance will never be ended. (Isa. 51:4-6)

Psalm

Psalm 121
The Lord watches over you

Additional Reading

Luke 7:1-10
Room at the table of Abraham

Hymn: O God of Light, ELW 507

God of salvation, there is nowhere that your presence is not felt. Your teachings have shown us the way throughout the generations. Shed the light of your justice on us and all people. Deliver us forever and ever.

Sunday, March 16, 2014

Second Sunday in Lent

John 3:1-17

The mission of Christ: saving the world

"And just as Moses lifted up the serpent in the wilderness, so must the Son of Man be lifted up, that whoever believes in him may have eternal life.

"For God so loved the world that he gave his only Son, so that everyone who believes in him may not perish but may have eternal life.

"Indeed, God did not send the Son into the world to condemn the world, but in order that the world might be saved through him." (John 3:14-17)

Psalm

Psalm 121

The Lord watches over you

Additional Readings

Genesis 12:1-4a

The blessing of God upon Abram

Romans 4:1-5, 13-17

The promise to those of Abraham's faith

Hymn: God Loved the World, ELW 323

O God, our leader and guide, in the waters of baptism you bring us to new birth to live as your children. Strengthen our faith in your promises, that by your Spirit we may lift up your life to all the world through your Son, Jesus Christ, our Savior and Lord, who lives and reigns with you and the Holy Spirit, one God, now and forever.

Monday, March 17, 2014

Week of Lent 2

Patrick, bishop, missionary to Ireland, died 461

Psalm 128
God promises life

Happy is everyone who fears the LORD,
    who walks in his ways.
You shall eat the fruit of the labor of your hands;
    you shall be happy, and it shall go well with you.

Your wife will be like a fruitful vine
    within your house;
your children will be like olive shoots
    around your table.
Thus shall the man be blessed
    who fears the LORD. (Ps. 128:1-4)

Additional Readings
Numbers 21:4-9   Hebrews 3:1-6
Moses lifts up the serpent   *Moses the servant, Christ the son*

Hymn: What a Fellowship, What a Joy Divine, ELW 774

O Lord, you have blessed us with your ways and you desire our happiness. You give us work to help us find meaning for our lives. Give us family and friends with whom we can share the fruits of our labors.

Tuesday, March 18, 2014

Week of Lent 2

Isaiah 65:17-25
God promises a new creation

For I am about to create new heavens
and a new earth;
the former things shall not be remembered
or come to mind.
But be glad and rejoice forever
in what I am creating;
for I am about to create Jerusalem as a joy,
and its people as a delight.
I will rejoice in Jerusalem,
and delight in my people;
no more shall the sound of weeping be heard in it,
or the cry of distress. (Isa. 65:17-19)

Psalm
Psalm 128
God promises life

Additional Reading
Romans 4:6-13
Abraham saved through faith

Hymn: Jerusalem, My Happy Home, ELW 628

God of creation, you made everything and you declared it all good, and yet you have not stopped creating. Draw us into your new creation and make us a delight in your eyes for all the world.

Wednesday, March 19, 2014

Joseph, Guardian of Jesus

Matthew 1:16, 18-21, 24a
The Lord appears to Joseph in a dream

Now the birth of Jesus the Messiah took place in this way. When his mother Mary had been engaged to Joseph, but before they lived together, she was found to be with child from the Holy Spirit. Her husband Joseph, being a righteous man and unwilling to expose her to public disgrace, planned to dismiss her quietly. But just when he had resolved to do this, an angel of the Lord appeared to him in a dream and said, "Joseph, son of David, do not be afraid to take Mary as your wife, for the child conceived in her is from the Holy Spirit. She will bear a son, and you are to name him Jesus, for he will save his people from their sins." (Matt. 1:18-21)

Psalm
Psalm 89:1-29
The Lord's steadfast love is established forever

Additional Readings
2 Samuel 7:4, 8-16
God makes a covenant with David

Romans 4:13-18
The promise to those who share Abraham's faith

Hymn: By All Your Saints, ELW 420 (stanza 9)

O God, from the family of your servant David you raised up Joseph to be the guardian of your incarnate Son and the husband of his blessed mother. Give us grace to imitate his uprightness of life and his obedience to your commands, through Jesus Christ, our Savior and Lord, who lives and reigns with you and the Holy Spirit, one God, now and forever.

Thursday, March 20, 2014

Week of Lent 2

Psalm 95
The rock of our salvation

O come, let us sing to the LORD;
   let us make a joyful noise to the rock of our salvation!
Let us come into his presence with thanksgiving;
   let us make a joyful noise to him with songs of praise!
For the LORD is a great God,
   and a great King above all gods.
In his hand are the depths of the earth;
   the heights of the mountains are his also.
The sea is his, for he made it,
   and the dry land, which his hands have formed. (Ps. 95:1-5)

Additional Readings
Exodus 16:1-8
Israel complains of hunger in the wilderness

Colossians 1:15-23
Christ, the reconciliation of all things

Hymn: Let All Things Now Living, ELW 881

O Lord our great God, you have held us in your hands since the beginning of time. Hear the song on our lips and the praise in our hearts. Let our joyful noise resound throughout your creation.

Friday, March 21, 2014

Week of Lent 2

Thomas Cranmer, Bishop of Canterbury, martyr, died 1556

Ephesians 2:11-22

Christ, the reconciliation of Jew and Gentile

So then, remember that at one time you Gentiles by birth, called "the uncircumcision" by those who are called "the circumcision"—a physical circumcision made in the flesh by human hands—remember that you were at that time without Christ, being aliens from the commonwealth of Israel, and strangers to the covenants of promise, having no hope and without God in the world. But now in Christ Jesus you who once were far off have been brought near by the blood of Christ. For he is our peace; in his flesh he has made both groups into one and has broken down the dividing wall, that is, the hostility between us. (Eph. 2:11-14)

Psalm

Psalm 95

The rock of our salvation

Additional Reading

Exodus 16:9-21

God gives manna and quail

Hymn: We Are Called, ELW 720

God of unity, through Christ you have made us one with your chosen people, Israel. Continue to show us the common faith we share in you that we may together bear witness to your peace in all the earth.

Saturday, March 22, 2014

Week of Lent 2

Jonathan Edwards, teacher, missionary to American Indians, died 1758

Exodus 16:27-35

Manna and the sabbath

On the seventh day some of the people went out to gather [manna], and they found none. The Lord said to Moses, "How long will you refuse to keep my commandments and instructions? See! The Lord has given you the sabbath, therefore on the sixth day he gives you food for two days; each of you stay where you are; do not leave your place on the seventh day." So the people rested on the seventh day. (Exod. 16:27-30)

Psalm

Psalm 95

The rock of our salvation

Additional Reading

John 4:1-6

Jesus travels to Jacob's well in Samaria

Hymn: O Day of Rest and Gladness, ELW 521

O God our provider, you meet our needs and you call us to Sabbath rest. Inspire our trust in you and joy in your abundance. Open our eyes to the opportunities to rest and to share what you have given us.

Sunday, March 23, 2014

Third Sunday in Lent

John 4:5-42

The woman at the well

Jesus said to [the Samaritan woman], "Everyone who drinks of this water will be thirsty again, but those who drink of the water that I will give them will never be thirsty. The water that I will give will become in them a spring of water gushing up to eternal life." The woman said to him, "Sir, give me this water, so that I may never be thirsty or have to keep coming here to draw water." (John 4:13-15)

Psalm

Psalm 95

The rock of our salvation

Additional Readings

Exodus 17:1-7

Water from the rock

Romans 5:1-11

Reconciled to God by Christ's death

Hymn: Come to Me, All Pilgrims Thirsty, ELW 777

Merciful God, the fountain of living water, you quench our thirst and wash away our sin. Give us this water always. Bring us to drink from the well that flows with the beauty of your truth through Jesus Christ, our Savior and Lord, who lives and reigns with you and the Holy Spirit, one God, now and forever.

Monday, March 24, 2014

Week of Lent 3

Oscar Arnulfo Romero, Bishop of El Salvador, martyr, died 1980

Psalm 81

We drink from the rock

"But my people did not listen to my voice;
   Israel would not submit to me.
So I gave them over to their stubborn hearts,
   to follow their own counsels.
O that my people would listen to me,
   that Israel would walk in my ways!
Then I would quickly subdue their enemies,
   and turn my hand against their foes.
Those who hate the LORD would cringe before him,
   and their doom would last forever.
I would feed you with the finest of the wheat,
   and with honey from the rock I would satisfy you." (Ps. 81:11-16)

Additional Readings

Genesis 24:1-27
Rebekah at the well

2 John 1-13
A woman reminded to abide in Christ

Hymn: You Satisfy the Hungry Heart, ELW 484

O Lord, you have been faithful to us and you desire our obedience. Open our ears and soften our hearts. Guide us in your ways and keep us safe from those who would harm us.

Tuesday, March 25, 2014

Annunciation of Our Lord

Luke 1:26-38
The angel greets Mary

In the sixth month the angel Gabriel was sent by God to a town in Galilee called Nazareth, to a virgin engaged to a man whose name was Joseph, of the house of David. The virgin's name was Mary. And he came to her and said, "Greetings, favored one! The Lord is with you." But she was much perplexed by his words and pondered what sort of greeting this might be. The angel said to her, "Do not be afraid, Mary, for you have found favor with God. And now, you will conceive in your womb and bear a son, and you will name him Jesus." (Luke 1:26-31)

Psalm
Psalm 45
Your name will be remembered

Additional Readings
Isaiah 7:10-14
A young woman will bear a son

Hebrews 10:4-10
The offering of Jesus' body sanctifies us

Hymn: The Only Son from Heaven, ELW 309

Pour your grace into our hearts, O God, that we who have known the incarnation of your Son, Jesus Christ, announced by an angel, may by his cross and passion be brought to the glory of his resurrection; for he lives and reigns with you, in the unity of the Holy Spirit, one God, now and forever.

Wednesday, March 26, 2014

Week of Lent 3

John 7:14-31, 37-39

Drink of Jesus, the Messiah

On the last day of the festival, the great day, while Jesus was standing there, he cried out, "Let anyone who is thirsty come to me, and let the one who believes in me drink. As the scripture has said, 'Out of the believer's heart shall flow rivers of living water.'" Now he said this about the Spirit, which believers in him were to receive; for as yet there was no Spirit, because Jesus was not yet glorified. (John 7:37-39)

Psalm

Psalm 81

We drink from the rock

Additional Reading

Jeremiah 2:4-13

God, the living water

Hymn: Shall We Gather at the River, ELW 423

God our living water, you have quenched our thirsty souls with the spirit of your love. Continue to pour your living water into our hearts that it may run over from our lives into our parched world.

Thursday, March 27, 2014

Week of Lent 3

Psalm 23
My head anointed with oil

Even though I walk through the darkest valley,
  I fear no evil;
for you are with me;
  your rod and your staff—
  they comfort me.

You prepare a table before me
  in the presence of my enemies;
you anoint my head with oil;
  my cup overflows.
Surely goodness and mercy shall follow me
  all the days of my life,
and I shall dwell in the house of the LORD
  my whole life long. (Ps. 23:4-6)

Additional Readings
1 Samuel 15:10-21
The prophet Samuel confronts the king

Ephesians 4:25-32
Called to honesty and forbearance

Hymn: My Shepherd, You Supply My Need, ELW 782

Lord our shepherd, you have anointed our heads with oil and claimed us as your daughters and sons. Lead us to your banquet table where we may share your goodness and mercy with our enemies and friends.

Friday, March 28, 2014

Week of Lent 3

Ephesians 5:1-9

Now in the Lord you are light

Let no one deceive you with empty words, for because of these things the wrath of God comes on those who are disobedient. Therefore do not be associated with them. For once you were darkness, but now in the Lord you are light. Live as children of light—for the fruit of the light is found in all that is good and right and true. (Eph. 5:6-9)

Psalm

Psalm 23

My head anointed with oil

Additional Reading

1 Samuel 15:22-31

The king confesses his sinful disobedience

Hymn: I Want to Walk as a Child of the Light, ELW 815

Good and honest Lord, your word casts light into the dark corners of our lives. Give us words that are not empty but full of your light for all those living in darkness.

Saturday, March 29, 2014

Week of Lent 3

Hans Nielsen Hauge, renewer of the church, died 1824

1 Samuel 15:32-34
Samuel grieves over Saul

Then Samuel said, "Bring Agag king of the Amalekites here to me."
And Agag came to him haltingly. Agag said, "Surely this is the
bitterness of death." But Samuel said,
  "As your sword has made women childless,
    so your mother shall be childless among women."
And Samuel hewed Agag in pieces before the LORD in Gilgal.

Then Samuel went to Ramah; and Saul went up to his house in
Gibeah of Saul. (1 Sam. 15:32-34)

Psalm
Psalm 23
My head anointed with oil

Additional Reading
John 1:1-9
Christ comes with light and life

Hymn: In All Our Grief, ELW 615

*Righteous God, you stand with us in our pain and help us to find ways
to deal with the grief and loss in our lives. When we are angered by
injustice, help us to hand it all over to you.*

Sunday, March 30, 2014

Fourth Sunday in Lent

John 9:1-41
The man born blind

Jesus heard that they had driven [out the man who had been blind], and when he found him, he said, "Do you believe in the Son of Man?" He answered, "And who is he, sir? Tell me, so that I may believe in him." Jesus said to him, "You have seen him, and the one speaking with you is he." He said, "Lord, I believe." And he worshiped him. Jesus said, "I came into this world for judgment so that those who do not see may see, and those who do see may become blind." (John 9:35-39)

Psalm
Psalm 23
My head anointed with oil

Additional Readings
1 Samuel 16:1-13
David is chosen and anointed

Ephesians 5:8-14
Live as children of light

Hymn: O Christ, Our Light, O Radiance True, ELW 675

Bend your ear to our prayers, Lord Christ, and come among us. By your gracious life and death for us, bring light into the darkness of our hearts, and anoint us with your Spirit, for you live and reign with the Father and the Holy Spirit, one God, now and forever.

Monday, March 31, 2014

Week of Lent 4

John Donne, poet, died 1631

Psalm 146
God opens the eyes of the blind

The LORD sets the prisoners free;
    the LORD opens the eyes of the blind.
The LORD lifts up those who are bowed down;
    the LORD loves the righteous.
The LORD watches over the strangers;
    he upholds the orphan and the widow,
    but the way of the wicked he brings to ruin.

The LORD will reign forever,
    your God, O Zion, for all generations.
Praise the LORD! (Ps. 146:7c-10)

Additional Readings
Isaiah 59:9-19   Acts 9:1-20
The blindness of injustice   *Saul is baptized, his sight restored*

Hymn: Praise the One Who Breaks the Darkness, ELW 843

Lord of our freedom and strength, you see all those in need we often overlook. Open our eyes to see the need in the world. Guide us in our caring response to all we see through your eyes.

_____

_____

_____

_____

_____

_____

_____

_____

_____

_____

_____

_____

Tuesday, April 1, 2014

Week of Lent 4

Isaiah 42:14-21
God will heal the blind

For a long time I have held my peace,
    I have kept still and restrained myself;
now I will cry out like a woman in labor,
    I will gasp and pant.
I will lay waste mountains and hills,
    and dry up all their herbage;
I will turn the rivers into islands,
    and dry up the pools.
I will lead the blind
    by a road they do not know,
by paths they have not known
    I will guide them.
I will turn the darkness before them into light,
    the rough places into level ground.
These are the things I will do,
    and I will not forsake them. (Isa. 42:14-16)

Psalm
Psalm 146
God opens the eyes of the blind

Additional Reading
Colossians 1:9-14
The inheritance of the saints in light

Hymn: In Deepest Night, ELW 699

O God, give us courageous and bold spirits, willing to cry out for those in our communities who have no voice, and to name the powers of darkness so all might walk on level ground. We pray this through Christ our Lord.

Wednesday, April 2, 2014

Week of Lent 4

Matthew 9:27-34
Jesus heals the blind

As Jesus went on from there, two blind men followed him, crying loudly, "Have mercy on us, Son of David!" When he entered the house, the blind men came to him; and Jesus said to them, "Do you believe that I am able to do this?" They said to him, "Yes, Lord." Then he touched their eyes and said, "According to your faith let it be done to you." And their eyes were opened. Then Jesus sternly ordered them, "See that no one knows of this." But they went away and spread the news about him throughout that district. (Matt. 9:27-31)

Psalm
Psalm 146
God opens the eyes of the blind

Additional Reading
Isaiah 60:17-22
God our light

Hymn: You Are Mine, ELW 581

Healer of the world, it is only you who makes the blind to see. Have mercy on us. Touch our eyes and hearts, casting away our blindness so we might see others and ourselves through your gracious and loving spirit.

Thursday, April 3, 2014

Week of Lent 4

Psalm 130
Mercy and redemption

Out of the depths I cry to you, O LORD.
    LORD, hear my voice!
Let your ears be attentive
    to the voice of my supplications!

If you, O LORD, should mark iniquities,
    Lord, who could stand?
But there is forgiveness with you,
    so that you may be revered. (Ps. 130:1-4)

Additional Readings
Ezekiel 1:1-3; 2:8—3:3
The word of God: lamentation and sweetness

Revelation 10:1-11
The word of God: bitter and sweet

Hymn: Out of the Depths I Cry to You, ELW 600

Creator of the universe, there is no place we can go in which you will not hear our cries. From out of the depths we cry for your mercy and ask for your forgiveness. Thank you for your attentive ears.

Friday, April 4, 2014

Week of Lent 4

Benedict the African, confessor, died 1589

Revelation 11:15-19

The word of God: thanksgiving and singing

Then the twenty-four elders who sit on their thrones before God fell
on their faces and worshiped God, singing,
   "We give you thanks, Lord God Almighty,
      who are and who were,
   for you have taken your great power
      and begun to reign.
   The nations raged,
      but your wrath has come,
      and the time for judging the dead,
   for rewarding your servants, the prophets
      and saints and all who fear your name,
      both small and great,
   and for destroying those who destroy the earth."

Then God's temple in heaven was opened, and the ark of his covenant
was seen within his temple; and there were flashes of lightning,
rumblings, peals of thunder, an earthquake, and heavy hail.
(Rev. 11:16-19)

Psalm	Additional Reading
Psalm 130	Ezekiel 33:10-16
Mercy and redemption	*The word of God: repent and live*

Hymn: Blessing and Honor, ELW 854

*God almighty, we join those who sing your praises and give glory to your
majestic reign. And yet, we your humble servants drop to our knees in
awe not only of your power to destroy, but also of your great capacity to
forgive us through Christ Jesus.*

Saturday, April 5, 2014

Week of Lent 4

Ezekiel 36:8-15

Blessings upon Israel

But you, O mountains of Israel, shall shoot out your branches, and yield your fruit to my people Israel; for they shall soon come home. See now, I am for you; I will turn to you, and you shall be tilled and sown; and I will multiply your population, the whole house of Israel, all of it; the towns shall be inhabited and the waste places rebuilt; and I will multiply human beings and animals upon you. They shall increase and be fruitful; and I will cause you to be inhabited as in your former times, and will do more good to you than ever before. Then you shall know that I am the LORD. I will lead people upon you—my people Israel—and they shall possess you, and you shall be their inheritance. No longer shall you bereave them of children. (Ezek. 36:8-12)

Psalm

Psalm 130

Mercy and redemption

Additional Reading

Luke 24:44-53

Jesus blesses the disciples

Hymn: Open Now Thy Gates of Beauty, ELW 533

Source of life, your message of hope resounds through the prophets of old. Bless us and strengthen our faith so we might fully trust in the promises of a new life and homecoming in Christ Jesus, who lives and reigns with you.

Sunday, April 6, 2014

Fifth Sunday in Lent

**Albrecht Dürer, died 1528; Matthias Grünewald, died 1529;
Lucas Cranach, died 1553; artists**

John 11:1-45
The raising of Lazarus

And Jesus looked upward and said, "Father, I thank you for having heard me. I knew that you always hear me, but I have said this for the sake of the crowd standing here, so that they may believe that you sent me." When he had said this, he cried with a loud voice, "Lazarus, come out!" The dead man came out, his hands and feet bound with strips of cloth, and his face wrapped in a cloth. Jesus said to them, "Unbind him, and let him go."

Many of the Jews therefore, who had come with Mary and had seen what Jesus did, believed in him. (John 11:41b-45)

Psalm	Additional Readings	
Psalm 130	Ezekiel 37:1-14	Romans 8:6-11
Mercy and redemption	*The dry bones of Israel*	*Life in the Spirit*

Hymn: When We Are Living, ELW 639

Almighty God, your Son came into the world to free us all from sin and death. Breathe upon us the power of your Spirit, that we may be raised to new life in Christ and serve you in righteousness all our days, through Jesus Christ, our Savior and Lord, who lives and reigns with you and the Holy Spirit, one God, now and forever.

Monday, April 7, 2014

Week of Lent 5

Psalm 143
Save me from death

Save me, O LORD, from my enemies;
    I have fled to you for refuge.
Teach me to do your will,
    for you are my God.
Let your good spirit lead me
    on a level path.

For your name's sake, O LORD, preserve my life.
    In your righteousness bring me out of trouble.
In your steadfast love cut off my enemies,
    and destroy all my adversaries,
    for I am your servant. (Ps. 143:9-12)

Additional Readings
1 Kings 17:17-24
Elijah raises the widow's son

Acts 20:7-12
Paul raises a young man

Hymn: Lord of Our Life, ELW 766

Gracious God, countless have cried out to you. Include us in those who turn to you for guidance on daily paths of discipleship. Teach us to do your will and live lives pleasing to you, for we desire to serve you alone.

Tuesday, April 8, 2014

Week of Lent 5

2 Kings 4:18-37
Elisha raises a child from death

When Elisha came into the house, he saw the child lying dead on his bed. So he went in and closed the door on the two of them, and prayed to the LORD. Then he got up on the bed and lay upon the child, putting his mouth upon his mouth, his eyes upon his eyes, and his hands upon his hands; and while he lay bent over him, the flesh of the child became warm. He got down, walked once to and fro in the room, then got up again and bent over him; the child sneezed seven times, and the child opened his eyes. Elisha summoned Gehazi and said, "Call the Shunammite woman." So he called her. When she came to him, he said, "Take your son." She came and fell at his feet, bowing to the ground; then she took her son and left. (2 Kings 4:32-37)

Psalm
Psalm 143
Save me from death

Additional Reading
Ephesians 2:1-10
Alive in Christ

Hymn: O God beyond All Praising, ELW 880

Fount of everlasting life, we stand in awe of your great power to bring the dead to life. Remember us in your abundant mercy and include us in your promise of eternal life through Jesus Christ.

Wednesday, April 9, 2014

Week of Lent 5

Dietrich Bonhoeffer, theologian, died 1945

Jeremiah 32:1-9, 36-41
Jeremiah buys a field

Jeremiah said, The word of the LORD came to me: Hanamel son of your uncle Shallum is going to come to you and say, "Buy my field that is at Anathoth, for the right of redemption by purchase is yours." Then my cousin Hanamel came to me in the court of the guard, in accordance with the word of the LORD, and said to me, "Buy my field that is at Anathoth in the land of Benjamin, for the right of possession and redemption is yours; buy it for yourself." Then I knew that this was the word of the LORD. (Jer. 32:6-8)

Psalm
Psalm 143
Save me from death

Additional Reading
Matthew 22:23-33
God of the living

Hymn: Jesus, Priceless Treasure, ELW 775

O source of wisdom and light, speak your word and inspire us once more. May your word come to us, becoming bread for our day and a light for our path.

Thursday, April 10, 2014

Week of Lent 5

Mikael Agricola, Bishop of Turku, died 1557

Psalm 31:9-16
I commend my spirit

Be gracious to me, O Lord, for I am in distress;
   my eye wastes away from grief,
   my soul and body also.
For my life is spent with sorrow,
   and my years with sighing;
my strength fails because of my misery,
   and my bones waste away. . . .

But I trust in you, O Lord;
   I say, "You are my God."
My times are in your hand;
   deliver me from the hand of my enemies and persecutors.
Let your face shine upon your servant;
   save me in your steadfast love. (Ps. 31:9-10, 14-16)

Additional Readings
1 Samuel 16:11-13
Samuel anoints David

Philippians 1:1-11
Encouraged to follow Christ's righteousness

Hymn: Jesus, Still Lead On, ELW 624

O God, be gracious to us especially when distress, despair, and grief touch our lives. Embrace us with your steadfast love and grant us grace sufficient for our deepest sighs and sorrows. Empower us in our darkest hours to proclaim, "You are my God."

Friday, April 11, 2014

Week of Lent 5

Philippians 1:21-30

Seeing Christ in this life

Only, live your life in a manner worthy of the gospel of Christ, so that, whether I come and see you or am absent and hear about you, I will know that you are standing firm in one spirit, striving side by side with one mind for the faith of the gospel, and are in no way intimidated by your opponents. For them this is evidence of their destruction, but of your salvation. And this is God's doing. For he has graciously granted you the privilege not only of believing in Christ, but of suffering for him as well—since you are having the same struggle that you saw I had and now hear that I still have. (Phil. 1:27-30)

Psalm

Psalm 31:9-16

I commend my spirit

Additional Reading

Job 13:13-19

A servant keeps silence

Hymn: Give Thanks for Saints, ELW 428

Gracious God, inspire us through your Holy Spirit to live a life worthy of the gospel of Christ. We choose to live such a life not out of fear of punishment, but as a response to your lavish love toward us as seen through Jesus Christ.

Saturday, April 12, 2014

Week of Lent 5

Mark 10:32-34

Going up to Jerusalem

They were on the road, going up to Jerusalem, and Jesus was walking ahead of them; they were amazed, and those who followed were afraid. He took the twelve aside again and began to tell them what was to happen to him, saying, "See, we are going up to Jerusalem, and the Son of Man will be handed over to the chief priests and the scribes, and they will condemn him to death; then they will hand him over to the Gentiles; they will mock him, and spit upon him, and flog him, and kill him; and after three days he will rise again." (Mark 10:32-34)

Psalm
Psalm 31:9-16
I commend my spirit

Additional Reading
Lamentations 3:55-66
A cry for help

Hymn: Tree of Life and Awesome Mystery, ELW 334

Almighty God, you were with Jesus as he walked to Jerusalem and to his own death on a cross. Do not forsake us in our journeys on this earth, but give us strength to live this day with our eyes toward you.

Holy Week

On the Sunday of the Passion, Christians enter into Holy Week. This day opens before the Christian community the final period of preparation before the celebration of the Three Days of the Lord's passion, death, and resurrection.

In many churches, palm branches will be given to worshipers for the procession into the worship space. Following an ancient custom, many Christians bring their palms home and place them in the household prayer center, behind a cross or sacred image, or above the indoor lintel of the entryway.

At sunset on Maundy Thursday, Lent comes to an end as the church begins the celebration of the events through which Christ has become the life and the resurrection for all who believe.

Prayer for Placing Palms in the Home

Use this blessing when placing palms in the home after the Palm Sunday liturgy.

Blessed is the One who comes in the name of the Lord!
May we who place these palms receive Christ into our midst
with the joy that marked the entrance to Jerusalem.
May we hold no betrayal in our hearts,
but peacefully welcome Christ,
who lives and reigns with you and the Holy Spirit,
one God, now and forever. Amen.

Sunday, April 13, 2014

Sunday of the Passion
Palm Sunday

Matthew 26:14—27:66
The passion and death of Jesus

Then Jesus cried again with a loud voice and breathed his last. At that moment the curtain of the temple was torn in two, from top to bottom. The earth shook, and the rocks were split. The tombs also were opened, and many bodies of the saints who had fallen asleep were raised. After his resurrection they came out of the tombs and entered the holy city and appeared to many. Now when the centurion and those with him, who were keeping watch over Jesus, saw the earthquake and what took place, they were terrified and said, "Truly this man was God's Son!" (Matt. 27:50-54)

Psalm
Psalm 31:9-16
I commend my spirit

Additional Readings
Isaiah 50:4-9a
The servant submits to suffering

Philippians 2:5-11
Death on a cross

Hymn: Sing, My Tongue, ELW 355/356

Everlasting God, in your endless love for the human race you sent our Lord Jesus Christ to take on our nature and to suffer death on the cross. In your mercy enable us to share in his obedience to your will and in the glorious victory of his resurrection, who lives and reigns with you and the Holy Spirit, one God, now and forever.

Monday, April 14, 2014

Monday in Holy Week

Psalm 36:5-11
Refuge under the shadow of your wings

Your steadfast love, O LORD, extends to the heavens,
  your faithfulness to the clouds.
Your righteousness is like the mighty mountains,
  your judgments are like the great deep;
  you save humans and animals alike, O LORD.

How precious is your steadfast love, O God!
  All people may take refuge in the shadow of your wings.
They feast on the abundance of your house,
  and you give them drink from the river of your delights.
For with you is the fountain of life;
  in your light we see light. (Ps. 36:5-9)

Additional Readings

Isaiah 42:1-9	Hebrews 9:11-15	John 12:1-11
The servant brings forth justice	*The blood of Christ redeems for eternal life*	*Mary of Bethany anoints Jesus*

Hymn: My Song Is Love Unknown, ELW 343

O God, your Son chose the path that led to pain before joy and to the cross before glory. Plant his cross in our hearts, so that in its power and love we may come at last to joy and glory, through Jesus Christ, our Savior and Lord, who lives and reigns with you and the Holy Spirit, one God, now and forever.

Tuesday, April 15, 2014

Tuesday in Holy Week

1 Corinthians 1:18-31

The cross of Christ reveals God's power and wisdom

Where is the one who is wise? Where is the scribe? Where is the debater of this age? Has not God made foolish the wisdom of the world? For since, in the wisdom of God, the world did not know God through wisdom, God decided, through the foolishness of our proclamation, to save those who believe. For Jews demand signs and Greeks desire wisdom, but we proclaim Christ crucified, a stumbling block to Jews and foolishness to Gentiles, but to those who are the called, both Jews and Greeks, Christ the power of God and the wisdom of God. For God's foolishness is wiser than human wisdom, and God's weakness is stronger than human strength. (1 Cor. 1:20-25)

Psalm

Psalm 71:1-14

From my mother's womb you have been my strength

Additional Readings

Isaiah 49:1-7

The servant brings salvation to earth's ends

John 12:20-36

Jesus speaks of his death

Hymn: Jesus, Keep Me Near the Cross, ELW 335

Lord Jesus, you have called us to follow you. Grant that our love may not grow cold in your service, and that we may not fail or deny you in the time of trial, for you live and reign with the Father and the Holy Spirit, one God, now and forever.

Wednesday, April 16, 2014

Wednesday in Holy Week

Isaiah 50:4-9a

The servant is vindicated by God

The Lord GOD has opened my ear,
and I was not rebellious, I did not turn backward.
I gave my back to those who struck me,
and my cheeks to those who pulled out the beard;
I did not hide my face from insult and spitting.

The Lord GOD helps me;
therefore I have not been disgraced;
therefore I have set my face like flint,
and I know that I shall not be put to shame;
he who vindicates me is near.
Who will contend with me?
Let us stand up together.
Who are my adversaries?
Let them confront me.
It is the Lord GOD who helps me;
who will declare me guilty? (Isa. 50:5-9a)

Psalm

Psalm 70

Be pleased, O God, to deliver me

Additional Readings

Hebrews 12:1-3

Look to Jesus, who endured the cross

John 13:21-32

Jesus foretells his betrayal

Hymn: Ah, Holy Jesus, ELW 349

Almighty God, your Son our Savior suffered at human hands and endured the shame of the cross. Grant that we may walk in the way of his cross and find it the way of life and peace, through Jesus Christ, our Savior and Lord, who lives and reigns with you and the Holy Spirit, one God, now and forever.

The Three Days

As the sun sets on Maundy Thursday, so Lent ends and the Three Days begin, ending with sunset on Easter Day. During these central days, Christians prepare to celebrate God's gift of new life given in baptism. Indeed, the readings of the Three Days move toward the baptismal font where new brothers and sisters are born of water and the Spirit, and where the baptized renew their baptismal promises.

In the home and in the church community, special attention is given to these days through prayer and the keeping of greater silence until the great Vigil of Easter is celebrated. Many Christians keep a fast from food, work, and entertainment on Good Friday and Holy Saturday. In the home, preparations can be made for the celebration of Easter: cleaning, coloring eggs, baking Easter breads, gathering greens or flowers to adorn crosses and sacred images. In those communities where baptisms will be celebrated, prayers may be offered for those to be received into the church.

Table Prayer for the Three Days

Blessed are you, O Lord our God.
With this food strengthen us on our journey from death to life.
We glory in the cross of Christ.
Raise us, with him, to the joy of the resurrection,
through Jesus Christ our Lord. Amen.

Thursday, April 17, 2014

Maundy Thursday

John 13:1-17, 31b-35
The service of Christ: footwashing and meal

After [Jesus] had washed their feet, had put on his robe, and had returned to the table, he said to them, "Do you know what I have done to you? You call me Teacher and Lord—and you are right, for that is what I am. So if I, your Lord and Teacher, have washed your feet, you also ought to wash one another's feet. For I have set you an example, that you also should do as I have done to you." (John 13:12-15)

Psalm	Additional Readings	
Psalm 116:1-2, 12-19	Exodus 12:1-4 [5-10]	1 Corinthians 11:
The cup of salvation	11-14	23-26
	The passover of the Lord	*Proclaim the Lord's death*

Hymn: Great God, Your Love Has Called Us, ELW 358

Holy God, source of all love, on the night of his betrayal, Jesus gave us a new commandment, to love one another as he loves us. Write this commandment in our hearts, and give us the will to serve others as he was the servant of all, your Son, Jesus Christ, our Savior and Lord, who lives and reigns with you and the Holy Spirit, one God, now and forever.

Friday, April 18, 2014

Good Friday

John 18:1—19:42

The passion and death of Jesus

When Jesus saw his mother and the disciple whom he loved standing beside her, he said to his mother, "Woman, here is your son." Then he said to the disciple, "Here is your mother." And from that hour the disciple took her into his own home.

After this, when Jesus knew that all was now finished, he said (in order to fulfill the scripture), "I am thirsty." A jar full of sour wine was standing there. So they put a sponge full of the wine on a branch of hyssop and held it to his mouth. When Jesus had received the wine, he said, "It is finished." Then he bowed his head and gave up his spirit. (John 19:26-30)

Psalm	**Additional Readings**	
Psalm 22	Isaiah 52:13—53:12	Hebrews 10:16-25
Why have you forsaken me?	*The suffering servant*	*The way to God is opened*

Hymn: There in God's Garden, ELW 342

Almighty God, look with loving mercy on your family, for whom our Lord Jesus Christ was willing to be betrayed, to be given over to the hands of sinners, and to suffer death on the cross; who now lives and reigns with you and the Holy Spirit, one God, now and forever.

Saturday, April 19, 2014

Resurrection of Our Lord
Vigil of Easter

Olavus Petri, priest, died 1552; Laurentius Petri, Bishop of Uppsala, died 1573; renewers of the church

Romans 6:3-11
Dying and rising with Christ

Do you not know that all of us who have been baptized into Christ Jesus were baptized into his death? Therefore we have been buried with him by baptism into death, so that, just as Christ was raised from the dead by the glory of the Father, so we too might walk in newness of life.

For if we have been united with him in a death like his, we will certainly be united with him in a resurrection like his. (Rom. 6:3-5)

Psalm
Isaiah 12:2-6
With joy you will draw water from the wells of salvation

Additional Readings
Isaiah 55:1-11
Salvation freely offered to all

John 20:1-18
Seeing the risen Christ

Hymn: Come, You Faithful, Raise the Strain, ELW 363

Eternal giver of life and light, this holy night shines with the radiance of the risen Christ. Renew your church with the Spirit given us in baptism, that we may worship you in sincerity and truth and may shine as a light in the world, through your Son, Jesus Christ our Lord, who lives and reigns with you and the Holy Spirit, one God, now and forever.

Sunday, April 20, 2014

Resurrection of Our Lord
Easter Day

Matthew 28:1-10
Proclaim the resurrection

But the angel said to the women, "Do not be afraid; I know that you are looking for Jesus who was crucified. He is not here; for he has been raised, as he said. Come, see the place where he lay. Then go quickly and tell his disciples, 'He has been raised from the dead, and indeed he is going ahead of you to Galilee; there you will see him.' This is my message for you." So they left the tomb quickly with fear and great joy, and ran to tell his disciples. (Matt. 28:5-8)

Psalm

Psalm 118:1-2, 14-24
On this day God has acted

Additional Readings

Acts 10:34-43
God raised Jesus on the third day

Colossians 3:1-4
Raised with Christ

Hymn: Christ Has Arisen, Alleluia, ELW 364

O God, you gave your only Son to suffer death on the cross for our redemption, and by his glorious resurrection you delivered us from the power of death. Make us die every day to sin, that we may live with him forever in the joy of the resurrection, through your Son, Jesus Christ our Lord, who lives and reigns with you and the Holy Spirit, one God, now and forever.

EASTER

The Three Days flow into the rejoicing of the fifty days of Easter. During this "week of weeks," Christians explore the meaning of the central actions of baptism for daily life: renouncing evil and professing faith, washing in water, being marked with the cross, being clothed in the white robe, receiving the light of the paschal/Easter candle, and eating and drinking the bread of life and the cup of salvation.

The fifty days were once called *Pentecost*, Greek for "fifty." On the fiftieth day of Easter, Christians celebrate the pentecostal mystery of the risen Christ breathing on the church the breath, the wind, and the fire of the Holy Spirit.

Table Prayer for the Season of Easter

O God of our risen Lord, we praise you, we bless you,
we worship you for the gifts of life you give us.
Always you offer us life, and for this we bless your holy name.
And we ask you,
give your life also to all who know only hunger and the pangs of death.
So may the whole world be raised to life,
through Jesus Christ, our Savior and Lord. Amen.

Monday, April 21, 2014

Week of Easter 1

Anselm, Bishop of Canterbury, died 1109

Psalm 118:1-2, 14-24
On this day God has acted

The stone that the builders rejected
   has become the chief cornerstone.
This is the LORD's doing;
   it is marvelous in our eyes.
This is the day that the LORD has made;
   let us rejoice and be glad in it. (Ps. 118:22-24)

Additional Readings
Exodus 14:10-31; 15:20-21
Israel crosses over the sea

Colossians 3:5-11
The new life in Christ

Hymn: Now All the Vault of Heaven Resounds, ELW 367

Creator of all, this is the day that you have made. No matter what happens today, help us to find ways to rejoice and be glad in it. Enable our joy of living this day to reflect your glory and marvelous ways.

Tuesday, April 22, 2014

Week of Easter 1

Colossians 3:12-17

The new life in Christ

As God's chosen ones, holy and beloved, clothe yourselves with compassion, kindness, humility, meekness, and patience. Bear with one another and, if anyone has a complaint against another, forgive each other; just as the Lord has forgiven you, so you also must forgive. Above all, clothe yourselves with love, which binds everything together in perfect harmony. And let the peace of Christ rule in your hearts, to which indeed you were called in the one body. And be thankful. (Col. 3:12-15)

Psalm

Psalm 118:1-2, 14-24
On this day God has acted

Additional Reading

Exodus 15:1-18
Song at the sea

Hymn: Christ Is Risen! Shout Hosanna! ELW 383

Holy God, clothe us today with your compassion, kindness, humility, meekness, and patience. Let the peace of Christ enfold us and remain in our hearts and our lives now and forever.

Wednesday, April 23, 2014

Week of Easter 1

Toyohiko Kagawa, renewer of society, died 1960

Matthew 28:1-10

Proclaim the resurrection

The angel said to the women, "Do not be afraid; I know that you
are looking for Jesus who was crucified. He is not here; for he has
been raised, as he said. Come, see the place where he lay. Then go
quickly and tell his disciples, 'He has been raised from the dead, and
indeed he is going ahead of you to Galilee; there you will see him.'
This is my message for you." So they left the tomb quickly with fear
and great joy, and ran to tell his disciples. Suddenly Jesus met them
and said, "Greetings!" And they came to him, took hold of his feet,
and worshiped him. Then Jesus said to them, "Do not be afraid;
go and tell my brothers to go to Galilee; there they will see me."
(Matt. 28:5-10)

Psalm

Psalm 118:1-2, 14-24
On this day God has acted

Additional Reading

Joshua 3:1-17
Israel crosses into the promised land

Hymn: The Day of Resurrection! ELW 361

*O God, you sent an angel to proclaim, "Do not be afraid." Yet fear comes
and overwhelms us. Cast out our fear and free us to join the women at
the tomb to be your witnesses of the good news.*

Thursday, April 24, 2014

Week of Easter 1

Psalm 16
Fullness of joy

I bless the LORD who gives me counsel;
 in the night also my heart instructs me.
I keep the LORD always before me;
 because he is at my right hand, I shall not be moved.

Therefore my heart is glad, and my soul rejoices;
 my body also rests secure.
For you do not give me up to Sheol,
 or let your faithful one see the Pit.

You show me the path of life.
 In your presence there is fullness of joy;
 in your right hand are pleasures forevermore. (Ps. 16:7-11)

Additional Readings
Song of Solomon 2:8-15
Arise, for the winter is past

Colossians 4:2-5
The new life in Christ

Hymn: In Thee Is Gladness, ELW 867

In your presence there is a fullness of joy beyond words. Gracious God, it is you who can show us the path of life and love. Counsel and instruct us on this day so we might rest securely in your grace.

Friday, April 25, 2014

Mark, Evangelist

Mark 1:1-15
The beginning of the gospel of Jesus Christ

The beginning of the good news of Jesus Christ, the Son of God.
As it is written in the prophet Isaiah,
"See, I am sending my messenger ahead of you,
who will prepare your way;
the voice of one crying out in the wilderness:
'Prepare the way of the Lord,
make his paths straight,'"
John the baptizer appeared in the wilderness, proclaiming a baptism of repentance for the forgiveness of sins. And people from the whole Judean countryside and all the people of Jerusalem were going out to him, and were baptized by him in the river Jordan, confessing their sins. (Mark 1:1-5)

Psalm
Psalm 57
Be merciful to me, O God

Additional Readings
Isaiah 52:7-10
The messenger announces salvation

2 Timothy 4:6-11, 18
The good fight of faith

Hymn: Open Your Ears, O Faithful People, ELW 519

Almighty God, you have enriched your church with Mark's proclamation of the gospel. Give us grace to believe firmly in the good news of salvation and to walk daily in accord with it, through Jesus Christ, our Savior and Lord, who lives and reigns with you and the Holy Spirit, one God, now and forever.

Saturday, April 26, 2014

Week of Easter 1

Song of Solomon 8:6-7

Love is strong as death

Set me as a seal upon your heart,
   as a seal upon your arm;
for love is strong as death,
   passion fierce as the grave.
Its flashes are flashes of fire,
   a raging flame.
Many waters cannot quench love,
   neither can floods drown it.
If one offered for love
   all the wealth of one's house,
   it would be utterly scorned. (Song of Sol. 8:6-7)

Psalm
Psalm 16
Fullness of joy

Additional Reading
John 20:11-20
The witness of Mary Magdalene

Hymn: Come, My Way, My Truth, My Life, ELW 816

O God, bless us with your love and grace. For your love is stronger than death or anything else encountered in our journeys on earth. Bless us with relationships that open the door to share your love with others.

Sunday, April 27, 2014

Second Sunday of Easter

John 20:19-31

Beholding the wounds of the risen Christ

A week later [Jesus'] disciples were again in the house, and Thomas was with them. Although the doors were shut, Jesus came and stood among them and said, "Peace be with you." Then he said to Thomas, "Put your finger here and see my hands. Reach out your hand and put it in my side. Do not doubt but believe." Thomas answered him, "My Lord and my God!" Jesus said to him, "Have you believed because you have seen me? Blessed are those who have not seen and yet have come to believe." (John 20:26-29)

Psalm	Additional Readings	
Psalm 16	**Acts 2:14a, 22-32**	**1 Peter 1:3-9**
Fullness of joy	*God fulfills the promise to David*	*New birth to a living hope*

Hymn: The Risen Christ, ELW 390

Almighty and eternal God, the strength of those who believe and the hope of those who doubt, may we, who have not seen, have faith in you and receive the fullness of Christ's blessing, who lives and reigns with you and the Holy Spirit, one God, now and forever.

Monday, April 28, 2014

Week of Easter 2

Psalm 114
God saves through water

Why is it, O sea, that you flee?
    O Jordan, that you turn back?
O mountains, that you skip like rams?
    O hills, like lambs?

Tremble, O earth, at the presence of the LORD,
    at the presence of the God of Jacob,
who turns the rock into a pool of water,
    the flint into a spring of water. (Ps. 114:5-8)

Additional Readings

Judges 6:36-40
Gideon and the fleece

1 Corinthians 15:12-20
Paul teaches the resurrection

Hymn: We Know That Christ Is Raised, ELW 449

O Creator of all, when we ask, "Why this?" we demonstrate that we have many questions with few places to turn for answers. You who brought creation into being and who restores life from death are present with us while we pause in our wonder.

Tuesday, April 29, 2014

Week of Easter 2

Catherine of Siena, theologian, died 1380

1 Corinthians 15:19-28
Paul teaches the resurrection

For since death came through a human being, the resurrection of the dead has also come through a human being; for as all die in Adam, so all will be made alive in Christ. But each in his own order: Christ the first fruits, then at his coming those who belong to Christ. Then comes the end, when he hands over the kingdom to God the Father, after he has destroyed every ruler and every authority and power. For he must reign until he has put all his enemies under his feet. (1 Cor. 15:21-25)

Psalm
Psalm 114
God saves through water

Additional Reading
Jonah 1:1-17
Jonah saved from the sea

Hymn: This Joyful Eastertide, ELW 391

Almighty God, we celebrate the first fruits of Christ and the victory of his resurrection. Give us patience to wait faithfully until the reign of Christ is fully realized and the resurrection of the dead shall come to pass. Remember us when that final day comes.

Wednesday, April 30, 2014

Week of Easter 2

Matthew 12:38-42

Jesus speaks of the sign of Jonah

Then some of the scribes and Pharisees said to him, "Teacher, we wish to see a sign from you." But he answered them, "An evil and adulterous generation asks for a sign, but no sign will be given to it except the sign of the prophet Jonah. For just as Jonah was three days and three nights in the belly of the sea monster, so for three days and three nights the Son of Man will be in the heart of the earth. The people of Nineveh will rise up at the judgment with this generation and condemn it, because they repented at the proclamation of Jonah, and see, something greater than Jonah is here! The queen of the South will rise up at the judgment with this generation and condemn it, because she came from the ends of the earth to listen to the wisdom of Solomon, and see, something greater than Solomon is here!" (Matt. 12:38-42)

Psalm

Psalm 114

God saves through water

Additional Reading

Jonah 2:1-10

Jonah's praise for deliverance

Hymn: The Strife Is O'er, the Battle Done, ELW 366

O God, no more signs are needed. We give you thanks and praise for raising Jesus from death on the first Easter Day. The power of death is defeated. Resurrection is the final sign! Amen! Alleluia! It shall be so!

PRAYER LIST FOR MAY

_____

_____

_____

_____

_____

_____

_____

_____

_____

_____

_____

Thursday, May 1, 2014

Philip and James, Apostles

John 14:8-14
The Son and the Father are one

Philip said to him, "Lord, show us the Father, and we will be satisfied." Jesus said to him, "Have I been with you all this time, Philip, and you still do not know me? Whoever has seen me has seen the Father. How can you say, 'Show us the Father'? Do you not believe that I am in the Father and the Father is in me? The words that I say to you I do not speak on my own; but the Father who dwells in me does his works." (John 14:8-10)

Psalm
Psalm 44:1-3, 20-26
Save us for the sake of your love

Additional Readings
Isaiah 30:18-21
God's mercy and justice

2 Corinthians 4:1-6
Proclaiming Jesus Christ as Lord

Hymn: Thine Is the Glory, ELW 376

Almighty God, you gave to your apostles Philip and James grace and strength to bear witness to your Son. Grant that we, remembering their victory of faith, may glorify in life and death the name of our Lord Jesus Christ, who lives and reigns with you and the Holy Spirit, one God, now and forever.

Friday, May 2, 2014

Week of Easter 2

Athanasius, Bishop of Alexandria, died 373

Psalm 116:1-4, 12-19
I will call upon God

I love the LORD, because he has heard
  my voice and my supplications.
Because he inclined his ear to me,
  therefore I will call on him as long as I live.
The snares of death encompassed me;
  the pangs of Sheol laid hold on me;
  I suffered distress and anguish.
Then I called on the name of the LORD:
  "O LORD, I pray, save my life!" (Ps. 116:1-4)

Additional Readings
Isaiah 26:1-4
God sets up victory like bulwarks

1 Peter 1:13-16
A holy life

Hymn: Dear Christians, One and All, Rejoice, ELW 594

Everlasting God, you bend your ear to us and hear our cries. In the midst of our distress and suffering, we will faithfully call upon your name and trust in the hope of your unchanging grace.

Saturday, May 3, 2014

Week of Easter 2

Luke 14:12-14

Welcome those in need to your table

[Jesus] said also to the one who had invited him, "When you give a luncheon or a dinner, do not invite your friends or your brothers or your relatives or rich neighbors, in case they may invite you in return, and you would be repaid. But when you give a banquet, invite the poor, the crippled, the lame, and the blind. And you will be blessed, because they cannot repay you, for you will be repaid at the resurrection of the righteous." (Luke 14:12-14)

Psalm

Psalm 116:1-4, 12-19

I will call upon God

Additional Reading

Isaiah 25:6-9

The feast for all peoples

Hymn: Let Us Go Now to the Banquet, ELW 523

Lord of grace, you wipe away the tears from every face and welcome all people to your banquet table. Fill us with compassion and the courage to step away from our comfort zones, reaching out to any in need.

Sunday, May 4, 2014

Third Sunday of Easter

Monica, mother of Augustine, died 387

Luke 24:13-35

Eating with the risen Christ

As they came near the village to which they were going, [Jesus] walked ahead as if he were going on. But they urged him strongly, saying, "Stay with us, because it is almost evening and the day is now nearly over." So he went in to stay with them. When he was at the table with them, he took bread, blessed and broke it, and gave it to them. Then their eyes were opened, and they recognized him; and he vanished from their sight. They said to each other, "Were not our hearts burning within us while he was talking to us on the road, while he was opening the scriptures to us?" (Luke 24:28-32)

Psalm

Psalm 116:1-4, 12-19

I will call upon God

Additional Readings

Acts 2:14a, 36-41

Receiving God's promise through baptism

1 Peter 1:17-23

Born anew

Hymn: Day of Arising, ELW 374

O God, your Son makes himself known to all his disciples in the breaking of bread. Open the eyes of our faith, that we may see him in his redeeming work, who lives and reigns with you and the Holy Spirit, one God, now and forever.

Monday, May 5, 2014

Week of Easter 3

Psalm 134
Praise God day and night

Come, bless the LORD, all you servants of the LORD,
    who stand by night in the house of the LORD!
Lift up your hands to the holy place,
    and bless the LORD.

May the LORD, maker of heaven and earth,
    bless you from Zion. (Ps. 134:1-3)

Additional Readings
Genesis 18:1-14
Abraham and Sarah eat with God

1 Peter 1:23-25
The word of God endures

Hymn: The Trumpets Sound, the Angels Sing, ELW 531

Maker of heaven and earth, you listen to the desires of our hearts and bless us with unexpected gifts. Help us to recognize when you draw near and to believe in your promises for our future.

Tuesday, May 6, 2014

Week of Easter 3

1 Peter 2:1-3
Long for the pure spiritual milk

Rid yourselves, therefore, of all malice, and all guile, insincerity, envy, and all slander. Like newborn infants, long for the pure, spiritual milk, so that by it you may grow into salvation—if indeed you have tasted that the Lord is good. (1 Peter 2:1-3)

Psalm
Psalm 134
Praise God day and night

Additional Reading
Proverbs 8:32—9:6
Wisdom serves a meal

Hymn: All Who Hunger, Gather Gladly, ELW 461

Wise One, you have instructed us to lay aside immaturity, rid ourselves of all malice and insincerity, and approach life with the fresh outlook of a newborn. Guide us as we grow into your wisdom and keep your ways.

Wednesday, May 7, 2014

Week of Easter 3

Exodus 24:1-11
Moses and the elders eat with God

Then Moses and Aaron, Nadab, and Abihu, and seventy of the elders of Israel went up, and they saw the God of Israel. Under his feet there was something like a pavement of sapphire stone, like the very heaven for clearness. God did not lay his hand on the chief men of the people of Israel; also they beheld God, and they ate and drank. (Exod. 24:9-11)

Psalm
Psalm 134
Praise God day and night

Additional Reading
John 21:1-14
The risen Christ eats with the disciples

Hymn: At the Lamb's High Feast We Sing, ELW 362

Lord, we are nourished by your presence just as Moses and the elders were, receiving all that is needful to sustain us along our journey. Open our eyes to your miraculous touch upon our lives and give us thankful hearts.

Thursday, May 8, 2014

Week of Easter 3

Julian of Norwich, renewer of the church, died around 1416

Psalm 23
God our shepherd

Even though I walk through the darkest valley,
    I fear no evil;
for you are with me;
    your rod and your staff—
    they comfort me.

You prepare a table before me
    in the presence of my enemies;
you anoint my head with oil;
    my cup overflows.
Surely goodness and mercy shall follow me
    all the days of my life,
and I shall dwell in the house of the LORD
    my whole life long. (Ps. 23:4-6)

Additional Readings
Exodus 2:15b-25   1 Peter 2:9-12
Moses the shepherd   *Living as God's people*

Hymn: Shepherd Me, O God, ELW 780

Good Shepherd, you have walked beside us through dark times, comforting us, restoring us, and leading us with your goodness and mercy. We will not fear when you are with us and when we are filled to overflowing with your love.

Friday, May 9, 2014

Week of Easter 3

**Nicolaus Ludwig von Zinzendorf, renewer of the church,
hymnwriter, died 1760**

1 Peter 2:13-17
Living honorably in the world

For the Lord's sake accept the authority of every human institution,
whether of the emperor as supreme, or of governors, as sent by him
to punish those who do wrong and to praise those who do right. For
it is God's will that by doing right you should silence the ignorance
of the foolish. As servants of God, live as free people, yet do not use
your freedom as a pretext for evil. Honor everyone. Love the family of
believers. Fear God. Honor the emperor. (1 Peter 2:13-17)

Psalm
Psalm 23
God our shepherd

Additional Reading
Exodus 3:16-22; 4:18-20
Moses the shepherd of Israel

Hymn: What God Ordains Is Good Indeed, ELW 776

*God, as you led your people out of Egypt, so you continue to light our
way through a world filled with ignorance. Fill us with courage to follow
your will, to live as free people, doing what is honorable and right.*

Saturday, May 10, 2014

Week of Easter 3

Ezekiel 34:1-16

God gathers the scattered flock

For thus says the Lord GOD: I myself will search for my sheep, and will seek them out. As shepherds seek out their flocks when they are among their scattered sheep, so I will seek out my sheep. I will rescue them from all the places to which they have been scattered on a day of clouds and thick darkness. I will bring them out from the peoples and gather them from the countries, and will bring them into their own land; and I will feed them on the mountains of Israel, by the watercourses, and in all the inhabited parts of the land. I will feed them with good pasture, and the mountain heights of Israel shall be their pasture; there they shall lie down in good grazing land, and they shall feed on rich pasture on the mountains of Israel. I myself will be the shepherd of my sheep, and I will make them lie down, says the Lord GOD. (Ezek. 34:11-15)

Psalm

Psalm 23

God our shepherd

Additional Reading

Luke 15:1-7

Parable of the lost sheep

Hymn: Savior, like a Shepherd Lead Us, ELW 789

Lord God, like lost sheep we are scattered throughout the world, wandering in dangerous and lonely places, but you seek us out, searching until we have been found. Gather us together and we will lie down in your good pasture.

Blessing for Mother's Day (May 11)

Under your wings, O Lord, you have held us,
as a mother holds her young.
Look with favor on all those women
who have sheltered children in their loving care.
Guide that they may lead;
strengthen that they may be tender;
grant wisdom that the people may live;
and hold all in your loving gaze
until we see you face-to-face.
Amen.

Sunday, May 11, 2014

Fourth Sunday of Easter

John 10:1-10
Christ the shepherd

So again Jesus said to them, "Very truly, I tell you, I am the gate for the sheep. All who came before me are thieves and bandits; but the sheep did not listen to them. I am the gate. Whoever enters by me will be saved, and will come in and go out and find pasture. The thief comes only to steal and kill and destroy. I came that they may have life, and have it abundantly." (John 10:7-10)

Psalm

Psalm 23
God our shepherd

Additional Readings

Acts 2:42-47
The believers' common life

1 Peter 2:19-25
Follow the shepherd, even in suffering

Hymn: The Lord's My Shepherd, ELW 778

O God our shepherd, you know your sheep by name and lead us to safety through the valleys of death. Guide us by your voice, that we may walk in certainty and security to the joyous feast prepared in your house, through Jesus Christ, our Savior and Lord, who lives and reigns with you and the Holy Spirit, one God, now and forever.

Monday, May 12, 2014

Week of Easter 4

Psalm 100

We are the sheep of God's pasture

Make a joyful noise to the LORD, all the earth.
  Worship the LORD with gladness;
  come into his presence with singing.

Know that the LORD is God.
  It is he that made us, and we are his;
  we are his people, and the sheep of his pasture.

Enter his gates with thanksgiving,
  and his courts with praise.
  Give thanks to him, bless his name.

For the LORD is good;
  his steadfast love endures forever,
  and his faithfulness to all generations. (Ps. 100:1-5)

Additional Readings

Ezekiel 34:17-23
God the true shepherd

1 Peter 5:1-5
Tend the flock of God

Hymn: All People That on Earth Do Dwell, ELW 883

Faithful God, you made us and we are yours. You fill us with gladness and we sing for joy. Your steadfast love and grace endure forever and we come into your presence with humility, thanks, and praise.

Tuesday, May 13, 2014

Week of Easter 4

Hebrews 13:20-21

God's blessing through Christ the shepherd

Now may the God of peace, who brought back from the dead our
Lord Jesus, the great shepherd of the sheep, by the blood of the eternal
covenant, make you complete in everything good so that you may
do his will, working among us that which is pleasing in his sight,
through Jesus Christ, to whom be the glory forever and ever. Amen.
(Heb. 13:20-21)

Psalm
Psalm 100
We are the sheep of God's pasture

Additional Reading
Ezekiel 34:23-31
God provides perfect pasture

Hymn: Go, My Children, with My Blessing, ELW 543

*Great Shepherd, you provide us with everything we need to live
abundant and complete lives, filled with your peace and love. Guide
our efforts into your vision for us, so that our work is pleasing in your
sight.*

Wednesday, May 14, 2014

Matthias, Apostle

Luke 6:12-16

Jesus calls the Twelve

Now during those days he went out to the mountain to pray; and he spent the night in prayer to God. And when day came, he called his disciples and chose twelve of them, whom he also named apostles: Simon, whom he named Peter, and his brother Andrew, and James, and John, and Philip, and Bartholomew, and Matthew, and Thomas, and James son of Alphaeus, and Simon, who was called the Zealot, and Judas son of James, and Judas Iscariot, who became a traitor. (Luke 6:12-16)

Psalm

Psalm 56

I am bound by the vow I made to you

Additional Readings

Isaiah 66:1-2

Heaven is God's throne, earth is God's footstool

Acts 1:15-26

The apostles cast lots for Matthias

Hymn: The Church of Christ, in Every Age, ELW 729

Almighty God, you chose your faithful servant Matthias to be numbered among the twelve. Grant that your church may always be taught and guided by faithful and true pastors, through Jesus Christ our shepherd, who lives and reigns with you and the Holy Spirit, one God, now and forever.

Thursday, May 15, 2014

Week of Easter 4

Psalm 31:1-5, 15-16
I commend my spirit

In you, O LORD, I seek refuge;
    do not let me ever be put to shame;
    in your righteousness deliver me.
Incline your ear to me;
    rescue me speedily.
Be a rock of refuge for me,
    a strong fortress to save me.

You are indeed my rock and my fortress;
    for your name's sake lead me and guide me,
take me out of the net that is hidden for me,
    for you are my refuge.
Into your hand I commit my spirit;
    you have redeemed me, O LORD, faithful God. (Ps. 31:1-5)

Additional Readings
Genesis 12:1-3   **Acts 6:8-15**
The call of Abram   *Stephen is arrested*

Hymn: Shout to the Lord, ELW 821

Rock and Fortress, your strength surrounds us as we face the perils of this sin-filled world. Bend your ear to us and hear us in our time of need as we commit our lives into your strong hands.

Friday, May 16, 2014

Week of Easter 4

Exodus 3:1-12

Moses at the burning bush

When the LORD saw that [Moses] had turned aside to see, God called to him out of the bush, "Moses, Moses!" And he said, "Here I am." Then he said, "Come no closer! Remove the sandals from your feet, for the place on which you are standing is holy ground." He said further, "I am the God of your father, the God of Abraham, the God of Isaac, and the God of Jacob." And Moses hid his face, for he was afraid to look at God. (Exod. 3:4-6)

Psalm

Psalm 31:1-5, 15-16

I commend my spirit

Additional Reading

Acts 7:1-16

Stephen addresses the council

Hymn: Christ Is Risen! Alleluia! ELW 382

Our refuge, you call us in the midst of everyday life, reaching through our fears and drawing us into your holy presence. Be with us as we go where you send us, for our times are in your hands.

Saturday, May 17, 2014

Week of Easter 4

Jeremiah 26:20-24

A prophet of the Lord persecuted

There was another man prophesying in the name of the LORD, Uriah son of Shemaiah from Kiriath-jearim. He prophesied against this city and against this land in words exactly like those of Jeremiah. And when King Jehoiakim, with all his warriors and all the officials, heard his words, the king sought to put him to death; but when Uriah heard of it, he was afraid and fled and escaped to Egypt. Then King Jehoiakim sent Elnathan son of Achbor and men with him to Egypt, and they took Uriah from Egypt and brought him to King Jehoiakim, who struck him down with the sword and threw his dead body into the burial place of the common people.

But the hand of Ahikam son of Shaphan was with Jeremiah so that he was not given over into the hands of the people to be put to death. (Jer. 26:20-24)

Psalm	**Additional Reading**
Psalm 31:1-5, 15-16	John 8:48-59
I commend my spirit	*Jesus the greater prophet*

Hymn: Faith of Our Fathers, ELW 812/813

Faithful God, you sent your Son and the prophets into danger to speak the truth, challenging the authorities of their day. Give us courage when we face opposition in your name, knowing you go before us to light the way.

Sunday, May 18, 2014

Fifth Sunday of Easter

Erik, King of Sweden, martyr, died 1160

John 14:1-14
Christ the way, truth, life

Philip said to [Jesus], "Lord, show us the Father, and we will be satisfied." Jesus said to him, "Have I been with you all this time, Philip, and you still do not know me? Whoever has seen me has seen the Father. How can you say, 'Show us the Father'? Do you not believe that I am in the Father and the Father is in me? The words that I say to you I do not speak on my own; but the Father who dwells in me does his works. Believe me that I am in the Father and the Father is in me; but if you do not, then believe me because of the works themselves. Very truly, I tell you, the one who believes in me will also do the works that I do and, in fact, will do greater works than these, because I am going to the Father." (John 14:8-12)

Psalm
Psalm 31:1-5, 15-16
I commend my spirit

Additional Readings
Acts 7:55-60
Martyrdom of Stephen

1 Peter 2:2-10
God's chosen people

Hymn: You Are the Way, ELW 758

Almighty God, your Son Jesus Christ is the way, the truth, and the life. Give us grace to love one another, to follow in the way of his commandments, and to share his risen life with all the world, for he lives and reigns with you and the Holy Spirit, one God, now and forever.

Monday, May 19, 2014

Week of Easter 5

Psalm 102:1-17

Prayer for deliverance

But you, O Lord, are enthroned forever;
    your name endures to all generations.
You will rise up and have compassion on Zion,
    for it is time to favor it;
    the appointed time has come.
For your servants hold its stones dear,
    and have pity on its dust.
The nations will fear the name of the Lord,
    and all the kings of the earth your glory.
For the Lord will build up Zion;
    he will appear in his glory. (Ps. 102:12-16)

Additional Readings

Exodus 13:17-22
God leads the way

Acts 7:17-40
Stephen addresses the council

Hymn: O God of Every Nation, ELW 713

In our loneliness and distress we cry out to you, Lord, and your compassion washes over us. We know the time has come to make changes and we trust in your strength to lead us out of the wilderness.

Tuesday, May 20, 2014

Week of Easter 5

Proverbs 3:5-12

God, the truth and life

Trust in the LORD with all your heart,
    and do not rely on your own insight.
In all your ways acknowledge him,
    and he will make straight your paths.
Do not be wise in your own eyes;
    fear the LORD, and turn away from evil.
It will be a healing for your flesh
    and a refreshment for your body. (Prov. 3:5-8)

Psalm

Psalm 102:1-17

Prayer for deliverance

Additional Reading

Acts 7:44-56

Stephen confronts the council

Hymn: All My Hope on God Is Founded, ELW 757

God of truth, you remind us that as a father disciplines his child, so you reprove those you love, encouraging us to give up our stubbornness, rely only on your wisdom, and trust in you with our whole hearts.

Wednesday, May 21, 2014

Week of Easter 5

Helena, mother of Constantine, died around 330

John 8:31-38
Jesus, the truth of God

Jesus answered them, "Very truly, I tell you, everyone who commits sin is a slave to sin. The slave does not have a permanent place in the household; the son has a place there forever. So if the Son makes you free, you will be free indeed. I know that you are descendants of Abraham; yet you look for an opportunity to kill me, because there is no place in you for my word. I declare what I have seen in the Father's presence; as for you, you should do what you have heard from the Father." (John 8:34-38)

Psalm
Psalm 102:1-17
Prayer for deliverance

Additional Reading
Proverbs 3:13-18
God, the truth and life

Hymn: Awake, My Heart, with Gladness, ELW 378

Lord, in your word is the truth that makes us free, yet sometimes that freedom is only superficial and underneath our façades we are still in bondage to sin. Help us search diligently for your truth and then to live it.

Thursday, May 22, 2014

Week of Easter 5

Psalm 66:8-20
Be joyful in God, all you lands

Bless our God, O peoples,
    let the sound of his praise be heard,
who has kept us among the living,
    and has not let our feet slip.
For you, O God, have tested us;
    you have tried us as silver is tried.
You brought us into the net;
    you laid burdens on our backs;
you let people ride over our heads;
    we went through fire and through water;
yet you have brought us out to a spacious place. (Ps. 66:8-12)

Additional Readings
Genesis 6:5-22   Acts 27:1-12
God's command to Noah   *Paul sails for Rome*

Hymn: Christ Jesus Lay in Death's Strong Bands, ELW 370

Our pilot, when life's journeys take us through trials and the wind blows against us, you guide us to safe harbor and never let our feet slip. Fill us with hope as we make our way home to you.

Friday, May 23, 2014

Week of Easter 5

Genesis 7:1-24
The great flood

Then the LORD said to Noah, "Go into the ark, you and all your household, for I have seen that you alone are righteous before me in this generation. Take with you seven pairs of all clean animals, the male and its mate; and a pair of the animals that are not clean, the male and its mate; and seven pairs of the birds of the air also, male and female, to keep their kind alive on the face of all the earth. For in seven days I will send rain on the earth for forty days and forty nights; and every living thing that I have made I will blot out from the face of the ground." And Noah did all that the LORD had commanded him. (Gen. 7:1-5)

Psalm
Psalm 66:8-20
Be joyful in God, all you lands

Additional Reading
Acts 27:13-38
Paul survives shipwreck

Hymn: Thy Holy Wings, ELW 613

Mighty God, you pay close attention to all that we do upon this earth and guide us when the storms of life assail us. Keep us safe and encourage us as we heed your prophetic words.

Saturday, May 24, 2014

Week of Easter 5

Nicolaus Copernicus, died 1543; Leonhard Euler, died 1783; scientists

John 14:27-29
Peace I leave with you

"Peace I leave with you; my peace I give to you. I do not give to you as the world gives. Do not let your hearts be troubled, and do not let them be afraid. You heard me say to you, 'I am going away, and I am coming to you.' If you loved me, you would rejoice that I am going to the Father, because the Father is greater than I. And now I have told you this before it occurs, so that when it does occur, you may believe." (John 14:27-29)

Psalm
Psalm 66:8-20
Be joyful in God, all you lands

Additional Reading
Genesis 8:13-19
The flood waters subside

Hymn: Alleluia! Sing to Jesus, ELW 392

With your peace filling our hearts, Lord, we can face any fear, hurdle every obstacle, and rejoice in your plans, even when we don't understand fully. Increase our trust in your promises as we walk with you into the future.

Sunday, May 25, 2014

Sixth Sunday of Easter

John 14:15-21

Christ our advocate

"If you love me, you will keep my commandments. And I will ask the Father, and he will give you another Advocate, to be with you forever. This is the Spirit of truth, whom the world cannot receive, because it neither sees him nor knows him. You know him, because he abides with you, and he will be in you." (John 14:15-17)

Psalm

Psalm 66:8-20

Be joyful in God, all you lands

Additional Readings

Acts 17:22-31

Paul's message to the Athenians

1 Peter 3:13-22

The days of Noah, a sign of baptism

Hymn: O Spirit of Life, ELW 405

Almighty and ever-living God, you hold together all things in heaven and on earth. In your great mercy receive the prayers of all your children, and give to all the world the Spirit of your truth and peace, through Jesus Christ, our Savior and Lord, who lives and reigns with you and the Holy Spirit, one God, now and forever.

Monday, May 26, 2014

Psalm 93
God reigns above the floods

The LORD is king, he is robed in majesty;
    the LORD is robed, he is girded with strength.
He has established the world; it shall never be moved;
    your throne is established from of old;
    you are from everlasting.

The floods have lifted up, O LORD,
    the floods have lifted up their voice;
    the floods lift up their roaring.
More majestic than the thunders of mighty waters,
    more majestic than the waves of the sea,
    majestic on high is the LORD!

Your decrees are very sure;
    holiness befits your house,
    O LORD, forevermore. (Ps. 93:1-5)

Additional Readings
Genesis 9:8-17
Sign of the covenant

Acts 27:39-44
Paul and companions come safely to land

Hymn: Come, Thou Almighty King, ELW 408

After the thunderous, crashing waves of the mighty seas and the roar of floodwaters abate comes the quiet and profound realization that your majesty extends far beyond our comprehension. Ground us deeply in this awareness of your holiness and strength.

Tuesday, May 27, 2014

Week of Easter 6

John Calvin, renewer of the church, died 1564

1 Peter 3:8-12

Seek peace and pursue it

Finally, all of you, have unity of spirit, sympathy, love for one another, a tender heart, and a humble mind. Do not repay evil for evil or abuse for abuse; but, on the contrary, repay with a blessing. It is for this that you were called—that you might inherit a blessing. For

"Those who desire life
    and desire to see good days,
let them keep their tongues from evil
    and their lips from speaking deceit;
let them turn away from evil and do good;
    let them seek peace and pursue it.
For the eyes of the Lord are on the righteous,
    and his ears are open to their prayer.
But the face of the Lord is against those who do evil." (1 Peter 3:8-12)

Psalm

Psalm 93
God reigns above the floods

Additional Reading

Deuteronomy 5:22-33
Moses delivers God's commandments

Hymn: We Are Called, ELW 720

O God, with your mighty voice in our ears and your consuming presence in our lives, you establish your will, calling us to have tender hearts and humble minds. Mold us into people who seek peace and do good, not evil.

Wednesday, May 28, 2014

Week of Easter 6

John 16:16-24

A little while, and you shall see

[Jesus said,] "A little while, and you will no longer see me, and again a little while, and you will see me." Then some of his disciples said to one another, "What does he mean by saying to us, 'A little while, and you will no longer see me, and again a little while, and you will see me'; and 'Because I am going to the Father'?" They said, "What does he mean by this 'a little while'? We do not know what he is talking about." Jesus knew that they wanted to ask him, so he said to them, "Are you discussing among yourselves what I meant when I said, 'A little while, and you will no longer see me, and again a little while, and you will see me'? Very truly, I tell you, you will weep and mourn, but the world will rejoice; you will have pain, but your pain will turn into joy." (John 16:16-20)

Psalm
Psalm 93
God reigns above the floods

Additional Reading
Deuteronomy 31:1-13
Moses promises God's presence

Hymn: Lord, Thee I Love with All My Heart, ELW 750

You go before us, Lord, leading the way, and have promised never to fail or forsake us. Even when we are mystified by your words, strengthen us, embolden us, and fill us with joy as we carry out your mission.

Thursday, May 29, 2014

Ascension of Our Lord

Jiří Tranovský, hymnwriter, died 1637

Luke 24:44-53
Christ present in all times and places

Then [Jesus] opened their minds to understand the scriptures, and he said to them, "Thus it is written, that the Messiah is to suffer and to rise from the dead on the third day, and that repentance and forgiveness of sins is to be proclaimed in his name to all nations, beginning from Jerusalem. You are witnesses of these things. And see, I am sending upon you what my Father promised; so stay here in the city until you have been clothed with power from on high." (Luke 24:45-49)

Psalm

Psalm 47
God has gone up with a shout

Additional Readings

Acts 1:1-11
Jesus sends the apostles

Ephesians 1:15-23
Seeing the risen and ascended Christ

Hymn: A Hymn of Glory Let Us Sing! ELW 393

Almighty God, your only Son was taken into the heavens and in your presence intercedes for us. Receive us and our prayers for all the world, and in the end bring everything into your glory, through Jesus Christ, our Sovereign and Lord, who lives and reigns with you and the Holy Spirit, one God, now and forever.

Friday, May 30, 2014

Week of Easter 6

Ephesians 2:1-7
Seated in the heavenly places with Christ

But God, who is rich in mercy, out of the great love with which he loved us even when we were dead through our trespasses, made us alive together with Christ—by grace you have been saved—and raised us up with him and seated us with him in the heavenly places in Christ Jesus, so that in the ages to come he might show the immeasurable riches of his grace in kindness toward us in Christ Jesus. (Eph. 2:4-7)

Psalm
Psalm 93
Praise to God who reigns

Additional Reading
2 Kings 2:1-12
Elijah ascends in a chariot of fire

Hymn: Rejoice, for Christ Is King! ELW 430

Merciful God, the extravagance of your kindness and love reminds us that you will never leave us and will always meet us where we are. Our hearts are filled with wonder and gratitude for this grace in which we stand.

Saturday, May 31, 2014

Visit of Mary to Elizabeth

Luke 1:39-57
Mary greets Elizabeth

In those days Mary set out and went with haste to a Judean town in the hill country, where she entered the house of Zechariah and greeted Elizabeth. When Elizabeth heard Mary's greeting, the child leaped in her womb. And Elizabeth was filled with the Holy Spirit and exclaimed with a loud cry, "Blessed are you among women, and blessed is the fruit of your womb." (Luke 1:39-42)

Psalm

Psalm 113
God, the helper of the needy

Additional Readings

1 Samuel 2:1-10
Hannah's thanksgiving

Romans 12:9-16b
Rejoice with those who rejoice

Hymn: Unexpected and Mysterious, ELW 258

Mighty God, by whose grace Elizabeth rejoiced with Mary and greeted her as the mother of the Lord: look with favor on your lowly servants that, with Mary, we may magnify your holy name and rejoice to acclaim her Son as our Savior, who lives and reigns with you and the Holy Spirit, one God, now and forever.

Sunday, June 1, 2014

Seventh Sunday of Easter

Justin, martyr at Rome, died around 165

John 17:1-11
Christ's prayer for his disciples

"I have made your name known to those whom you gave me from the world. They were yours, and you gave them to me, and they have kept your word. Now they know that everything you have given me is from you; for the words that you gave to me I have given to them, and they have received them and know in truth that I came from you; and they have believed that you sent me. I am asking on their behalf; I am not asking on behalf of the world, but on behalf of those whom you gave me, because they are yours. All mine are yours, and yours are mine; and I have been glorified in them. And now I am no longer in the world, but they are in the world, and I am coming to you. Holy Father, protect them in your name that you have given me, so that they may be one, as we are one." (John 17:6-11)

Psalm
Psalm 68:1-10, 32-35
Sing to God

Additional Readings
Acts 1:6-14
Jesus' companions at prayer

1 Peter 4:12-14;
5:6-11
God sustains those who suffer

Hymn: Lord, Who the Night You Were Betrayed, ELW 463

O God of glory, your Son Jesus Christ suffered for us and ascended to your right hand. Unite us with Christ and each other in suffering and in joy, that all the world may be drawn into your bountiful presence, through Jesus Christ, our Savior and Lord, who lives and reigns with you and the Holy Spirit, one God, now and forever.

Monday, June 2, 2014

Week of Easter 7

Psalm 99
Priests and people praise God

The LORD is king; let the peoples tremble!
　He sits enthroned upon the cherubim; let the earth quake!
The LORD is great in Zion;
　he is exalted over all the peoples.
Let them praise your great and awesome name.
　Holy is he!
Mighty King, lover of justice,
　you have established equity;
you have executed justice
　and righteousness in Jacob.
Extol the LORD our God;
　worship at his footstool.
　Holy is he! (Ps. 99:1-5)

Additional Readings
Leviticus 9:1-11, 22-24　　　　　　1 Peter 4:1-6
The high priest Aaron offers sacrifice　　*Live by the will of God*

Hymn: Oh, Worship the King, ELW 842

Everlasting God, in the resurrection of your Son you have made all things new. May your praise be our constant song as we remember your mighty deeds and rejoice in your reign of justice and righteousness.

Tuesday, June 3, 2014

Week of Easter 7

The Martyrs of Uganda, died 1886
John XXIII, Bishop of Rome, died 1963

1 Peter 4:7-11
Be good stewards of grace

The end of all things is near; therefore be serious and discipline yourselves for the sake of your prayers. Above all, maintain constant love for one another, for love covers a multitude of sins. Be hospitable to one another without complaining. Like good stewards of the manifold grace of God, serve one another with whatever gift each of you has received. Whoever speaks must do so as one speaking the very words of God; whoever serves must do so with the strength that God supplies, so that God may be glorified in all things through Jesus Christ. To him belong the glory and the power forever and ever. Amen. (1 Peter 4:7-11)

Psalm	**Additional Reading**
Psalm 99	Numbers 16:41-50
Priests and people praise God	*The high priest Aaron makes atonement*

Hymn: We All Are One in Mission, ELW 576

God of boundless grace, keep us mindful of the special gifts you have given us for your service. Keep our hearts centered in you through prayer so that our unique abilities may glorify you in your Son, through your Spirit.

Wednesday, June 4, 2014

Week of Easter 7

1 Kings 8:54-65
Solomon offers sacrifice

Then the king, and all Israel with him, offered sacrifice before the LORD. Solomon offered as sacrifices of well-being to the LORD twenty-two thousand oxen and one hundred twenty thousand sheep. So the king and all the people of Israel dedicated the house of the LORD. The same day the king consecrated the middle of the court that was in front of the house of the LORD; for there he offered the burnt offerings and the grain offerings and the fat pieces of the sacrifices of well-being, because the bronze altar that was before the LORD was too small to receive the burnt offerings and the grain offerings and the fat pieces of the sacrifices of well-being.

So Solomon held the festival at that time, and all Israel with him—a great assembly, people from Lebo-hamath to the Wadi of Egypt—before the LORD our God, seven days. (1 Kings 8:62-65)

Psalm
Psalm 99
Priests and people praise God

Additional Reading
John 3:31-36
The Son and the Father

Hymn: Jesus Shall Reign, ELW 434

God of our ancestors, remind us of our need to listen to you and to recall all that you have taught us. Help us to know that joy springs from the brokenness of contrite hearts.

Thursday, June 5, 2014

Week of Easter 7

Boniface, Bishop of Mainz, missionary to Germany, martyr, died 754

Psalm 33:12-22
Our help and our shield

Truly the eye of the LORD is on those who fear him,
  on those who hope in his steadfast love,
to deliver their soul from death,
  and to keep them alive in famine.
Our soul waits for the LORD;
  he is our help and shield.
Our heart is glad in him,
  because we trust in his holy name.
Let your steadfast love, O LORD, be upon us,
  even as we hope in you. (Ps. 33:18-22)

Additional Readings
Exodus 19:1-9a
The covenant at Sinai

Acts 2:1-11
The giving of the Spirit

Hymn: Jesus Lives, My Sure Defense, ELW 621

God of the cosmos, you are sculptor not only of heaven and earth but of the beauty of our inner landscapes. Kindle the fire of your love in our hearts so that we may await your coming in confidence.

Friday, June 6, 2014

Week of Easter 7

Romans 8:14-17

Led by the Spirit of God

For all who are led by the Spirit of God are children of God. For you did not receive a spirit of slavery to fall back into fear, but you have received a spirit of adoption. When we cry, "Abba! Father!" it is that very Spirit bearing witness with our spirit that we are children of God, and if children, then heirs, heirs of God and joint heirs with Christ—if, in fact, we suffer with him so that we may also be glorified with him. (Rom. 8:14-17)

Psalm

Psalm 33:12-22

Our help and our shield

Additional Reading

Exodus 19:16-25

Moses and Aaron meet the Lord

Hymn: We All Believe in One True God, ELW 411

God our protector, when we cry "Abba!" we confess our perfect love and utter trust in you. Strengthen our faith so that we may be purified in our suffering for the sake of your Son.

Saturday, June 7, 2014

Vigil of Pentecost

Seattle, chief of the Duwamish Confederacy, died 1866

John 7:37-39

Jesus, the true living water

On the last day of the festival, the great day, while Jesus was standing there, he cried out, "Let anyone who is thirsty come to me, and let the one who believes in me drink. As the scripture has said, 'Out of the believer's heart shall flow rivers of living water.'" Now he said this about the Spirit, which believers in him were to receive; for as yet there was no Spirit, because Jesus was not yet glorified. (John 7:37-39)

Psalm	Additional Readings	
Psalm 33:12-22	Exodus 19:1-9	Romans 8:14-17, 22-27
Our help and our shield	*The covenant at Sinai*	*Praying with the Spirit*

Hymn: Come, Holy Ghost, God and Lord, ELW 395

Almighty and ever-living God, you fulfilled the promise of Easter by sending the gift of your Holy Spirit. Look upon your people gathered in prayer, open to receive the Spirit's flame. May it come to rest in our hearts and heal the divisions of word and tongue, that with one voice and one song we may praise your name in joy and thanksgiving; through Jesus Christ, our Savior and Lord, who lives and reigns with you and the Holy Spirit, one God, now and forever.

Pentecost

Christians pray to God "in the power of the Spirit." The gifts of the Spirit are faith, hope, and love. Whenever two or more gather in Jesus' name, the Spirit is present. At every baptism and communion, we pray for the Spirit's presence to forgive and strengthen, inspire and refresh. In the household, we pray for the Spirit's guidance, for the deepening of faith, hope, and love, for the patience and wisdom to live in peace with each other and our neighbors.

Table Prayer for Pentecost

Blessed are you, O Lord our God,
who gathers the whole world into the Spirit of your Son.
You have given us food for another day:
blessed be God forever!
We beg you to pour out food for the needy,
that all peoples and languages may praise your name,
through Jesus Christ our Lord.
Amen.

Thanksgiving for the Holy Spirit
Use this prayer during the week following Pentecost Sunday.

O Spirit of God, seek us;
Good Spirit, pray with us;
Spirit of counsel, inform us;
Spirit of might, free us;
Spirit of truth, enlighten us;
Spirit of Christ, raise us;
O Holy Spirit, dwell in us. Amen.

Sunday, June 8, 2014

Day of Pentecost

John 20:19-23

The Spirit poured out

When it was evening on that day, the first day of the week, and the doors of the house where the disciples had met were locked for fear of the Jews, Jesus came and stood among them and said, "Peace be with you." After he said this, he showed them his hands and his side. Then the disciples rejoiced when they saw the Lord. Jesus said to them again, "Peace be with you. As the Father has sent me, so I send you." When he had said this, he breathed on them and said to them, "Receive the Holy Spirit. If you forgive the sins of any, they are forgiven them; if you retain the sins of any, they are retained." (John 20:19-23)

Psalm

Psalm 104:24-34, 35b

Renewing the face of the earth

Additional Readings

Acts 2:1-21

Filled with the Spirit

I Corinthians 12:3b-13

Varieties of gifts, the same Spirit

Hymn: O Day Full of Grace, ELW 627

O God, on this day you open the hearts of your faithful people by sending into us your Holy Spirit. Direct us by the light of that Spirit, that we may have a right judgment in all things and rejoice at all times in your peace, through Jesus Christ, your Son and our Lord, who lives and reigns with you and the Holy Spirit, one God, now and forever.

Monday, June 9, 2014

Time after Pentecost

Columba, died 597; Aidan, died 651; Bede, died 735; renewers of the church

Psalm 104:24-34, 35b
Renewing the face of the earth

O LORD, how manifold are your works!
  In wisdom you have made them all;
  the earth is full of your creatures. . . .

These all look to you
  to give them their food in due season;
when you give to them, they gather it up;
  when you open your hand, they are filled with good things.
When you hide your face, they are dismayed;
  when you take away their breath, they die
  and return to their dust.
When you send forth your spirit, they are created;
  and you renew the face of the ground. (Ps. 104:24, 27-30)

Additional Readings
Joel 2:18-29
The promised spirit of God

Romans 8:18-24
We have the first fruits of the Spirit

Hymn: All Creatures, Worship God Most High! ELW 835

O God, author of heaven and earth, you sustain us with a dazzling abundance of good things. Renew us with your saving breath and remind us that we begin each day as your new creation.

Tuesday, June 10, 2014

Time after Pentecost

Romans 8:26-27
Praying in the Spirit

Likewise the Spirit helps us in our weakness; for we do not know how to pray as we ought, but that very Spirit intercedes with sighs too deep for words. And God, who searches the heart, knows what is the mind of the Spirit, because the Spirit intercedes for the saints according to the will of God. (Rom. 8:26-27)

Psalm
Psalm 104:24-34, 35b
Renewing the face of the earth

Additional Reading
Ezekiel 39:7-8, 21-29
The promised spirit of God

Hymn: Healer of Our Every Ill, ELW 612

God of grace, cultivate in our hearts the awareness of your constant presence and the desire for a closer relationship with you. Help us learn to approach you freely and without fear through your Spirit.

Wednesday, June 11, 2014

Barnabas, Apostle

Acts 11:19-30; 13:1-3
Barnabas and Saul are set apart

Now in the church at Antioch there were prophets and teachers: Barnabas, Simeon who was called Niger, Lucius of Cyrene, Manaen a member of the court of Herod the ruler, and Saul. While they were worshiping the Lord and fasting, the Holy Spirit said, "Set apart for me Barnabas and Saul for the work to which I have called them." Then after fasting and praying they laid their hands on them and sent them off. (Acts 13:1-3)

Psalm
Psalm 112
Happy are the God-fearing

Additional Readings
Isaiah 42:5-12
The Lord calls us in righteousness

Matthew 10:7-16
Jesus sends out the Twelve

Hymn: Spread, Oh, Spread, Almighty Word, ELW 663

We praise you, O God, for the life of your faithful servant Barnabas, who, seeking not his own renown but the well-being of your church, gave generously of his life and possessions for the relief of the poor and the spread of the gospel. Grant that we may follow his example and by our actions give glory to you, Father, Son, and Holy Spirit, now and forever.

Thursday, June 12, 2014

Time after Pentecost

Psalm 8
How exalted is your name

O LORD, our Sovereign,
    how majestic is your name in all the earth!

You have set your glory above the heavens.
    Out of the mouths of babes and infants
you have founded a bulwark because of your foes,
    to silence the enemy and the avenger.

When I look at your heavens, the work of your fingers,
    the moon and the stars that you have established;
what are human beings that you are mindful of them,
    mortals that you care for them?

Yet you have made them a little lower than God,
    and crowned them with glory and honor. (Ps. 8:1-5)

Additional Readings
Job 38:1-11
Creation story from Job

2 Timothy 1:8-12a
Grace revealed in Christ

Hymn: Many and Great, O God, ELW 837

God of majesty, help us to be good stewards of your marvelous creation. Restrain our impulses to use the things of this earth for our own gain, and help us to see that in caring for them we worship you.

Friday, June 13, 2014

Time after Pentecost

2 Timothy 1:12b-14
The treasure of the triune God

I am not ashamed, for I know the one in whom I have put my trust, and I am sure that he is able to guard until that day what I have entrusted to him. Hold to the standard of sound teaching that you have heard from me, in the faith and love that are in Christ Jesus. Guard the good treasure entrusted to you, with the help of the Holy Spirit living in us. (2 Tim. 1:12b-14)

Psalm
Psalm 8
How exalted is your name

Additional Reading
Job 38:12-21
Creation story from Job

Hymn: Praise the Almighty! ELW 877

God of glory, thank you for leading us in your way, imperfect as we are. Help us to be prophetic signs of your love and mercy to the world as we live out our holy calling in faith and trust in you.

Saturday, June 14, 2014

Time after Pentecost

Basil the Great, Bishop of Caesarea, died 379;
Gregory, Bishop of Nyssa, died around 385;
Gregory of Nazianzus, Bishop of Constantinople, died around 389;
Macrina, teacher, died around 379

John 14:15-17
Father, Son, Spirit

"If you love me, you will keep my commandments. And I will ask the Father, and he will give you another Advocate, to be with you forever. This is the Spirit of truth, whom the world cannot receive, because it neither sees him nor knows him. You know him, because he abides with you, and he will be in you." (John 14:15-17)

Psalm
Psalm 8
How exalted is your name

Additional Reading
Job 38:22-38
Creation story from Job

Hymn: Father Most Holy, ELW 415

God of mercy, though we love you, we also disobey in many ways. Perfect our hearts so that we may love our brothers and sisters as we love you. Remind us that in acts of love we are joined with you.

SUMMER

The weeks and months following the Day of Pentecost coincide with the natural seasons of summer, autumn, and late autumn/November. Christian communities refer to this time in different ways. Whatever time is used to describe the many weeks between Pentecost and Christ the King (the last Sunday of the year), the seasons and calendars of North America offer some distinctive periods by which we may shape prayer in the household.

The Day of Pentecost is celebrated close to the end of the school year. A connection exists between graduations/new beginnings and our prayer for the Spirit's guidance in new endeavors. For many people, the months of June, July, and August signal a slightly altered schedule attuned to the weather, harvests, and vacations. Summer months offer their unique grace to those who spend time in discerning the many images that link the scriptures and the patient growth of the seed in the soil.

Table Prayer for Summer

O God of wonder,
the whole earth is full of your glory.
We give you thanks for the gifts of summer
and the blessings of this meal.
Teach us to share what we have received,
for you are the giver of all good things.
We ask this through Christ our Lord. Amen.

Blessing for Father's Day (June 15)

As a loving father cares for his children,
so you, O God, have compassion for us.
Look with favor on all those men
who guide and protect their children.
Hold them in your good care
and strengthen them for the holy task
that you have entrusted to them,
that all your children may flourish
in an atmosphere of wise love. Amen.

Sunday, June 15, 2014

The Holy Trinity

Matthew 28:16-20

Living in the community of the Trinity

Now the eleven disciples went to Galilee, to the mountain to which Jesus had directed them. When they saw him, they worshiped him; but some doubted. And Jesus came and said to them, "All authority in heaven and on earth has been given to me. Go therefore and make disciples of all nations, baptizing them in the name of the Father and of the Son and of the Holy Spirit, and teaching them to obey everything that I have commanded you. And remember, I am with you always, to the end of the age." (Matt. 28:16-20)

Psalm

Psalm 8

How exalted is your name

Additional Readings

Genesis 1:1—2:4a

Creation of the heavens and the earth

2 Corinthians 13:11-13

Paul's farewell

Hymn: Come, Join the Dance of Trinity, ELW 412

Almighty Creator and ever-living God: we worship your glory, eternal Three-in-One, and we praise your power, majestic One-in-Three. Keep us steadfast in this faith, defend us in all adversity, and bring us at last into your presence, where you live in endless joy and love, Father, Son, and Holy Spirit, one God, now and forever.

Monday, June 16, 2014

Time after Pentecost

Psalm 29
Praise the glory of God

Ascribe to the LORD, O heavenly beings,
    ascribe to the LORD glory and strength.
Ascribe to the LORD the glory of his name;
    worship the LORD in holy splendor. . . .

The LORD sits enthroned over the flood;
    the LORD sits enthroned as king forever.
May the LORD give strength to his people!
    May the LORD bless his people with peace! (Ps. 29:1-2, 10-11)

Additional Readings
Job 38:39—39:12
Creation story from Job

I Corinthians 12:1-3
Faith is a gift of the Spirit

Hymn: Oh, That I Had a Thousand Voices, ELW 833

God of the dawn, awaken us to the splendor of your marvelous creation all around us. Help us to hear it as a mighty hymn that proclaims your glory from age to age.

Tuesday, June 17, 2014

Time after Pentecost

1 Corinthians 12:4-13
The Spirit in the community

Now there are varieties of gifts, but the same Spirit; and there are varieties of services, but the same Lord; and there are varieties of activities, but it is the same God who activates all of them in everyone. To each is given the manifestation of the Spirit for the common good. (1 Cor. 12:4-7)

Psalm
Psalm 29
Praise the glory of God

Additional Reading
Job 39:13-25
Creation story from Job

Hymn: O Living Breath of God, ELW 407

Loving God, teach us to recognize the unique abilities of service that your Spirit has entrusted to us. Teach us to refrain from envy of others so that we may treasure our special gifts just as you do.

Wednesday, June 18, 2014

Time after Pentecost

John 14:25-26

Father, Son, Spirit

"I have said these things to you while I am still with you. But the Advocate, the Holy Spirit, whom the Father will send in my name, will teach you everything, and remind you of all that I have said to you." (John 14:25-26)

Psalm

Psalm 29

Praise the glory of God

Additional Reading

Job 39:26—40:5

Creation story from Job; Job's response

Hymn: Come, Gracious Spirit, Heavenly Dove, ELW 404

God of wisdom, show us how to embrace the winds of your Holy Spirit that blow through our lives. Give us the discipline to love and recall your holy scriptures so that we may always cling to your word.

Thursday, June 19, 2014

Time after Pentecost

Psalm 69:7-10 [11-15] 16-18
Draw near to me

Answer me, O LORD, for your steadfast love is good;
    according to your abundant mercy, turn to me.
Do not hide your face from your servant,
    for I am in distress—make haste to answer me.
Draw near to me, redeem me,
    set me free because of my enemies. (Ps. 69:16-18)

Additional Readings

Jeremiah 18:12-17
Israel's stubborn idolatry

Hebrews 2:5-9
Exaltation through abasement

Hymn: What Wondrous Love Is This, ELW 666

God of mercy, we often find that in being faithful to you, evil is mobilized against us. In those hard times let us never lose sight of you, and remind us of your steadfast love which never fails.

Friday, June 20, 2014

Time after Pentecost

Jeremiah 18:18-23

A plot against Jeremiah

Give heed to me, O Lord,
  and listen to what my adversaries say!
Is evil a recompense for good?
  Yet they have dug a pit for my life.
Remember how I stood before you to speak good for them,
  to turn away your wrath from them.
Therefore give their children over to famine;
  hurl them out to the power of the sword,
let their wives become childless and widowed.
  May their men meet death by pestilence,
  their youths be slain by the sword in battle.
May a cry be heard from their houses,
  when you bring the marauder suddenly upon them!
For they have dug a pit to catch me,
  and laid snares for my feet.
Yet you, O Lord, know all their plotting to kill me.
Do not forgive their iniquity,
  do not blot out their sin from your sight.
Let them be tripped up before you;
  deal with them while you are angry. (Jer. 18:19-23)

Psalm
Psalm 69:7-10 [11-15] 16-18
Draw near to me

Additional Reading
Acts 5:17-26
The apostles are persecuted

Hymn: Forgive Our Sins As We Forgive, ELW 605

Gracious God, give us grace-filled hearts in the face of our adversaries. Help us to seek mercy for them, instead of revenge, just as you are merciful to us. Lead us into the light of your boundless compassion.

Saturday, June 21, 2014

Time after Pentecost

Onesimos Nesib, translator, evangelist, died 1931

Luke 11:53—12:3
What is secret will become known

When [Jesus] went outside, the scribes and the Pharisees began to be very hostile toward him and to cross-examine him about many things, lying in wait for him, to catch him in something he might say.

Meanwhile, when the crowd gathered by the thousands, so that they trampled on one another, he began to speak first to his disciples, "Beware of the yeast of the Pharisees, that is, their hypocrisy. Nothing is covered up that will not be uncovered, and nothing secret that will not become known. Therefore whatever you have said in the dark will be heard in the light, and what you have whispered behind closed doors will be proclaimed from the housetops. (Luke 11:53—12:3)

Psalm	Additional Reading
Psalm 69:7-10 [11-15] 16-18	Jeremiah 20:1-6
Draw near to me	*Jeremiah persecuted by Pashhur*

Hymn: Christ, Be Our Light, ELW 715

God of truth, we know that when we say one thing yet do another, the evil effect multiplies in ways we cannot fathom. Keep us faithful to you and steadfast in all seasons of life.

Sunday, June 22, 2014

Time after Pentecost

Matthew 10:24-39

The cost of discipleship

[Jesus said,] "Whoever loves father or mother more than me is not worthy of me; and whoever loves son or daughter more than me is not worthy of me; and whoever does not take up the cross and follow me is not worthy of me. Those who find their life will lose it, and those who lose their life for my sake will find it." (Matt. 10:37-39)

Psalm

Psalm 69:7-10 [11-15]
16-18
Draw near to me

Additional Readings

Jeremiah 20:7-13
The prophet must speak

Romans 6:1b-11
Buried and raised with Christ in baptism

Hymn: Take Up Your Cross, the Savior Said, ELW 667

Teach us, good Lord God, to serve you as you deserve, to give and not to count the cost, to fight and not to heed the wounds, to toil and not to seek for rest, to labor and not to ask for reward, except that of knowing that we do your will, through Jesus Christ, our Savior and Lord.

Monday, June 23, 2014

Time after Pentecost

Psalm 6
Prayer for deliverance

O Lord, do not rebuke me in your anger,
  or discipline me in your wrath.
Be gracious to me, O Lord, for I am languishing;
  O Lord, heal me, for my bones are shaking with terror.
My soul also is struck with terror,
  while you, O Lord—how long?

Turn, O Lord, save my life;
  deliver me for the sake of your steadfast love.
For in death there is no remembrance of you;
  in Sheol who can give you praise? (Ps. 6:1-5)

Additional Readings

Micah 7:1-7
The corruption of the people

Revelation 2:1-7
Remember from what you have fallen

Hymn: O God, Our Help in Ages Past, ELW 632

Merciful God, come to us in the midst of our affliction with signs of your gracious love. When we find ourselves on the brink of desperation, remind us that you are always there to catch us if we begin to fall.

Tuesday, June 24, 2014

John the Baptist

Luke 1:57-67 [68-80]
The birth and naming of John

On the eighth day [Elizabeth and her neighbors and relatives] came to circumcise the child, and they were going to name him Zechariah after his father. But his mother said, "No; he is to be called John." They said to her, "None of your relatives has this name." Then they began motioning to his father to find out what name he wanted to give him. He asked for a writing tablet and wrote, "His name is John." And all of them were amazed. Immediately his mouth was opened and his tongue freed, and he began to speak, praising God. (Luke 1:59-64)

Psalm
Psalm 141
My eyes are turned to God

Additional Readings
Malachi 3:1-4
My messenger, a refiner and purifier

Acts 13:13-26
The gospel for the descendents of Abraham

Hymn: Blessed Be the God of Israel, ELW 250

Almighty God, by your gracious providence your servant John the Baptist was born to Elizabeth and Zechariah. Grant to your people the wisdom to see your purpose and the openness to hear your will, that the light of Christ may increase in us, through Jesus Christ, our Savior and Lord, who lives and reigns with you and the Holy Spirit, one God, now and forever.

Wednesday, June 25, 2014

Time after Pentecost

Presentation of the Augsburg Confession, 1530
Philipp Melanchthon, renewer of the church, died 1560

Matthew 10:5-23
Jesus speaks about persecution

"See, I am sending you out like sheep into the midst of wolves; so be wise as serpents and innocent as doves. Beware of them, for they will hand you over to councils and flog you in their synagogues; and you will be dragged before governors and kings because of me, as a testimony to them and the Gentiles. When they hand you over, do not worry about how you are to speak or what you are to say; for what you are to say will be given to you at that time; for it is not you who speak, but the Spirit of your Father speaking through you." (Matt. 10:16-20)

Psalm
Psalm 6
Prayer for deliverance

Additional Reading
Jeremiah 38:1-13
Jeremiah imprisoned and released

Hymn: O God, My Faithful God, ELW 806

Lord Jesus, the path of discipleship is fraught with danger. Keep our minds clear and our hearts pure so that we may be worthy instruments of the Holy Spirit. Give us the power of endurance in your name.

Thursday, June 26, 2014

Time after Pentecost

Psalm 89:1-4, 15-18
I sing of your love

I will sing of your steadfast love, O LORD, forever;
    with my mouth I will proclaim your faithfulness to all generations.
I declare that your steadfast love is established forever;
    your faithfulness is as firm as the heavens.
You said, "I have made a covenant with my chosen one,
    I have sworn to my servant David:
'I will establish your descendants forever,
    and build your throne for all generations.'" (Ps. 89:1-4)

Additional Readings
Jeremiah 25:1-7
Israel provokes God's anger

Galatians 5:2-6
The nature of Christian freedom

Hymn: Golden Breaks the Dawn, ELW 852

God of glory, you have carried us through adversity into the light of your love. Give us hands to praise you and hearts to worship you so that we may sing of your salvation in all that we do.

Friday, June 27, 2014

Time after Pentecost

Cyril, Bishop of Alexandria, died 444

Galatians 5:7-12
Beware of false teachers

You were running well; who prevented you from obeying the truth? Such persuasion does not come from the one who calls you. A little yeast leavens the whole batch of dough. I am confident about you in the Lord that you will not think otherwise. But whoever it is that is confusing you will pay the penalty. But my friends, why am I still being persecuted if I am still preaching circumcision? In that case the offense of the cross has been removed. I wish those who unsettle you would castrate themselves! (Gal. 5:7-12)

Psalm
Psalm 89:1-4, 15-18
I sing of your love

Additional Reading
Jeremiah 25:8-14
Captivity of Israel foretold

Hymn: Strengthen for Service, Lord, ELW 497

Triune God, it is so easy for us to give in to temptations that take us away from you. Keep us focused on you alone so that we may resist confusion and distraction and remain grounded in your word.

Saturday, June 28, 2014

Time after Pentecost

Irenaeus, Bishop of Lyons, died around 202

Jeremiah 28:1-4
Hananiah prophesies falsely

In that same year, at the beginning of the reign of King Zedekiah of Judah, in the fifth month of the fourth year, the prophet Hananiah son of Azzur, from Gibeon, spoke to me in the house of the LORD, in the presence of the priests and all the people, saying, "Thus says the LORD of hosts, the God of Israel: I have broken the yoke of the king of Babylon. Within two years I will bring back to this place all the vessels of the LORD's house, which King Nebuchadnezzar of Babylon took away from this place and carried to Babylon. I will also bring back to this place King Jeconiah son of Jehoiakim of Judah, and all the exiles from Judah who went to Babylon, says the LORD, for I will break the yoke of the king of Babylon." (Jer. 28:1-4)

Psalm
Psalm 89:1-4, 15-18
I sing of your love

Additional Reading
Luke 17:1-4
Causing little ones to stumble

Hymn: God of Grace and God of Glory, ELW 705

God of our ancestors, help us to discern the falsehoods spoken by self-appointed prophets who neither hear nor heed you, and give us the courage to stand up to them. Make us standard-bearers of your truth.

Sunday, June 29, 2014

Time after Pentecost

Peter and Paul, Apostles (transferred to June 30)

Matthew 10:40-42

Welcome Christ in those Christ sends

"Whoever welcomes you welcomes me, and whoever welcomes me welcomes the one who sent me. Whoever welcomes a prophet in the name of a prophet will receive a prophet's reward; and whoever welcomes a righteous person in the name of a righteous person will receive the reward of the righteous; and whoever gives even a cup of cold water to one of these little ones in the name of a disciple—truly I tell you, none of these will lose their reward." (Matt. 10:40-42)

Psalm

Psalm 89:1-4, 15-18

I sing of your love

Additional Readings

Jeremiah 28:5-9

Test of a true prophet

Romans 6:12-23

No longer under law but under grace

Hymn: O Christ, Your Heart, Compassionate, ELW 722

O God, you direct our lives by your grace, and your words of justice and mercy reshape the world. Mold us into a people who welcome your word and serve one another, through Jesus Christ, our Savior and Lord.

Monday, June 30, 2014

Peter and Paul, Apostles (*transferred*)

John 21:15-19
Jesus says to Peter: Tend my sheep

When they had finished breakfast, Jesus said to Simon Peter, "Simon son of John, do you love me more than these?" He said to him, "Yes, Lord; you know that I love you." Jesus said to him, "Feed my lambs." A second time he said to him, "Simon son of John, do you love me?" He said to him, "Yes, Lord; you know that I love you." Jesus said to him, "Tend my sheep." He said to him the third time, "Simon son of John, do you love me?" Peter felt hurt because he said to him the third time, "Do you love me?" And he said to him, "Lord, you know everything; you know that I love you." Jesus said to him, "Feed my sheep. Very truly, I tell you, when you were younger, you used to fasten your own belt and to go wherever you wished. But when you grow old, you will stretch out your hands, and someone else will fasten a belt around you and take you where you do not wish to go." (He said this to indicate the kind of death by which he would glorify God.) After this he said to him, "Follow me." (John 21:15-19)

Psalm	Additional Readings	
Psalm 87:1-3, 5-7	Acts 12:1-11	2 Timothy 4:6-8,
Glorious things are spoken of you	*Peter released from prison*	17-18
		The good fight of faith

Hymn: Lord, You Give the Great Commission, ELW 579

Almighty God, we praise you that your blessed apostles Peter and Paul glorified you by their martyrdoms. Grant that your church throughout the world may always be instructed by their teaching and example, be knit together in unity by your Spirit, and ever stand firm upon the one foundation who is Jesus Christ our Lord, for he lives and reigns with you and the Holy Spirit, one God, now and forever.

PRAYER LIST FOR JULY

_____

_____

_____

_____

_____

_____

_____

_____

_____

_____

Tuesday, July 1, 2014

Time after Pentecost

Catherine Winkworth, died 1878; John Mason Neale, died 1866; hymn translators

1 John 4:1-6
Testing the spirits

Beloved, do not believe every spirit, but test the spirits to see whether they are from God; for many false prophets have gone out into the world. By this you know the Spirit of God: every spirit that confesses that Jesus Christ has come in the flesh is from God, and every spirit that does not confess Jesus is not from God. And this is the spirit of the antichrist, of which you have heard that it is coming; and now it is already in the world. (1 John 4:1-3)

Psalm
Psalm 119:161-168
Loving God's law

Additional Reading
1 Kings 21:17-29
Elijah confronts Ahab

Hymn: Let Us Ever Walk with Jesus, ELW 802

God of truth, too many dubious persuasions confront us, couched in convincing images and clever spin. How shall we test the spirits in our world of twisted words, endlessly repeated? Steady us in Christ Jesus, coming from you, your way, your life.

Wednesday, July 2, 2014

Time after Pentecost

Matthew 11:20-24

Jesus prophesies against the cities

Then he began to reproach the cities in which most of his deeds of power had been done, because they did not repent. "Woe to you, Chorazin! Woe to you, Bethsaida! For if the deeds of power done in you had been done in Tyre and Sidon, they would have repented long ago in sackcloth and ashes. But I tell you, on the day of judgment it will be more tolerable for Tyre and Sidon than for you. And you, Capernaum,

will you be exalted to heaven?

No, you will be brought down to Hades.

For if the deeds of power done in you had been done in Sodom, it would have remained until this day. But I tell you that on the day of judgment it will be more tolerable for the land of Sodom than for you." (Matt. 11:20-24)

Psalm

Psalm 119:161-168

Loving God's law

Additional Reading

Jeremiah 18:1-11

Jeremiah at the potter's wheel

Hymn: Mine Eyes Have Seen the Glory, ELW 890

Sackcloth is not in style, God. Repentance is considered weak or mocked as insecure. We desire our own deeds of power. Reproach us until our illusions fall away and we turn toward your grace in Jesus Christ.

Thursday, July 3, 2014

Thomas, Apostle

John 14:1-7

Jesus, the way, the truth, the life

Thomas said to [Jesus], "Lord, we do not know where you are going. How can we know the way?" Jesus said to him, "I am the way, and the truth, and the life. No one comes to the Father except through me. If you know me, you will know my Father also. From now on you do know him and have seen him." (John 14:5-7)

Psalm

Psalm 136:1-4, 23-26
God's mercy endures forever

Additional Readings

Judges 6:36-40
God affirms Gideon's calling

Ephesians 4:11-16
The body of Christ has various gifts

Hymn: Come, My Way, My Truth, My Life, ELW 816

Ever-living God, you strengthened your apostle Thomas with firm and certain faith in the resurrection of your Son. Grant that we too may confess our faith in Jesus Christ, our Lord and our God, who lives and reigns with you and the Holy Spirit, one God, now and forever.

Friday, July 4, 2014

Time after Pentecost

Psalm 145:8-14
God is full of compassion

The LORD is gracious and merciful,
    slow to anger and abounding in steadfast love.
The LORD is good to all,
    and his compassion is over all that he has made.

All your works shall give thanks to you, O LORD,
    and all your faithful shall bless you.
They shall speak of the glory of your kingdom,
    and tell of your power,
to make known to all people your mighty deeds,
    and the glorious splendor of your kingdom. (Ps. 145:8-12)

Additional Readings
Zechariah 2:6-13
Exiles are the apple of God's eye

Romans 7:7-20
Sin and the law kill us

Hymn: Let Streams of Living Justice, ELW 710

Dios, Gott, Baba, Allah, God—however we speak your name—you are the all-compassionate one, slow to anger and abounding in steadfast love. Remake us in Christ, so our lives proclaim your gracious realm and all peoples bless you.

Saturday, July 5, 2014

Time after Pentecost

Luke 10:21-24
Jesus rejoices in the Holy Spirit

At that same hour Jesus rejoiced in the Holy Spirit and said, "I thank you, Father, Lord of heaven and earth, because you have hidden these things from the wise and the intelligent and have revealed them to infants; yes, Father, for such was your gracious will. All things have been handed over to me by my Father; and no one knows who the Son is except the Father, or who the Father is except the Son and anyone to whom the Son chooses to reveal him."

Then turning to the disciples, Jesus said to them privately, "Blessed are the eyes that see what you see! For I tell you that many prophets and kings desired to see what you see, but did not see it, and to hear what you hear, but did not hear it." (Luke 10:21-24)

Psalm
Psalm 145:8-14
God is full of compassion

Additional Reading
Zechariah 4:1-7
By my Spirit, says God

Hymn: O God of Mercy, God of Light, ELW 714

Too much remains hidden and mysterious, God. Send your Spirit: opening our eyes to see the wonders of grace and our ears to hear your word of love so we rejoice with your beloved, Jesus Christ.

Sunday, July 6, 2014

Time after Pentecost

Jan Hus, martyr, died 1415

Matthew 11:16-19, 25-30

The yoke of discipleship

"Come to me, all you that are weary and are carrying heavy burdens, and I will give you rest. Take my yoke upon you, and learn from me; for I am gentle and humble in heart, and you will find rest for your souls. For my yoke is easy, and my burden is light." (Matt. 11:28-30)

Psalm

Psalm 145:8-14

God is full of compassion

Additional Readings

Zechariah 9:9-12

The king comes in peace

Romans 7:15-25a

The struggle within the self

Hymn: Softly and Tenderly Jesus Is Calling, ELW 608

You are great, O God, and greatly to be praised. You have made us for yourself, and our hearts are restless until they rest in you. Grant that we may believe in you, call upon you, know you, and serve you, through your Son, Jesus Christ, our Savior and Lord.

Monday, July 7, 2014

Time after Pentecost

Psalm 131
I rest like a weaned child on God

O LORD, my heart is not lifted up,
 my eyes are not raised too high;
I do not occupy myself with things
 too great and too marvelous for me.
But I have calmed and quieted my soul,
 like a weaned child with its mother;
 my soul is like the weaned child that is with me.

O Israel, hope in the LORD
 from this time on and forevermore. (Ps. 131:1-3)

Additional Readings
Jeremiah 27:1-11, 16-22
Jeremiah wears the evil yoke

Romans 1:18-25
The guilt of humankind

Hymn: Come Down, O Love Divine, ELW 804

No longer suckling at your breast, God, but needing your arms around us to quiet our fears, we relax in your care, finding a peace that passes understanding, a hope that sustains us through every trouble, through Jesus Christ.

Tuesday, July 8, 2014

Time after Pentecost

Jeremiah 28:10-17

Hananiah breaks Jeremiah's yoke

Then the prophet Hananiah took the yoke from the neck of the prophet Jeremiah, and broke it. And Hananiah spoke in the presence of all the people, saying, "Thus says the LORD: This is how I will break the yoke of King Nebuchadnezzar of Babylon from the neck of all the nations within two years." At this, the prophet Jeremiah went his way.

Sometime after the prophet Hananiah had broken the yoke from the neck of the prophet Jeremiah, the word of the LORD came to Jeremiah: Go, tell Hananiah, Thus says the LORD: You have broken wooden bars only to forge iron bars in place of them! For thus says the LORD of hosts, the God of Israel: I have put an iron yoke on the neck of all these nations so that they may serve King Nebuchadnezzar of Babylon, and they shall indeed serve him; I have even given him the wild animals. (Jer. 28:10-14)

Psalm	Additional Reading
Psalm 131	Romans 3:1-8
I rest like a weaned child on God	*The faithfulness of God*

Hymn: O God of Every Nation, ELW 713

The slavery continues, God. Wood, iron, confiscated passports, people traffickers, withheld wages, the constant need to make oneself invisible: the yoke of exile is hard. Release your people. Free the oppressed according to the promise of your beloved, Jesus Christ.

Wednesday, July 9, 2014

Time after Pentecost

Jeremiah 13:1-11
Jeremiah's loincloth

Then the word of the LORD came to me: Thus says the LORD: Just so I will ruin the pride of Judah and the great pride of Jerusalem. This evil people, who refuse to hear my words, who stubbornly follow their own will and have gone after other gods to serve them and worship them, shall be like this loincloth, which is good for nothing. For as the loincloth clings to one's loins, so I made the whole house of Israel and the whole house of Judah cling to me, says the LORD, in order that they might be for me a people, a name, a praise, and a glory. But they would not listen. (Jer. 13:8-11)

Psalm
Psalm 131
I rest like a weaned child on God

Additional Reading
John 13:1-17
Jesus washes the disciples' feet

Hymn: Abide with Me, ELW 629

Your word is as near to us as an intimate garment, O God, but too often we ignore it. Cling to us. Do not let us go until we are covered with and respond to your love through Christ Jesus.

Thursday, July 10, 2014

Time after Pentecost

Psalm 65:[1-8] 9-13
Your paths overflow with plenty

You visit the earth and water it,
    you greatly enrich it;
the river of God is full of water;
    you provide the people with grain,
    for so you have prepared it.
You water its furrows abundantly,
    settling its ridges,
softening it with showers,
    and blessing its growth.
You crown the year with your bounty;
    your wagon tracks overflow with richness.
The pastures of the wilderness overflow,
    the hills gird themselves with joy,
the meadows clothe themselves with flocks,
    the valleys deck themselves with grain,
    they shout and sing together for joy. (Ps. 65:9-13)

Additional Readings
Isaiah 48:1-5
What God declared long ago

Romans 2:12-16
God judges the secret thoughts

Hymn: This Is My Father's World, ELW 824

You offer abundant harvest and abundant life, O God. Crown our voices so we sing and shout together with the trees, rivers, and hills, rejoicing in your goodness through Jesus Christ.

Friday, July 11, 2014

Time after Pentecost

Benedict of Nursia, Abbot of Monte Cassino, died around 540

Romans 15:14-21
Sanctified by the Holy Spirit

I myself feel confident about you, my brothers and sisters, that you yourselves are full of goodness, filled with all knowledge, and able to instruct one another. Nevertheless on some points I have written to you rather boldly by way of reminder, because of the grace given me by God to be a minister of Christ Jesus to the Gentiles in the priestly service of the gospel of God, so that the offering of the Gentiles may be acceptable, sanctified by the Holy Spirit. In Christ Jesus, then, I have reason to boast of my work for God. (Rom. 15:14-17)

Psalm
Psalm 65:[1-8] 9-13
Your paths overflow with plenty

Additional Reading
Isaiah 48:6-11
You will hear new, hidden things

Hymn: The Son of God, Our Christ, ELW 584

Although we are full of goodness, filled with knowledge, and able to instruct one another, stretch us beyond what we know, God, so your love in Jesus Christ is shared with those whose values and culture are different from ours.

Saturday, July 12, 2014

Time after Pentecost

Nathan Söderblom, Bishop of Uppsala, died 1931

Isaiah 52:1-6
Sold, redeemed without money

For thus says the LORD: You were sold for nothing, and you shall be redeemed without money. For thus says the Lord GOD: Long ago, my people went down into Egypt to reside there as aliens; the Assyrian, too, has oppressed them without cause. Now therefore what am I doing here, says the LORD, seeing that my people are taken away without cause? Their rulers howl, says the LORD, and continually, all day long, my name is despised. Therefore my people shall know my name; therefore in that day they shall know that it is I who speak; here am I. (Isa. 52:3-6)

Psalm
Psalm 65:[1-8] 9-13
Your paths overflow with plenty

Additional Reading
John 12:44-50
I have come as light into the world

Hymn: When the Poor Ones, ELW 725

Really, God, without money? You save us without money, without price—no coupons, no credit cards, no bar codes necessary for your redeeming love? How odd to get something free that isn't a come-on. Thank you.

Sunday, July 13, 2014

Time after Pentecost

Matthew 13:1-9, 18-23

The parable of the sower and the seed

[Jesus] told them many things in parables, saying: "Listen! A sower went out to sow. And as he sowed, some seeds fell on the path, and the birds came and ate them up. Other seeds fell on rocky ground, where they did not have much soil, and they sprang up quickly, since they had no depth of soil. But when the sun rose, they were scorched; and since they had no root, they withered away. Other seeds fell among thorns, and the thorns grew up and choked them. Other seeds fell on good soil and brought forth grain, some a hundredfold, some sixty, some thirty. Let anyone with ears listen!" (Matt. 13:3-9)

Psalm

Psalm 65:[1-8] 9-13

Your paths overflow with plenty

Additional Readings

Isaiah 55:10-13

The growth of the word

Romans 8:1-11

Living according to the Spirit

Hymn: Lord, Let My Heart Be Good Soil, ELW 512

Almighty God, we thank you for planting in us the seed of your word. By your Holy Spirit help us to receive it with joy, live according to it, and grow in faith and hope and love, through Jesus Christ, our Savior and Lord.

Monday, July 14, 2014

Time after Pentecost

Psalm 92
The righteous as a tree

The righteous flourish like the palm tree,
　　and grow like a cedar in Lebanon.
They are planted in the house of the LORD;
　　they flourish in the courts of our God.
In old age they still produce fruit;
　　they are always green and full of sap,
showing that the LORD is upright;
　　he is my rock, and there is no unrighteousness in him. (Ps. 92:12-15)

Additional Readings
Leviticus 26:3-20   **1 Thessalonians 4:1-8**
A rich and a poor harvest   *A life pleasing to God*

Hymn: My Hope Is Built on Nothing Less, ELW 596/597

"Full of sap" describes the elders of our church, God. They flourish in your courts, cleaning, teaching, baking, fixing, praying, weeding, and singing. They show us what you are like: full of gentle care and upright love.

Tuesday, July 15, 2014

Time after Pentecost

Ephesians 4:17—5:2
The old life and the new

Let no evil talk come out of your mouths, but only what is useful
for building up, as there is need, so that your words may give grace
to those who hear. And do not grieve the Holy Spirit of God, with
which you were marked with a seal for the day of redemption. Put
away from you all bitterness and wrath and anger and wrangling
and slander, together with all malice, and be kind to one another,
tenderhearted, forgiving one another, as God in Christ has forgiven
you. (Eph. 4:29-32)

Psalm
Psalm 92
The righteous as a tree

Additional Reading
Deuteronomy 28:1-14
The blessings of obedience

Hymn: God, When Human Bonds Are Broken, ELW 603

*Tenderness is a forgotten value, God, and kindness gets lost in the
vitriol of winning at all costs. Train our voices away from malice and
bitterness toward words that build up the community, heal hurt, and
offer the grace of Jesus Christ.*

Wednesday, July 16, 2014

Time after Pentecost

Proverbs 11:23-30
The fruit of righteousness

Whoever diligently seeks good seeks favor,
    but evil comes to the one who searches for it.
Those who trust in their riches will wither,
    but the righteous will flourish like green leaves.
Those who trouble their households will inherit wind,
    and the fool will be servant to the wise.
The fruit of the righteous is a tree of life,
    but violence takes lives away. (Prov. 11:27-30)

Psalm
Psalm 92
The righteous as a tree

Additional Reading
Matthew 13:10-17
The purpose of parable

Hymn: Be Thou My Vision, ELW 793

Gracious God, you offer us a tree of life, green leaves, and favor. How did we become a society of guns and violence, troubled households, a sick search for wealth? Turn us to a righteousness that does not inherit the wind.

Thursday, July 17, 2014

Time after Pentecost

Bartolomé de Las Casas, missionary to the Indies, died 1566

Psalm 86:11-17
Teach me your ways

Teach me your way, O Lord,
> that I may walk in your truth;
> give me an undivided heart to revere your name.
I give thanks to you, O Lord my God, with my whole heart,
> and I will glorify your name forever.
For great is your steadfast love toward me;
> you have delivered my soul from the depths of Sheol. (Ps. 86:11-13)

Additional Readings
Isaiah 41:21-29
The futility of idols

Hebrews 2:1-9
Warning to pay attention

Hymn: O Master, Let Me Walk with You, ELW 818

Teach us your way, O Lord, that we may walk in your truth; give us undivided hearts: hearts centered on your word, your love, your deliverance; hearts overflowing with thanks for your beloved, Jesus Christ.

Friday, July 18, 2014

Time after Pentecost

Hebrews 6:13-20
The certainty of God's promises

When God made a promise to Abraham, because he had no one greater by whom to swear, he swore by himself, saying, "I will surely bless you and multiply you." And thus Abraham, having patiently endured, obtained the promise. (Heb. 6:13-15)

Psalm
Psalm 86:11-17
Teach me your ways

Additional Reading
Isaiah 44:9-17
Those who make idols are nothing

Hymn: The God of Abraham Praise, ELW 831

Patience, perseverance, and endurance evade our twitter minds, gasping for the constant update. How shall we obtain your promise, God, if we are constantly distracted? How shall we hear your words of blessing if our ears are plugged with noise?

Saturday, July 19, 2014

Time after Pentecost

Matthew 7:15-20
A tree and its fruit

"Beware of false prophets, who come to you in sheep's clothing but inwardly are ravenous wolves. You will know them by their fruits. Are grapes gathered from thorns, or figs from thistles? In the same way, every good tree bears good fruit, but the bad tree bears bad fruit. A good tree cannot bear bad fruit, nor can a bad tree bear good fruit. Every tree that does not bear good fruit is cut down and thrown into the fire. Thus you will know them by their fruits." (Matt. 7:15-20)

Psalm
Psalm 86:11-17
Teach me your ways

Additional Reading
Isaiah 44:18-20
Idols do not know or comprehend

Hymn: If God My Lord Be for Me, ELW 788

We prefer our false prophets dressed as wolves, Jesus: feisty, combative, entertaining with stinging one-liners. Their fruits are advertising revenue and book contracts. Wean our culture away from its love of thorns to discover the good fruits: compassion and truth.

Sunday, July 20, 2014

Time after Pentecost

Matthew 13:24-30, 36-43
The parable of the weeds

He put before them another parable: "The kingdom of heaven may be compared to someone who sowed good seed in his field; but while everybody was asleep, an enemy came and sowed weeds among the wheat, and then went away. So when the plants came up and bore grain, then the weeds appeared as well. And the slaves of the householder came and said to him, 'Master, did you not sow good seed in your field? Where, then, did these weeds come from?' He answered, 'An enemy has done this.' The slaves said to him, 'Then do you want us to go and gather them?' But he replied, 'No; for in gathering the weeds you would uproot the wheat along with them. Let both of them grow together until the harvest; and at harvest time I will tell the reapers, Collect the weeds first and bind them in bundles to be burned, but gather the wheat into my barn.'" (Matt. 13:24-30)

Psalm
Psalm 86:11-17
Teach me your ways

Additional Readings
Isaiah 44:6-8
There is no other God

Romans 8:12-25
The revealing of the children of God

Hymn: Come, Ye Thankful People, Come, ELW 693

Faithful God, most merciful judge, you care for your children with firmness and compassion. By your Spirit nurture us who live in your kingdom, that we may be rooted in the way of your Son, Jesus Christ, our Savior and Lord.

Monday, July 21, 2014

Time after Pentecost

Psalm 75
God's judgment

We give thanks to you, O God;
  we give thanks; your name is near.
People tell of your wondrous deeds.

At the set time that I appoint
  I will judge with equity.
When the earth totters, with all its inhabitants,
  it is I who keep its pillars steady. (Ps. 75:1-3)

Additional Readings
Nahum 1:1-13   Revelation 14:12-20
The wrath and mercy of God   *The harvest at the end of time*

Hymn: How Great Thou Art, ELW 856

*Your name is near, God, on our lips and in our hearts. When our lives
totter and inequity rules, keep us steady in your justice and courageous
in faith through your pillar of love, Jesus Christ.*

Tuesday, July 22, 2014

Mary Magdalene, Apostle

John 20:1-2, 11-18
Mary Magdalene meets Jesus in the garden

Jesus said to [Mary Magdalene], "Woman, why are you weeping? Whom are you looking for?" Supposing him to be the gardener, she said to him, "Sir, if you have carried him away, tell me where you have laid him, and I will take him away." Jesus said to her, "Mary!" She turned and said to him in Hebrew, "Rabbouni!" (which means Teacher). Jesus said to her, "Do not hold on to me, because I have not yet ascended to the Father. But go to my brothers and say to them, 'I am ascending to my Father and your Father, to my God and your God.'" Mary Magdalene went and announced to the disciples, "I have seen the Lord"; and she told them that he had said these things to her. (John 20:15-18)

Psalm
Psalm 73:23-28
I will speak of all God's works

Additional Readings
Ruth 1:6-18
Ruth stays with Naomi

Acts 13:26-33a
The raising of Jesus fulfills God's promise

Hymn: Signs and Wonders, ELW 672

Almighty God, your Son first entrusted the apostle Mary Magdalene with the joyful news of his resurrection. Following the example of her witness, may we proclaim Christ as our living Lord and one day see him in glory, for he lives and reigns with you and the Holy Spirit, one God, now and forever.

Wednesday, July 23, 2014

Time after Pentecost

Birgitta of Sweden, renewer of the church, died 1373

Daniel 12:1-13
The righteous will shine

"At that time Michael, the great prince, the protector of your people, shall arise. There shall be a time of anguish, such as has never occurred since nations first came into existence. But at that time your people shall be delivered, everyone who is found written in the book. Many of those who sleep in the dust of the earth shall awake, some to everlasting life, and some to shame and everlasting contempt. Those who are wise shall shine like the brightness of the sky, and those who lead many to righteousness, like the stars forever and ever. But you, Daniel, keep the words secret and the book sealed until the time of the end. Many shall be running back and forth, and evil shall increase." (Dan. 12:1-4)

Psalm
Psalm 75
God's judgment

Additional Reading
Matthew 12:15-21
God's chosen servant

Hymn: I'm So Glad Jesus Lifted Me, ELW 860

Morning Star, leading to life; Wisdom, shining brighter than the sky: write our names in your book, so we trust in your deliverance and remain steadfast even when others are running back and forth because of the increase of evil.

Thursday, July 24, 2014

Time after Pentecost

Psalm 119:129-136
Light and understanding

Your decrees are wonderful;
  therefore my soul keeps them.
The unfolding of your words gives light;
  it imparts understanding to the simple.
With open mouth I pant,
  because I long for your commandments.
Turn to me and be gracious to me,
  as is your custom toward those who love your name.
Keep my steps steady according to your promise,
  and never let iniquity have dominion over me. (Ps. 119:129-133)

Additional Readings

1 Kings 1:28-37
Solomon designated as king

1 Corinthians 4:14-20
Reign of God depends not on talk but power

Hymn: Let All Things Now Living, ELW 881

Word by word, as it unfolds before our eyes, we see your light, God. Word by word we begin to understand your love for us. Word by word you show us the right path by your living Word, Jesus Christ.

Friday, July 25, 2014

James, Apostle

Mark 10:35-45

Whoever wishes to be great must serve

James and John, the sons of Zebedee, came forward to [Jesus] and said to him, "Teacher, we want you to do for us whatever we ask of you." And he said to them, "What is it you want me to do for you?" And they said to him, "Grant us to sit, one at your right hand and one at your left, in your glory." But Jesus said to them, "You do not know what you are asking. Are you able to drink the cup that I drink, or be baptized with the baptism that I am baptized with?" They replied, "We are able." Then Jesus said to them, "The cup that I drink you will drink; and with the baptism with which I am baptized, you will be baptized; but to sit at my right hand or at my left is not mine to grant, but it is for those for whom it has been prepared." (Mark 10:35-40)

Psalm

Psalm 7:1-10
God, my shield and defense

Additional Readings

1 Kings 19:9-18
Elijah hears God in the midst of silence

Acts 11:27—12:3a
James is killed by Herod

Hymn: Will You Let Me Be Your Servant, ELW 659

Gracious God, we remember before you today your servant and apostle James, the first among the twelve to be martyred for the name of Jesus Christ. Pour out on the leaders of your church that spirit of self-denying service which is the true mark of authority among your people, through Jesus Christ our servant, who lives and reigns with you and the Holy Spirit, one God, now and forever.

Saturday, July 26, 2014

Time after Pentecost

1 Kings 2:1-4

David's instructions to Solomon

When David's time to die drew near, he charged his son Solomon, saying: "I am about to go the way of all the earth. Be strong, be courageous, and keep the charge of the LORD your God, walking in his ways and keeping his statutes, his commandments, his ordinances, and his testimonies, as it is written in the law of Moses, so that you may prosper in all that you do and wherever you turn. Then the LORD will establish his word that he spoke concerning me: 'If your heirs take heed to their way, to walk before me in faithfulness with all their heart and with all their soul, there shall not fail you a successor on the throne of Israel.'" (1 Kings 2:1-4)

Psalm
Psalm 119:129-136
Light and understanding

Additional Reading
Matthew 12:38-42
Something greater than Solomon is here

Hymn: Lord of All Nations, Grant Me Grace, ELW 716

God of all generations, how shall we ensure that the children of our community learn your will? How do we hand on to others the goodness we have experienced from you? Instruct us so we might do a better job than David.

Sunday, July 27, 2014

Time after Pentecost

Matthew 13:31-33, 44-52
Parables of the reign of heaven

[Jesus] told them another parable: "The kingdom of heaven is like yeast that a woman took and mixed in with three measures of flour until all of it was leavened." . . .

"The kingdom of heaven is like treasure hidden in a field, which someone found and hid; then in his joy he goes and sells all that he has and buys that field.

"Again, the kingdom of heaven is like a merchant in search of fine pearls; on finding one pearl of great value, he went and sold all that he had and bought it." (Matt. 13:33, 44-46)

Psalm
Psalm 119:129-136
Light and understanding

Additional Readings
1 Kings 3:5-12
Solomon's prayer for wisdom

Romans 8:26-39
Nothing can separate us from God's love

Hymn: You Are the Way, ELW 758

Beloved and sovereign God, through the death and resurrection of your Son you bring us into your kingdom of justice and mercy. By your Spirit, give us your wisdom, that we may treasure the life that comes from Jesus Christ, our Savior and Lord.

Monday, July 28, 2014

Time after Pentecost

Johann Sebastian Bach, died 1750; Heinrich Schütz,
died 1672; George Frederick Handel, died 1759; musicians

Psalm 119:121-128
Give me understanding

I am your servant; give me understanding,
 so that I may know your decrees.
It is time for the LORD to act,
 for your law has been broken.
Truly I love your commandments
 more than gold, more than fine gold.
Truly I direct my steps by all your precepts;
 I hate every false way. (Ps. 119:125-128)

Additional Readings
1 Kings 3:16-28   James 3:13-18
Solomon's wisdom in judgment   *Two kinds of wisdom*

Hymn: Come with Us, O Blessed Jesus, ELW 501

It is time for you to act, God. The hungry still search for food. The homeless remain exposed. Those looked down upon wait for hope. It is time for us to act, God. Direct our steps to follow Jesus Christ.

Tuesday, July 29, 2014

Time after Pentecost

Mary, Martha, and Lazarus of Bethany
Olaf, King of Norway, martyr, died 1030

1 Kings 4:29-34
God gave Solomon wisdom

God gave Solomon very great wisdom, discernment, and breadth of understanding as vast as the sand on the seashore, so that Solomon's wisdom surpassed the wisdom of all the people of the east, and all the wisdom of Egypt. He was wiser than anyone else, wiser than Ethan the Ezrahite, and Heman, Calcol, and Darda, children of Mahol; his fame spread throughout all the surrounding nations. He composed three thousand proverbs, and his songs numbered a thousand and five. He would speak of trees, from the cedar that is in the Lebanon to the hyssop that grows in the wall; he would speak of animals, and birds, and reptiles, and fish. People came from all the nations to hear the wisdom of Solomon; they came from all the kings of the earth who had heard of his wisdom. (1 Kings 4:29-34)

Psalm
Psalm 119:121-128
Give me understanding

Additional Reading
Ephesians 6:10-18
The allegory of the armor of God

Hymn: Lord Jesus, You Shall Be My Song, ELW 808

Speak to us of trees, God, that we might discern the needs of the earth. Speak to us of animals and birds, so we attain a breadth of understanding. Give us wisdom—your word—speaking to us in Christ Jesus.

Wednesday, July 30, 2014

Time after Pentecost

Proverbs 1:1-7, 20-33

The call of wisdom

Wisdom cries out in the street;
  in the squares she raises her voice.
At the busiest corner she cries out;
  at the entrance of the city gates she speaks:
"How long, O simple ones, will you love being simple?
How long will scoffers delight in their scoffing
  and fools hate knowledge?
Give heed to my reproof;
I will pour out my thoughts to you;
  I will make my words known to you." (Prov. 1:20-23)

Psalm
Psalm 119:121-128
Give me understanding

Additional Reading
Mark 4:30-34
Jesus' use of parables

Hymn: We Eat the Bread of Teaching, ELW 518

Ever-expanding Wisdom, how long will the simple love their falsehoods, the scoffers delight in spreading innuendo and lies, the fools prefer prejudice to proof? Pour out your thoughts until we know you and live by your light, through Jesus Christ.

Thursday, July 31, 2014

Time after Pentecost

Psalm 145:8-9, 14-21

You open wide your hand

The LORD upholds all who are falling,
   and raises up all who are bowed down.
The eyes of all look to you,
   and you give them their food in due season.
You open your hand,
   satisfying the desire of every living thing. (Ps. 145:14-16)

Additional Readings

Proverbs 10:1-5

The righteous will not go hungry

Philippians 4:10-15

Being well fed and yet hungry

Hymn: O Bread of Life from Heaven, ELW 480

Open-handed God, ready to catch the falling, giving courage to the bent over and bowed down, holding the fragile: release all the clenched fists so the stranger is welcomed and the hungry fed, through Jesus Christ.

_____

_____

_____

_____

_____

_____

_____

_____

_____

_____

_____

Friday, August 1, 2014

Time after Pentecost

Isaiah 51:17-23
Drink no more from the bowl of wrath

Therefore hear this, you who are wounded,
   who are drunk, but not with wine:
Thus says your Sovereign, the LORD,
   your God who pleads the cause of his people:
See, I have taken from your hand the cup of staggering;
you shall drink no more
   from the bowl of my wrath.
And I will put it into the hand of your tormentors,
   who have said to you,
   "Bow down, that we may walk on you";
and you have made your back like the ground
   and like the street for them to walk on. (Isa. 51:21-23)

Psalm
Psalm 145:8-9, 14-21
You open wide your hand

Additional Reading
Romans 9:6-13
True descendants of Abraham

Hymn: All Are Welcome, ELW 641

Sovereign God, as you take away from us the cup of your wrath, so take away from our hands the cup of wrath we offer to our enemies and those who seek to do us harm. Let us instead drink deeply of the intoxicating draught of your love.

Saturday, August 2, 2014

Time after Pentecost

Isaiah 44:1-5

God's blessing on Israel

But now hear, O Jacob my servant,
   Israel whom I have chosen!
Thus says the LORD who made you,
   who formed you in the womb and will help you:
Do not fear, O Jacob my servant,
   Jeshurun whom I have chosen.
For I will pour water on the thirsty land,
   and streams on the dry ground;
I will pour my spirit upon your descendants,
   and my blessing on your offspring.
They shall spring up like a green tamarisk,
   like willows by flowing streams.
This one will say, "I am the LORD's,"
   another will be called by the name of Jacob,
yet another will write on the hand, "The LORD's,"
   and adopt the name of Israel. (Isa. 44:1-5)

Psalm

Psalm 145:8-9, 14-21
You open wide your hand

Additional Reading

Matthew 7:7-11
Bread and stones

Hymn: Bread of Life, Our Host and Meal, ELW 464

Eternal God, so blessed are we by your life-giving, spirit-restoring, heart-fulfilling grace that we become like trees in the desert lining the small streams of water. We belong to you.

Sunday, August 3, 2014

Time after Pentecost

Matthew 14:13-21

Jesus feeds 5000

Then [Jesus] ordered the crowds to sit down on the grass. Taking the five loaves and the two fish, he looked up to heaven, and blessed and broke the loaves, and gave them to the disciples, and the disciples gave them to the crowds. And all ate and were filled; and they took up what was left over of the broken pieces, twelve baskets full. And those who ate were about five thousand men, besides women and children. (Matt. 14:19-21)

Psalm

Psalm 145:8-9, 14-21
You open wide your hand

Additional Readings

Isaiah 55:1-5
Eat and drink what truly satisfies

Romans 9:1-5
The glory of God's people in Israel

Hymn: We Come to the Hungry Feast, ELW 479

Glorious God, your generosity waters the world with goodness, and you cover creation with abundance. Awaken in us a hunger for the food that satisfies both body and spirit, and with this food fill all the starving world, through your Son, Jesus Christ, our Savior and Lord.

Monday, August 4, 2014

Time after Pentecost

Psalm 78:1-8, 17-29
God fed the people with manna

Yet he commanded the skies above,
    and opened the doors of heaven;
he rained down on them manna to eat,
    and gave them the grain of heaven.
Mortals ate of the bread of angels;
    he sent them food in abundance. (Ps. 78:23-25)

Additional Readings
Deuteronomy 8:1-10   Romans 1:8-15
God will feed the people   *A harvest among the Gentiles*

Hymn: Break Now the Bread of Life, ELW 515

Holy One of Israel, as once you fed us in the wilderness and kept us alive for the journey, so feed us now in the starving times of our doubt and fear, that we may keep on walking in the path of your love, the healing of your world.

Tuesday, August 5, 2014

Time after Pentecost

Acts 2:37-47

The believers breaking bread

Awe came upon everyone, because many wonders and signs were being done by the apostles. All who believed were together and had all things in common; they would sell their possessions and goods and distribute the proceeds to all, as any had need. Day by day, as they spent much time together in the temple, they broke bread at home and ate their food with glad and generous hearts, praising God and having the goodwill of all the people. And day by day the Lord added to their number those who were being saved. (Acts 2:43-47)

Psalm

Psalm 78:1-8, 17-29

God fed the people with manna

Additional Reading

Deuteronomy 26:1-15

A tithe from God's harvest

Hymn: Draw Us in the Spirit's Tether, ELW 470

Faithful Lord of love: teach us to love, as you love us without reservation; teach us to share, as you share each day the abundance of your creation; teach us to give to others, so that they and we ourselves will have the fullness of joy.

Wednesday, August 6, 2014

Time after Pentecost

Exodus 16:2-15, 31-35
God feeds the people manna

The whole congregation of the Israelites complained against Moses and Aaron in the wilderness. The Israelites said to them, "If only we had died by the hand of the LORD in the land of Egypt, when we sat by the fleshpots and ate our fill of bread; for you have brought us out into this wilderness to kill this whole assembly with hunger."
Then the LORD said to Moses, "I am going to rain bread from heaven for you, and each day the people shall go out and gather enough for that day. In that way I will test them, whether they will follow my instruction or not." (Exod. 16:2-4)

Psalm
Psalm 78:1-8, 17-29
God fed the people with manna

Additional Reading
Matthew 15:32-39
Jesus feeds 4000

Hymn: Glorious Things of You Are Spoken, ELW 647

Give us this day the bread that we need. Take from us the worry that fills us about tomorrow. Remove from us our fussiness, our greed, our avarice, our over-wanting, and help us feast with joy upon the quietness of your presence, forever and ever.

Thursday, August 7, 2014

Time after Pentecost

Psalm 85:8-13
I will listen to God

Let me hear what God the LORD will speak,
  for he will speak peace to his people,
  to his faithful, to those who turn to him in their hearts.
Surely his salvation is at hand for those who fear him,
  that his glory may dwell in our land.

Steadfast love and faithfulness will meet;
  righteousness and peace will kiss each other.
Faithfulness will spring up from the ground,
  and righteousness will look down from the sky.
The LORD will give what is good,
  and our land will yield its increase.
Righteousness will go before him,
  and will make a path for his steps. (Ps. 85:8-13)

Additional Readings
1 Kings 18:1-16
God promises relief from drought

Acts 17:10-15
The good news is shared

Hymn: Lord, Speak to Us, That We May Speak, ELW 676

God of all creation, we know that the first thing is to listen, before we even say "Our Father." Bring us into the listening space of your presence, the realm of your company, the pleasure of your friendship. And keep us there—safe and sound—until we have heard.

Friday, August 8, 2014

Time after Pentecost

Dominic, founder of the Order of Preachers (Dominicans), died 1221

Acts 18:24-28
A new disciple preaches

Now there came to Ephesus a Jew named Apollos, a native of Alexandria. He was an eloquent man, well-versed in the scriptures. He had been instructed in the Way of the Lord; and he spoke with burning enthusiasm and taught accurately the things concerning Jesus, though he knew only the baptism of John. He began to speak boldly in the synagogue; but when Priscilla and Aquila heard him, they took him aside and explained the Way of God to him more accurately. And when he wished to cross over to Achaia, the believers encouraged him and wrote to the disciples to welcome him. On his arrival he greatly helped those who through grace had become believers, for he powerfully refuted the Jews in public, showing by the scriptures that the Messiah is Jesus. (Acts 18:24-28)

Psalm
Psalm 85:8-13
I will listen to God

Additional Reading
1 Kings 18:17-19, 30-40
God's flooded altar burns

Hymn: In Christ Called to Baptize, ELW 575

Eternal God, in the waters of baptism we learned how much we are welcomed into the family of faith. Swimming in those waters each day, help us see our sisters and our brothers, tend to their needs, bind up their wounds, and embrace them in the arms of Jesus' love.

Saturday, August 9, 2014

Time after Pentecost

1 Kings 18:41-46

From drought to heavy rain

Elijah said to Ahab, "Go up, eat and drink; for there is a sound of rushing rain." So Ahab went up to eat and to drink. Elijah went up to the top of Carmel; there he bowed himself down upon the earth and put his face between his knees. He said to his servant, "Go up now, look toward the sea." He went up and looked, and said, "There is nothing." Then he said, "Go again seven times." At the seventh time he said, "Look, a little cloud no bigger than a person's hand is rising out of the sea." Then he said, "Go say to Ahab, 'Harness your chariot and go down before the rain stops you.'" In a little while the heavens grew black with clouds and wind; there was a heavy rain. Ahab rode off and went to Jezreel. But the hand of the Lord was on Elijah; he girded up his loins and ran in front of Ahab to the entrance of Jezreel. (1 Kings 18:41-46)

Psalm
Psalm 85:8-13
I will listen to God

Additional Reading
Matthew 16:1-4
The sign of Jonah

Hymn: Crashing Waters at Creation, ELW 455

God of hope, rain can come from the smallest of clouds. Cities can blossom from the smallest of visions. Life in all its wonder and majesty can grow from the tiniest flicker of faith. Keep alive the glimmer of hope in us.

Sunday, August 10, 2014

Time after Pentecost

Lawrence, deacon, martyr, died 258

Matthew 14:22-33

Jesus walking on the sea

Immediately [Jesus] made the disciples get into the boat and go on ahead to the other side, while he dismissed the crowds. And after he had dismissed the crowds, he went up the mountain by himself to pray. When evening came, he was there alone, but by this time the boat, battered by the waves, was far from the land, for the wind was against them. And early in the morning he came walking toward them on the sea. But when the disciples saw him walking on the sea, they were terrified, saying, "It is a ghost!" And they cried out in fear. But immediately Jesus spoke to them and said, "Take heart, it is I; do not be afraid." (Matt. 14:22-27)

Psalm
Psalm 85:8-13
I will listen to God

Additional Readings
1 Kings 19:9-18
Elijah on Mount Horeb

Romans 10:5-15
The word of faith

Hymn: Calm to the Waves, ELW 794

O God our defender, storms rage around and within us and cause us to be afraid. Rescue your people from despair, deliver your sons and daughters from fear, and preserve us in the faith of your Son, Jesus Christ, our Savior and Lord.

Monday, August 11, 2014

Time after Pentecost

Clare, Abbess of San Damiano, died 1253

Psalm 18:1-19
God saves from the waters

He reached down from on high, he took me;
   he drew me out of mighty waters.
He delivered me from my strong enemy,
   and from those who hated me;
   for they were too mighty for me.
They confronted me in the day of my calamity;
   but the LORD was my support.
He brought me out into a broad place;
   he delivered me, because he delighted in me. (Ps. 18:16-19)

Additional Readings
Genesis 7:11—8:5
God saves Noah from the flood

2 Peter 2:4-10
God judges and rescues

Hymn: Eternal Father, Strong to Save, ELW 756

Help me, O God, to find your hand that reaches out when I am barely floating on the sea of chaos. Open my eyes that I may see. Open my ears that I may hear. Open my heart that I may love.

Tuesday, August 12, 2014

Time after Pentecost

Genesis 19:1-29

God saves Lot

Abraham went early in the morning to the place where he had stood before the LORD; and he looked down toward Sodom and Gomorrah and toward all the land of the Plain and saw the smoke of the land going up like the smoke of a furnace.

So it was that, when God destroyed the cities of the Plain, God remembered Abraham, and sent Lot out of the midst of the overthrow, when he overthrew the cities in which Lot had settled. (Gen. 19:27-29)

Psalm

Psalm 18:1-19

God saves from the waters

Additional Reading

Romans 9:14-29

God's wrath, God's mercy

Hymn: In All Our Grief, ELW 615

God of love, we know that you are not a God of anger, wrath, and destruction, though many of your enemies would have us believe otherwise. Help us to understand more completely the depth of your patience, compassion, and salvation.

Wednesday, August 13, 2014

Time after Pentecost

Florence Nightingale, died 1910; Clara Maass, died 1901;
renewers of society

Matthew 8:23-27

Jesus stills the storm

And when he got into the boat, his disciples followed him. A windstorm arose on the sea, so great that the boat was being swamped by the waves; but he was asleep. And they went and woke him up, saying, "Lord, save us! We are perishing!" And he said to them, "Why are you afraid, you of little faith?" Then he got up and rebuked the winds and the sea; and there was a dead calm. They were amazed, saying, "What sort of man is this, that even the winds and the sea obey him?" (Matt. 8:23-27)

Psalm

Psalm 18:1-19

God saves from the waters

Additional Reading

Job 36:24-33; 37:14-24

The waters of God's creation

Hymn: Jesus, Savior, Pilot Me, ELW 755

Jesus, Lamb of God, have mercy on us. When storms threaten and whirlwinds erase everything that is safe, come to us, sit next to us, and hold us close.

Thursday, August 14, 2014

Time after Pentecost

Maximilian Kolbe, died 1941; Kaj Munk, died 1944; martyrs

Psalm 67
Let all the peoples praise God

May God be gracious to us and bless us
    and make his face to shine upon us,
that your way may be known upon earth,
    your saving power among all nations.
Let the peoples praise you, O God;
    let all the peoples praise you.

Let the nations be glad and sing for joy,
    for you judge the peoples with equity
    and guide the nations upon earth.
Let the peoples praise you, O God;
    let all the peoples praise you. (Ps. 67:1-5)

Additional Readings
Isaiah 45:20-25
All the ends of the earth shall be saved

Revelation 15:1-4
All nations will worship God

Hymn: Praise to the Lord, the Almighty, ELW 858

Eternal God, the nations singing and laughing together is one picture of the reign of your love. As we crown you Lord of the nations, help us to join hands, sing, and laugh.

Friday, August 15, 2014

Mary, Mother of Our Lord

Luke 1:46-55

Mary's thanksgiving

And Mary said,
"My soul magnifies the Lord,
   and my spirit rejoices in God my Savior,
for he has looked with favor on the lowliness of his servant.
   Surely, from now on all generations will call me blessed;
for the Mighty One has done great things for me,
   and holy is his name." (Luke 1:46-49)

Psalm

Psalm 34:1-9
O magnify the Lord with me

Additional Readings

Isaiah 61:7-11
*God will cause
righteousness to spring up*

Galatians 4:4-7
*We are no longer slaves,
but children*

Hymn: Canticle of the Turning, 723

Almighty God, in choosing the virgin Mary to be the mother of your Son, you made known your gracious regard for the poor, the lowly, and the despised. Grant us grace to receive your word in humility, and so to be made one with your Son, Jesus Christ our Savior and Lord, who lives and reigns with you and the Holy Spirit, one God, now and forever.

Saturday, August 16, 2014

Time after Pentecost

Isaiah 56:1-5

A covenant for all who obey

Thus says the LORD:
Maintain justice, and do what is right,
for soon my salvation will come,
   and my deliverance be revealed.

Happy is the mortal who does this,
   the one who holds it fast,
who keeps the sabbath, not profaning it,
   and refrains from doing any evil.

Do not let the foreigner joined to the LORD say,
   "The LORD will surely separate me from his people";
and do not let the eunuch say,
   "I am just a dry tree." (Isa. 56:1-3)

Psalm

Psalm 67

Let all the peoples praise God

Additional Reading

Matthew 14:34-36

Jesus heals the sick

Hymn: Let Justice Flow like Streams, ELW 717

Holy One, it is not often hard to know what is the right thing to do. What is hard is to have the courage to do it. Fill our hearts and souls with courage and daring, that your kingdom of peace and justice may quickly come.

Sunday, August 17, 2014

Time after Pentecost

Matthew 15:[10-20] 21-28

The Canaanite woman's daughter is healed

[The Canaanite woman] came and knelt before [Jesus], saying, "Lord, help me." He answered, "It is not fair to take the children's food and throw it to the dogs." She said, "Yes, Lord, yet even the dogs eat the crumbs that fall from their masters' table." Then Jesus answered her, "Woman, great is your faith! Let it be done for you as you wish." And her daughter was healed instantly. (Matt. 15:25-28)

Psalm

Psalm 67
Let all the peoples praise God

Additional Readings

Isaiah 56:1, 6-8
A house of prayer for all people

Romans 11:1-2a, **29-32**
God's mercy to all, Jew and Gentile

Hymn: We Come to You for Healing, Lord, ELW 617

God of all peoples, your arms reach out to embrace all those who call upon you. Teach us as disciples of your Son to love the world with compassion and constancy, that your name may be known throughout the earth, through Jesus Christ, our Savior and Lord.

Monday, August 18, 2014

Time after Pentecost

Psalm 87
Foreigners praise God in Zion

On the holy mount stands the city he founded;
    the Lord loves the gates of Zion
    more than all the dwellings of Jacob.
Glorious things are spoken of you,
    O city of God.

Among those who know me I mention Rahab and Babylon;
    Philistia too, and Tyre, with Ethiopia—
    "This one was born there," they say.

And of Zion it shall be said,
    "This one and that one were born in it";
    for the Most High himself will establish it. (Ps. 87:1-5)

Additional Readings
2 Kings 5:1-14
The foreigner Naaman is healed

Acts 15:1-21
The believing Jews accept the Gentiles

Hymn: Come, We That Love the Lord, ELW 625

Sovereign God, our ancestors looked up to Zion and made their pilgrimages of faith. As we make our daily journeys of prayer, give us a vision of your city of love where hearts are open and you make peace among all your creatures.

Tuesday, August 19, 2014

Time after Pentecost

Romans 11:13-29
God saves Jews and Gentiles

So that you may not claim to be wiser than you are, brothers and sisters, I want you to understand this mystery: a hardening has come upon part of Israel, until the full number of the Gentiles has come in. And so all Israel will be saved; as it is written,

"Out of Zion will come the Deliverer;
    he will banish ungodliness from Jacob."
"And this is my covenant with them,
    when I take away their sins."

As regards the gospel they are enemies of God for your sake; but as regards election they are beloved, for the sake of their ancestors; for the gifts and the calling of God are irrevocable. (Rom. 11:25-29)

Psalm
Psalm 87
Foreigners praise God in Zion

Additional Reading
Isaiah 43:8-13
Let all the nations gather

Hymn: Alleluia! Sing to Jesus, ELW 392

Lord God, when we hear that your bread of life and cup of blessing are gifts for us as your people, move us also to be your gifts for the people we have yet to meet and understand. Help us to become your instruments of healing.

Wednesday, August 20, 2014

Time after Pentecost

Bernard, Abbot of Clairvaux, died 1153

Matthew 8:1-13

Jesus heals many people

When [Jesus] entered Capernaum, a centurion came to him, appealing to him and saying, "Lord, my servant is lying at home paralyzed, in terrible distress." And he said to him, "I will come and cure him." The centurion answered, "Lord, I am not worthy to have you come under my roof; but only speak the word, and my servant will be healed. For I also am a man under authority, with soldiers under me; and I say to one, 'Go,' and he goes, and to another, 'Come,' and he comes, and to my slave, 'Do this,' and the slave does it." When Jesus heard him, he was amazed and said to those who followed him, "Truly I tell you, in no one in Israel have I found such faith." (Matt. 8:5-10)

Psalm

Psalm 87

Foreigners praise God in Zion

Additional Reading

Isaiah 66:18-23

All nations shall come to worship

Hymn: O Christ, the Healer, We Have Come, ELW 610

Speak the word, dear God. Speak the word and we shall be healed. Speak the word and we can speak our words of healing to your children, all of them.

Thursday, August 21, 2014

Time after Pentecost

Psalm 138
Your love endures forever

All the kings of the earth shall praise you, O Lord,
    for they have heard the words of your mouth.
They shall sing of the ways of the Lord,
    for great is the glory of the Lord.
For though the Lord is high, he regards the lowly;
    but the haughty he perceives from far away.

Though I walk in the midst of trouble,
    you preserve me against the wrath of my enemies;
you stretch out your hand,
    and your right hand delivers me.
The Lord will fulfill his purpose for me;
    your steadfast love, O Lord, endures forever.
    Do not forsake the work of your hands. (Ps. 138:4-8)

Additional Readings
Ezekiel 28:11-19
Disobedience and the loss of Eden

I Corinthians 6:1-11
When believers disagree

Hymn: Holy God, Holy and Glorious, ELW 637

*How long is your love, O Lord, how long? How enduring is your
compassion for each one of us? Does it last beyond our sinning? Does it
remain beyond our doubts? Does it continue when we have given up?
Help us to trust your enduring yes.*

Friday, August 22, 2014

Time after Pentecost

Ezekiel 31:15-18

Israel like the cedars of Lebanon

Thus says the Lord GOD: On the day [Assyria] went down to Sheol I closed the deep over it and covered it; I restrained its rivers, and its mighty waters were checked. I clothed Lebanon in gloom for it, and all the trees of the field fainted because of it. I made the nations quake at the sound of its fall, when I cast it down to Sheol with those who go down to the Pit; and all the trees of Eden, the choice and best of Lebanon, all that were well watered, were consoled in the world below. They also went down to Sheol with it, to those killed by the sword, along with its allies, those who lived in its shade among the nations.

Which among the trees of Eden was like you in glory and in greatness? Now you shall be brought down with the trees of Eden to the world below; you shall lie among the uncircumcised, with those who are killed by the sword. This is Pharaoh and all his horde, says the Lord GOD. (Ezek. 31:15-18)

Psalm
Psalm 138
Your love endures forever

Additional Reading
2 Corinthians 10:12-18
Let those who boast, boast in the Lord

Hymn: Light Dawns on a Weary World, ELW 726

Eternal God, you are God of the living and the dead. Nowhere is there a time or place where your presence is not felt, your love not imagined. Come now into this place and this time. Come into our life and even our death.

Saturday, August 23, 2014

Time after Pentecost

Ezekiel 36:33-38
A desolate land becomes like Eden

Thus says the Lord GOD: On the day that I cleanse you from all your iniquities, I will cause the towns to be inhabited, and the waste places shall be rebuilt. The land that was desolate shall be tilled, instead of being the desolation that it was in the sight of all who passed by. And they will say, "This land that was desolate has become like the garden of Eden; and the waste and desolate and ruined towns are now inhabited and fortified." Then the nations that are left all around you shall know that I, the LORD, have rebuilt the ruined places, and replanted that which was desolate; I, the LORD, have spoken, and I will do it. (Ezek. 36:33-36)

Psalm
Psalm 138
Your love endures forever

Additional Reading
Matthew 16:5-12
Bread as a sign of other things

Hymn: Come, Ye Disconsolate, ELW 607

Lord God, as you have always done, bring about the rebuilding of what is broken, the mending of what is torn apart, the healing of what is wounded, and begin a new work with us.

Sunday, August 24, 2014

Time after Pentecost

Bartholomew, Apostle (transferred to August 25)

Matthew 16:13-20

The profession of Peter's faith

[Jesus] said to [the disciples], "But who do you say that I am?" Simon Peter answered, "You are the Messiah, the Son of the living God." And Jesus answered him, "Blessed are you, Simon son of Jonah! For flesh and blood has not revealed this to you, but my Father in heaven. And I tell you, you are Peter, and on this rock I will build my church, and the gates of Hades will not prevail against it. I will give you the keys of the kingdom of heaven, and whatever you bind on earth will be bound in heaven, and whatever you loose on earth will be loosed in heaven." (Matt. 16:15-19)

Psalm

Psalm 138

Your love endures forever

Additional Readings

Isaiah 51:1-6

God's enduring salvation

Romans 12:1-8

One body in Christ, with gifts that differ

Hymn: Built on a Rock, ELW 652

O God, with all your faithful followers of every age, we praise you, the rock of our life. Be our strong foundation and form us into the body of your Son, that we may gladly minister to all the world, through Jesus Christ, our Savior and Lord.

Monday, August 25, 2014

Bartholomew, Apostle (*transferred*)

John 1:43-51

Jesus says: Follow me

When Jesus saw Nathanael coming toward him, he said of him, "Here is truly an Israelite in whom there is no deceit!" Nathanael asked him, "Where did you get to know me?" Jesus answered, "I saw you under the fig tree before Philip called you." Nathanael replied, "Rabbi, you are the Son of God! You are the King of Israel!" Jesus answered, "Do you believe because I told you that I saw you under the fig tree? You will see greater things than these." And he said to him, "Very truly, I tell you, you will see heaven opened and the angels of God ascending and descending upon the Son of Man." (John 1:47-51)

Psalm

Psalm 12

A plea for help in evil times

Additional Readings

Exodus 19:1-6

Israel is God's priestly kingdom

1 Corinthians 12:27-31a

The body of Christ

Hymn: O God, My Faithful God, ELW 806

Almighty and everlasting God, you gave to your apostle Bartholomew grace truly to believe and courageously to preach your word. Grant that your church may proclaim the good news to the ends of the earth, through Jesus Christ, our Savior and Lord, who lives and reigns with you and the Holy Spirit, one God, now and forever.

Tuesday, August 26, 2014

Time after Pentecost

Psalm 18:1-3, 20-32
God the rock

I love you, O LORD, my strength.
The LORD is my rock, my fortress, and my deliverer,
   my God, my rock in whom I take refuge,
   my shield, and the horn of my salvation, my stronghold.
I call upon the LORD, who is worthy to be praised,
   so I shall be saved from my enemies. (Ps. 18:1-3)

Additional Readings
Deuteronomy 32:18-20, 28-39
Praise the rock that is God

Romans 11:33-36
The riches, wisdom, and knowledge of God

Hymn: He Comes to Us as One Unknown, ELW 737

Lord God of strength, you are worthy of praise and adoration now and always. You are the rock upon which stand and to which we cling in the changes of life. Thank you!

Wednesday, August 27, 2014

Time after Pentecost

Isaiah 28:14-22

God lays a cornerstone in Zion

Therefore hear the word of the Lord, you scoffers
  who rule this people in Jerusalem.
Because you have said, "We have made a covenant with death,
  and with Sheol we have an agreement;
when the overwhelming scourge passes through
  it will not come to us;
for we have made lies our refuge,
  and in falsehood we have taken shelter";
therefore thus says the Lord God,
See, I am laying in Zion a foundation stone,
  a tested stone,
a precious cornerstone, a sure foundation:
  "One who trusts will not panic." (Isa. 28:14-16)

Psalm
Psalm 18:1-3, 20-32
God the rock

Additional Reading
Matthew 26:6-13
A woman anoints Jesus

Hymn: Christ Is Made the Sure Foundation, ELW 645

*Dear God, when we make our allegiance with all that is wrong and un-
holy, you place before us a cornerstone to which we can cling: the story
and the love of your grace and forgiveness. Keep us steadfast.*

Thursday, August 28, 2014

Time after Pentecost

Augustine, Bishop of Hippo, died 430
Moses the Black, monk, martyr, died around 400

Psalm 26:1-8
Your love is before my eyes

Vindicate me, O Lord,
   for I have walked in my integrity,
   and I have trusted in the Lord without wavering.
Prove me, O Lord, and try me;
   test my heart and mind.
For your steadfast love is before my eyes,
   and I walk in faithfulness to you. (Ps. 26:1-3)

Additional Readings
Jeremiah 14:13-18
Denunciation of lying prophets

Ephesians 5:1-6
Do not be deceived by empty words

Hymn: We Praise You, O God, ELW 870

O God, hold out before our eyes the path that leads to your love. Let it be that upon which we focus every day and every night, forever and ever.

Friday, August 29, 2014

Time after Pentecost

2 Thessalonians 2:7-12

Refusal to love the truth

For the mystery of lawlessness is already at work, but only until the one who now restrains it is removed. And then the lawless one will be revealed, whom the Lord Jesus will destroy with the breath of his mouth, annihilating him by the manifestation of his coming. The coming of the lawless one is apparent in the working of Satan, who uses all power, signs, lying wonders, and every kind of wicked deception for those who are perishing, because they refused to love the truth and so be saved. For this reason God sends them a powerful delusion, leading them to believe what is false, so that all who have not believed the truth but took pleasure in unrighteousness will be condemned. (2 Thess. 2:7-12)

Psalm
Psalm 26:1-8
Your love is before my eyes

Additional Reading
Jeremiah 15:1-9
The consequences of sin

Hymn: Abide, O Dearest Jesus, ELW 539

Lord God, Satan is a tempter, a deceiver, and a fraud. Lead us not into deception but into the safe arms of your protecting care.

Saturday, August 30, 2014

Time after Pentecost

Jeremiah 15:10-14
Jeremiah's complaint to God

Woe is me, my mother, that you ever bore me, a man of strife and contention to the whole land! I have not lent, nor have I borrowed, yet all of them curse me. The LORD said: Surely I have intervened in your life for good, surely I have imposed enemies on you in a time of trouble and in a time of distress. Can iron and bronze break iron from the north?

Your wealth and your treasures I will give as plunder, without price, for all your sins, throughout all your territory. I will make you serve your enemies in a land that you do not know, for in my anger a fire is kindled that shall burn forever. (Jer. 15:10-14)

Psalm
Psalm 26:1-8
Your love is before my eyes

Additional Reading
Matthew 8:14-17
Jesus heals many at Peter's house

Hymn: If You But Trust in God to Guide You, ELW 769

Lord God, as Jeremiah complained and you sent him to speak in a foreign place, you were also with him. So be with us in the daring times when we obey your guidance; for we know you live among all who need to hear your words of promise.

Sunday, August 31, 2014

Time after Pentecost

Matthew 16:21-28
The rebuke to Peter

From that time on, Jesus began to show his disciples that he must go to Jerusalem and undergo great suffering at the hands of the elders and chief priests and scribes, and be killed, and on the third day be raised. And Peter took him aside and began to rebuke him, saying, "God forbid it, Lord! This must never happen to you." But he turned and said to Peter, "Get behind me, Satan! You are a stumbling block to me; for you are setting your mind not on divine things but on human things." (Matt. 16:21-23)

Psalm
Psalm 26:1-8
Your love is before my eyes

Additional Readings
Jeremiah 15:15-21
God fortifies the prophet

Romans 12:9-21
Live in harmony

Hymn: Take Up Your Cross, the Savior Said, ELW 667

O God, we thank you for your Son who chose the path of suffering for the sake of the world. Humble us by his example, point us to the path of obedience, and give us strength to follow your commands, through Jesus Christ, our Savior and Lord.

PRAYER LIST FOR SEPTEMBER

_____

_____

_____

_____

_____

_____

_____

_____

_____

_____

_____

_____

Time after Pentecost

Autumn

The days of early autumn (September and October) herald the resumption of a more regular schedule: school begins, church education programs commence, and the steady rhythms of work are accompanied by cooling breezes and the changing colors of the landscape. During these months, various crops are harvested and appear on roadside stands and in grocery stores. In many countries the harvest days of September and October are marked with prayer, feasting, and special care for the poor and hungry.

Table Prayer for Autumn

We praise you and bless you, O God,
for autumn days,
and for the gifts of this table.
Grant us grace to share your goodness,
until all people are fed by the harvest of the earth.
We ask this through Christ our Lord. Amen.

Monday, September 1, 2014

Time after Pentecost

Psalm 17

The righteous shall see God

I call upon you, for you will answer me, O God;
  incline your ear to me, hear my words.
Wondrously show your steadfast love,
  O savior of those who seek refuge
  from their adversaries at your right hand.

Guard me as the apple of the eye;
  hide me in the shadow of your wings,
from the wicked who despoil me,
  my deadly enemies who surround me. (Ps. 17:6-9)

Additional Readings

2 Samuel 11:2-26
David sins

Revelation 3:1-6
Wake up to your faithlessness

Hymn: What Wondrous Love Is This, ELW 666

Lord God, you promise to be near us in life and in death. Help us live faithfully and make that promise active in our daily lives, bringing healing, hope, and comfort to all in need.

Tuesday, September 2, 2014

Time after Pentecost

Nikolai Frederik Severin Grundtvig, bishop, renewer of the church,
died 1872

Revelation 3:7-13
Facing the hour of trial

"And to the angel of the church in Philadelphia write:
  These are the words of the holy one, the true one,
    who has the key of David,
  who opens and no one will shut,
    who shuts and no one opens:

. . . Because you have kept my word of patient endurance, I will keep
you from the hour of trial that is coming on the whole world to test
the inhabitants of the earth. I am coming soon; hold fast to what
you have, so that no one may seize your crown. If you conquer, I will
make you a pillar in the temple of my God; you will never go out of
it. I will write on you the name of my God, and the name of the city
of my God, the new Jerusalem that comes down from my God out of
heaven, and my own new name." (Rev. 3:7, 10-12)

Psalm	Additional Reading
Psalm 17	2 Samuel 11:27b—12:15
The righteous shall see God	*Nathan rebukes David*

Hymn: Just As I Am, without One Plea, ELW 592

*Gracious Lord, we admit to you our frailty and failings. Keep us faithful
in prayer and forgiveness. Give us courage to share your love with others
in need no matter the obstacles the world places in our paths.*

Wednesday, September 3, 2014

Time after Pentecost

Jeremiah 17:5-18
The vindication of the righteous

Thus says the LORD:
Cursed are those who trust in mere mortals
   and make mere flesh their strength,
   whose hearts turn away from the LORD.
They shall be like a shrub in the desert,
   and shall not see when relief comes.
They shall live in the parched places of the wilderness,
   in an uninhabited salt land.

Blessed are those who trust in the LORD,
   whose trust is the LORD.
They shall be like a tree planted by water,
   sending out its roots by the stream.
It shall not fear when heat comes,
   and its leaves shall stay green;
in the year of drought it is not anxious,
   and it does not cease to bear fruit. (Jer. 17:5-8)

Psalm
Psalm 17
The righteous shall see God

Additional Reading
Matthew 12:22-32
Jesus comes to cast out Satan

Hymn: Come to Me, All Pilgrims Thirsty, ELW 777

Merciful Lord, we are not always as brave as you call us to be. Forgive us. Open our eyes to see where your Spirit is at work even now in our world and send us there to serve.

Thursday, September 4, 2014

Time after Pentecost

Psalm 119:33-40
The path of your commandments

Teach me, O LORD, the way of your statutes,
> and I will observe it to the end.
Give me understanding, that I may keep your law
> and observe it with my whole heart.
Lead me in the path of your commandments,
> for I delight in it.
Turn my heart to your decrees,
> and not to selfish gain. (Ps. 119:33-36)

Additional Readings
Ezekiel 24:1-14
God judges unrepentant Israel

2 Corinthians 12:11-21
Sinners warned but unrepentant

Hymn: O God of Light, ELW 507

Holy Lord, forgive our stubborn and often foolish desires to go our own ways. Lead us to those sacred places and holy people who help us find again and follow your path, bringing love, mercy, grace, and hope.

Friday, September 5, 2014

Time after Pentecost

Romans 10:15b-21
God reaches out to erring Israel

As it is written, "How beautiful are the feet of those who bring good news!" But not all have obeyed the good news; for Isaiah says, "Lord, who has believed our message?" So faith comes from what is heard, and what is heard comes through the word of Christ. (Rom. 10:15b-17)

Psalm
Psalm 119:33-40
The path of your commandments

Additional Reading
Ezekiel 24:15-27
God opens the prophet's mouth

Hymn: God's Word Is Our Great Heritage, ELW 509

Gracious Lord, in your word you offer understanding and delight, a path that leads to you. Today, with your words in our mouths and your love for others in our hearts, give us opportunities to be messengers of peace.

Saturday, September 6, 2014

Time after Pentecost

Ezekiel 33:1-6

The prophet's vocation

The word of the Lord came to me: O Mortal, speak to your people and say to them, If I bring the sword upon a land, and the people of the land take one of their number as their sentinel; and if the sentinel sees the sword coming upon the land and blows the trumpet and warns the people; then if any who hear the sound of the trumpet do not take warning, and the sword comes and takes them away, their blood shall be upon their own heads. They heard the sound of the trumpet and did not take warning; their blood shall be upon themselves. But if they had taken warning, they would have saved their lives. But if the sentinel sees the sword coming and does not blow the trumpet, so that the people are not warned, and the sword comes and takes any of them, they are taken away in their iniquity, but their blood I will require at the sentinel's hand. (Ezek. 33:1-6)

Psalm
Psalm 119:33-40
The path of your commandments

Additional Reading
Matthew 23:29-36
The martyrdom of the prophets

Hymn: Lo! He Comes with Clouds Descending, ELW 435

Lord God, you call us to be your children in this world, here and now, this very day. You call us to speak out for those who cannot speak for themselves, to love the unlovable, faithfully proclaiming forgiveness and hope.

Sunday, September 7, 2014

Time after Pentecost

Matthew 18:15-20

Reconciliation in the community of faith

"If another member of the church sins against you, go and point out the fault when the two of you are alone. If the member listens to you, you have regained that one. But if you are not listened to, take one or two others along with you, so that every word may be confirmed by the evidence of two or three witnesses. If the member refuses to listen to them, tell it to the church; and if the offender refuses to listen even to the church, let such a one be to you as a Gentile and a tax collector." (Matt. 18:15-17)

Psalm

Psalm 119:33-40

The path of your commandments

Additional Readings

Ezekiel 33:7-11

The prophet's responsibility

Romans 13:8-14

Live honorably as in the day

Hymn: Forgive Our Sins As We Forgive, ELW 605

O Lord God, enliven and preserve your church with your perpetual mercy. Without your help, we mortals will fail; remove far from us everything that is harmful, and lead us toward all that gives life and salvation, through Jesus Christ, our Savior and Lord.

Monday, September 8, 2014

Time after Pentecost

Psalm 119:65-72
The law humbles me

You have dealt well with your servant,
　　O LORD, according to your word.
Teach me good judgment and knowledge,
　　for I believe in your commandments.
Before I was humbled I went astray,
　　but now I keep your word. (Ps. 119:65-67)

Additional Readings
Leviticus 4:27-31; 5:14-16
Atoning for sin in the community

1 Peter 2:11-17
Live as servants of God

Hymn: O Word of God Incarnate, ELW 514

Merciful Lord, you taught us that the last will be first, the first will be last, and that the greatest is the one who serves others. Help us today to pay close attention to your word as we serve the gospel.

Tuesday, September 9, 2014

Time after Pentecost

Peter Claver, priest, missionary to Colombia, died 1654

Romans 13:1-7

Obeying authority

Let every person be subject to the governing authorities; for there is no authority except from God, and those authorities that exist have been instituted by God. Therefore whoever resists authority resists what God has appointed, and those who resist will incur judgment. For rulers are not a terror to good conduct, but to bad. Do you wish to have no fear of the authority? Then do what is good, and you will receive its approval; for it is God's servant for your good. But if you do what is wrong, you should be afraid, for the authority does not bear the sword in vain! It is the servant of God to execute wrath on the wrongdoer. (Rom. 13:1-4)

Psalm

Psalm 119:65-72

The law humbles me

Additional Reading

Deuteronomy 17:2-13

Punishment for sin in community

Hymn: Let the Whole Creation Cry, ELW 876

Lord God, you made heaven and earth. We praise your name for this blessed gift. We ask your Spirit to fill us as we guide others to use your creation's gifts wisely for the sake of those to come.

Wednesday, September 10, 2014

Time after Pentecost

Matthew 21:18-22

Jesus teaches about praying in faith

In the morning, when [Jesus] returned to the city, he was hungry. And seeing a fig tree by the side of the road, he went to it and found nothing at all on it but leaves. Then he said to it, "May no fruit ever come from you again!" And the fig tree withered at once. When the disciples saw it, they were amazed, saying, "How did the fig tree wither at once?" Jesus answered them, "Truly I tell you, if you have faith and do not doubt, not only will you do what has been done to the fig tree, but even if you say to this mountain, 'Be lifted up and thrown into the sea,' it will be done. Whatever you ask for in prayer with faith, you will receive." (Matt. 21:18-22)

Psalm

Psalm 119:65-72

The law humbles me

Additional Reading

Leviticus 16:1-5, 20-28

The scapegoat cleanses the community

Hymn: Lord, Teach Us How to Pray Aright, ELW 745

Merciful Lord, you teach us to pray in faith, believing your promises to hear our prayers. Continually offer us opportunities to turn our prayers into service, our petitions into actions, and our thanksgivings into blessing, all in your name.

Thursday, September 11, 2014

Time after Pentecost

Psalm 103:[1-7] 8-13
God's compassion and mercy

The LORD is merciful and gracious,
    slow to anger and abounding in steadfast love.
He will not always accuse,
    nor will he keep his anger forever.
He does not deal with us according to our sins,
    nor repay us according to our iniquities.
For as the heavens are high above the earth,
    so great is his steadfast love toward those who fear him;
as far as the east is from the west,
    so far he removes our transgressions from us. (Ps. 103:8-12)

Additional Readings
Genesis 37:12-36   1 John 3:11-16
Joseph's brothers sin against him   *Love one another*

Hymn: Praise, My Soul, the God of Heaven, ELW 864

*Lord God, you forgive our sins. Thank you for your mercy. As we praise
your name, never let us forget our obligations to love one another, to
bring mercy, to forgive others as you forgive us, and to do so generously.*

Friday, September 12, 2014

Time after Pentecost

Genesis 41:53—42:17

Joseph acts harshly against his brothers

But Joseph said to [his brothers], "It is just as I have said to you; you are spies! Here is how you shall be tested: as Pharaoh lives, you shall not leave this place unless your youngest brother comes here! Let one of you go and bring your brother, while the rest of you remain in prison, in order that your words may be tested, whether there is truth in you; or else, as Pharaoh lives, surely you are spies." And he put them all together in prison for three days. (Gen. 42:14-17)

Psalm

Psalm 103:[1-7] 8-13

God's compassion and mercy

Additional Reading

Acts 7:9-16

Joseph's family is fed in Egypt

Hymn: Lord of Glory, You Have Bought Us, ELW 707

Generous Lord, bathed in baptismal waters, we feast at your table, serving your church and our world with the gifts you give us in our communities of faith. Bless us as we feed the hungry with food and mercy.

Saturday, September 13, 2014

Time after Pentecost

John Chrysostom, Bishop of Constantinople, died 407

Matthew 6:7-15

Forgiving one another

"Pray then in this way:
Our Father in heaven,
   hallowed be your name.
   Your kingdom come.
   Your will be done,
      on earth as it is in heaven.
   Give us this day our daily bread.
   And forgive us our debts,
      as we also have forgiven our debtors.
   And do not bring us to the time of trial,
      but rescue us from the evil one." (Matt. 6:9-13)

Psalm

Psalm 103:[1-7] 8-13
God's compassion and mercy

Additional Reading

Genesis 45:1-20
Joseph forgives his brothers

Hymn: Our Father, God in Heaven Above, ELW 746/747

Merciful Lord, when we forget how much you have forgiven us, remind us of your mercy through word, sacrament, prayer, and actions of love. Shower us with your Spirit, offering us new avenues to bring compassion into others' lives.

Sunday, September 14, 2014

Time after Pentecost

Holy Cross Day (transferred to September 15)

Matthew 18:21-35

A parable of forgiveness

Then Peter came and said to him, "Lord, if another member of the church sins against me, how often should I forgive? As many as seven times?" Jesus said to him, "Not seven times, but, I tell you, seventy-seven times." (Matt. 18:21-22)

Psalm

Psalm 103:[1-7] 8-13

God's compassion and mercy

Additional Readings

Genesis 50:15-21

Joseph reconciles with his brothers

Romans 14:1-12

When brothers and sisters judge each other

Hymn: Listen, God Is Calling, ELW 513

O Lord God, merciful judge, you are the inexhaustible fountain of forgiveness. Replace our hearts of stone with hearts that love and adore you, that we may delight in doing your will, through Jesus Christ, our Savior and Lord.

Monday, September 15, 2014

Holy Cross Day (*transferred*)

John 3:13-17
The Son of Man will be lifted up

[Jesus said,] "No one has ascended into heaven except the one who descended from heaven, the Son of Man. And just as Moses lifted up the serpent in the wilderness, so must the Son of Man be lifted up, that whoever believes in him may have eternal life.

"For God so loved the world that he gave his only Son, so that everyone who believes in him may not perish but may have eternal life.

"Indeed, God did not send the Son into the world to condemn the world, but in order that the world might be saved through him." (John 3:13-17)

Psalm
Psalm 98:1-4
The Lord has done marvelous things

Additional Readings
Numbers 21:4b-9
A bronze serpent in the wilderness

1 Corinthians 1:18-24
The cross is the power of God

Hymn: Lift High the Cross, ELW 660

Almighty God, your Son Jesus Christ was lifted high upon the cross so that he might draw the whole world to himself. To those who look upon the cross, grant your wisdom, healing, and eternal life, through Jesus Christ, our Savior and Lord, who lives and reigns with you and the Holy Spirit, one God, now and forever.

Tuesday, September 16, 2014

Time after Pentecost

Cyprian, Bishop of Carthage, martyr, died around 258

Psalm 133
How good it is to live in unity

How very good and pleasant it is
    when kindred live together in unity!
It is like the precious oil on the head,
    running down upon the beard,
on the beard of Aaron,
    running down over the collar of his robes.
It is like the dew of Hermon,
    which falls on the mountains of Zion.
For there the LORD ordained his blessing,
    life forevermore. (Ps. 133:1-3)

Additional Readings
Genesis 49:29—50:14   Romans 14:13—15:2
Honoring Jacob's burial wishes   *Building each other up*

Hymn: Beloved, God's Chosen, ELW 648

*Gracious Lord, you shower us with blessings; your goodness fills our
hearts with gladness. Help us work with others, not letting differences
divide us, but rather seeing where we have common purpose to help
others in need.*

Wednesday, September 17, 2014

Time after Pentecost

Hildegard, Abbess of Bingen, died 1179

Genesis 50:22-26
Joseph dies

So Joseph remained in Egypt, he and his father's household; and Joseph lived one hundred ten years. Joseph saw Ephraim's children of the third generation; the children of Machir son of Manasseh were also born on Joseph's knees.

Then Joseph said to his brothers, "I am about to die; but God will surely come to you, and bring you up out of this land to the land that he swore to Abraham, to Isaac, and to Jacob." So Joseph made the Israelites swear, saying, "When God comes to you, you shall carry up my bones from here." And Joseph died, being one hundred ten years old; he was embalmed and placed in a coffin in Egypt. (Gen. 50:22-26)

Psalm	Additional Reading
Psalm 133	Mark 11:20-25
How good it is to live in unity	*Forgiveness for those who forgive*

Hymn: Children of the Heavenly Father, ELW 781

Lord, you make us your children through our baptism into Christ. As you teach, admonish, and love us, strengthen us through our faith communities so to teach, forgive, admonish, and love one another that all people may know your peace.

Thursday, September 18, 2014

Time after Pentecost

Dag Hammarskjöld, renewer of society, died 1961

Psalm 145:1-8
God is slow to anger

I will extol you, my God and King,
    and bless your name forever and ever.
Every day I will bless you,
    and praise your name forever and ever.
Great is the LORD, and greatly to be praised;
    his greatness is unsearchable. . . .

The LORD is gracious and merciful,
    slow to anger and abounding in steadfast love. (Ps. 145:1-3, 8)

Additional Readings
Nahum 1:1, 14—2:2
God's wrath toward Nineveh

2 Corinthians 13:1-4
Dissent among believers

Hymn: Before You, Lord, We Bow, ELW 893

Gracious Lord, when we wander off, you find us. When we harden our hearts against our neighbors, you call us to account. When we hold back forgiveness, you send us in peace to love and serve all in need.

Friday, September 19, 2014

Time after Pentecost

2 Corinthians 13:5-10
Correction that builds up

But we pray to God that you may not do anything wrong—not that we may appear to have met the test, but that you may do what is right, though we may seem to have failed. For we cannot do anything against the truth, but only for the truth. For we rejoice when we are weak and you are strong. This is what we pray for, that you may become perfect. So I write these things while I am away from you, so that when I come, I may not have to be severe in using the authority that the Lord has given me for building up and not for tearing down. (2 Cor. 13:7-10)

Psalm
Psalm 145:1-8
God is slow to anger

Additional Reading
Nahum 2:3-13
Nineveh under siege

Hymn: Just a Closer Walk with Thee, ELW 697

O Lord our God, teach us to be as slow to anger as you are, admonishing one another in love to build up our communities of faith that our actions might give witness to your forgiveness and mercy.

Saturday, September 20, 2014

Time after Pentecost

Zephaniah 2:13-15

Judgment on Nineveh

And he will stretch out his hand against the north,
   and destroy Assyria;
and he will make Nineveh a desolation,
   a dry waste like the desert.
Herds shall lie down in it, every wild animal;
the desert owl and the screech owl shall lodge on its capitals;
the owl shall hoot at the window,
   the raven croak on the threshold;
   for its cedar work will be laid bare.
Is this the exultant city that lived secure,
that said to itself, "I am, and there is no one else"?
What a desolation it has become,
   a lair for wild animals!
Everyone who passes by it
   hisses and shakes the fist. (Zeph. 2:13-15)

Psalm
Psalm 145:1-8
God is slow to anger

Additional Reading
Matthew 19:23-30
The last will be first

Hymn: All Who Love and Serve Your City, ELW 724

Gracious Lord, continually guide us to pay attention and seek out the least among us, leading them to safety and giving them hope. So nurture and protect all who are in need that they might know they are first in your kingdom.

Sunday, September 21, 2014

Time after Pentecost

**Matthew, Apostle and Evangelist
(transferred to September 22)**

Matthew 20:1-16

The parable of the vineyard workers

"But [the landowner] replied to one of [the laborers], 'Friend, I am doing you no wrong; did you not agree with me for the usual daily wage? Take what belongs to you and go; I choose to give to this last the same as I give to you. Am I not allowed to do what I choose with what belongs to me? Or are you envious because I am generous?' So the last will be first, and the first will be last." (Matt. 20:13-16)

Psalm	**Additional Readings**	
Psalm 145:1-8	Jonah 3:10—4:11	Philippians 1:21-30
God is slow to anger	*God's concern for Nineveh*	*Standing firm in the gospel*

Hymn: Praise and Thanksgiving, ELW 689

Almighty and eternal God, you show perpetual lovingkindness to us your servants. Because we cannot rely on our own abilities, grant us your merciful judgment, and train us to embody the generosity of your Son, Jesus Christ, our Savior and Lord.

Monday, September 22, 2014

Matthew, Apostle and Evangelist (*transferred*)

Matthew 9:9-13

Jesus calls to Matthew: Follow me

As Jesus was walking along, he saw a man called Matthew sitting at the tax booth; and he said to him, "Follow me." And he got up and followed him.

And as he sat at dinner in the house, many tax collectors and sinners came and were sitting with him and his disciples. When the Pharisees saw this, they said to his disciples, "Why does your teacher eat with tax collectors and sinners?" But when he heard this, he said, "Those who are well have no need of a physician, but those who are sick. Go and learn what this means, 'I desire mercy, not sacrifice.' For I have come to call not the righteous but sinners." (Matt. 9:9-13)

Psalm	Additional Readings	
Psalm 119:33-40	Ezekiel 2:8—3:11	Ephesians 2:4-10
Give me understanding	*A prophet to the house of Israel*	*By grace you have been saved*

Hymn: Jesus Calls Us; o'er the Tumult, ELW 696

Almighty God, your Son our Savior called a despised tax collector to become one of his apostles. Help us, like Matthew, to respond to the transforming call of Jesus Christ, who lives and reigns with you and the Holy Spirit, one God, now and forever.

Tuesday, September 23, 2014

Time after Pentecost

Psalm 106:1-12
God's mercy

Praise the LORD!
   O give thanks to the LORD, for he is good;
   for his steadfast love endures forever.
Who can utter the mighty doings of the LORD,
   or declare all his praise?
Happy are those who observe justice,
   who do righteousness at all times.

Remember me, O LORD, when you show favor to your people;
   help me when you deliver them;
that I may see the prosperity of your chosen ones,
   that I may rejoice in the gladness of your nation,
   that I may glory in your heritage. (Ps. 106:1-5)

Additional Readings
Genesis 28:10-17
God blesses the runaway Jacob

Romans 16:17-20
A warning about troublemakers

Hymn: Lord, Take My Hand and Lead Me, ELW 767

Lord God, even as we sing praises to you, we know we need your steadfast love as we serve all people in need. Strengthen our efforts to bring justice, healing, blessing, and peace to your kingdom and into our troubled world.

Wednesday, September 24, 2014

Time after Pentecost

Matthew 18:1-5

True greatness

At that time the disciples came to Jesus and asked, "Who is the greatest in the kingdom of heaven?" He called a child, whom he put among them, and said, "Truly I tell you, unless you change and become like children, you will never enter the kingdom of heaven. Whoever becomes humble like this child is the greatest in the kingdom of heaven. Whoever welcomes one such child in my name welcomes me." (Matt. 18:1-5)

Psalm

Psalm 106:1-12

God's mercy

Additional Reading

Isaiah 41:1-13

God will be with the last

Hymn: Cradling Children in His Arm, ELW 444

Gracious Lord, keep us mindful of our call not only to welcome children, the least, the lonely, the unloved, and the outcast, but also to seek them out and offer them the blessings of life in your name and in your kingdom.

Thursday, September 25, 2014

Time after Pentecost

Psalm 25:1-9
God's compassion and love

Make me to know your ways, O LORD;
  teach me your paths.
Lead me in your truth, and teach me,
  for you are the God of my salvation;
  for you I wait all day long.

Be mindful of your mercy, O LORD, and of your steadfast love,
  for they have been from of old.
Do not remember the sins of my youth or my transgressions;
  according to your steadfast love remember me,
  for your goodness' sake, O LORD! (Ps. 25:4-7)

Additional Readings
Ezekiel 12:17-28   James 4:11-16
God's judgment is timely   *We do not know what tomorrow will bring*

Hymn: Rise Up, O Saints of God! ELW 669

Holy God, encourage us to pay close attention to the people and circumstances you place in front of us this day. Help us not to hang back but to rise up in loving service, empowered always by your Spirit.

Friday, September 26, 2014

Time after Pentecost

Ezekiel 18:5-18

Those who repent shall live

If a man is righteous and does what is lawful and right—if he does not eat upon the mountains or lift up his eyes to the idols of the house of Israel, does not defile his neighbor's wife or approach a woman during her menstrual period, does not oppress anyone, but restores to the debtor his pledge, commits no robbery, gives his bread to the hungry and covers the naked with a garment, does not take advance or accrued interest, withholds his hand from iniquity, executes true justice between contending parties, follows my statutes, and is careful to observe my ordinances, acting faithfully—such a one is righteous; he shall surely live, says the Lord God. (Ezek. 18:5-9)

Psalm

Psalm 25:1-9

God's compassion and love

Additional Reading

Acts 13:32-41

Through Jesus forgiveness is proclaimed

Hymn: Thy Strong Word, ELW 511

Lord God, by your word the universe lives. By your word you sustain us for daily life in your kingdom. Living in your word and putting our faith into action, we bring life, justice, and hope in your name.

Saturday, September 27, 2014

Time after Pentecost

Ezekiel 18:19-24

A child does not suffer for a parent's sin

Yet you say, "Why should not the son suffer for the iniquity of the father?" When the son has done what is lawful and right, and has been careful to observe all my statutes, he shall surely live. The person who sins shall die. A child shall not suffer for the iniquity of a parent, nor a parent suffer for the iniquity of a child; the righteousness of the righteous shall be his own, and the wickedness of the wicked shall be his own. (Ezek. 18:19-20)

Psalm

Psalm 25:1-9

God's compassion and love

Additional Reading

Mark 11:27-33

Jesus' authority is questioned

Hymn: Christ, Whose Glory Fills the Skies, ELW 553

Lord God, your grace frees us from judging others and from judging ourselves. Help us to hear your words of compassion that they might overflow our own lives and enable us to go and serve those in need.

Sunday, September 28, 2014

Time after Pentecost

Matthew 21:23-32

A parable of doing God's will

"What do you think? A man had two sons; he went to the first and said, 'Son, go and work in the vineyard today.' He answered, 'I will not'; but later he changed his mind and went. The father went to the second and said the same; and he answered, 'I go, sir'; but he did not go. Which of the two did the will of his father?" They said, "The first." Jesus said to them, "Truly I tell you, the tax collectors and the prostitutes are going into the kingdom of God ahead of you. For John came to you in the way of righteousness and you did not believe him, but the tax collectors and the prostitutes believed him; and even after you saw it, you did not change your minds and believe him." (Matt. 21:28-32)

Psalm

Psalm 25:1-9

God's compassion and love

Additional Readings

Ezekiel 18:1-4, 25-32

The fairness of God's way

Philippians 2:1-13

Christ humbled to the point of death

Hymn: All My Hope on God Is Founded, ELW 757

God of love, giver of life, you know our frailties and failings. Give us your grace to overcome them, keep us from those things that harm us, and guide us in the way of salvation, through Jesus Christ, our Savior and Lord.

Monday, September 29, 2014

Michael and All Angels

Revelation 12:7-12

Michael defeats Satan in a cosmic battle

And war broke out in heaven; Michael and his angels fought against the dragon. The dragon and his angels fought back, but they were defeated, and there was no longer any place for them in heaven. The great dragon was thrown down, that ancient serpent, who is called the Devil and Satan, the deceiver of the whole world—he was thrown down to the earth, and his angels were thrown down with him. (Rev. 12:7-9)

Psalm
Psalm 103:1-5, 20-22
Bless the Lord, you angels

Additional Readings
Daniel 10:10-14; 12:1-3
Michael shall arise

Luke 10:17-20
Jesus gives his followers authority

Hymn: Blessing and Honor, ELW 854

Everlasting God, you have wonderfully established the ministries of angels and mortals. Mercifully grant that as Michael and the angels contend against the cosmic forces of evil, so by your direction they may help and defend us here on earth, through your Son, Jesus Christ our Lord, who lives and reigns with you and the Holy Spirit, one God whom we worship and praise with angels and archangels and all the company of heaven, now and forever.

Tuesday, September 30, 2014

Time after Pentecost

Jerome, translator, teacher, died 420

Psalm 28

Prayer to do God's will

Blessed be the LORD,
  for he has heard the sound of my pleadings.
The LORD is my strength and my shield;
  in him my heart trusts;
so I am helped, and my heart exults,
  and with my song I give thanks to him.

The LORD is the strength of his people;
  he is the saving refuge of his anointed.
O save your people, and bless your heritage;
  be their shepherd, and carry them forever. (Ps. 28:6-9)

Additional Readings

Judges 16:1-22
Samson asked about his strength

Philippians 1:15-21
Christ is proclaimed regardless of the motive

Hymn: Jesus Lives, My Sure Defense, ELW 621

O Lord our God, ruler of the universe, we live in your blessings. We pray for courage to know your will and to put it into action in our daily lives, for the sake of our neighborhoods and your world.

_____

_____

_____

_____

_____

_____

_____

_____

_____

_____

_____

Wednesday, October 1, 2014

Time after Pentecost

Judges 16:23-31
Samson prays to do God's will

Then Samson called to the LORD and said, "Lord GOD, remember me and strengthen me only this once, O God, so that with this one act of revenge I may pay back the Philistines for my two eyes." And Samson grasped the two middle pillars on which the house rested, and he leaned his weight against them, his right hand on the one and his left hand on the other. Then Samson said, "Let me die with the Philistines." He strained with all his might; and the house fell on the lords and all the people who were in it. So those he killed at his death were more than those he had killed during his life. Then his brothers and all his family came down and took him and brought him up and buried him between Zorah and Eshtaol in the tomb of his father Manoah. He had judged Israel twenty years. (Judg. 16:28-31)

Psalm
Psalm 28
Prayer to do God's will

Additional Reading
Matthew 9:2-8
Jesus' authority to forgive and heal

Hymn: Lead On, O King Eternal! ELW 805

O God, when we face difficult decisions, start to give up hope, or are tempted to turn away from you, draw us back. Help us listen to your voice and lean on your Son, Jesus Christ, for direction and strength.

Thursday, October 2, 2014

Time after Pentecost

Psalm 80:7-15

Look down from heaven, O God

Restore us, O God of hosts;
    let your face shine, that we may be saved.

You brought a vine out of Egypt;
    you drove out the nations and planted it.
You cleared the ground for it;
    it took deep root and filled the land. . . .

Turn again, O God of hosts;
    look down from heaven, and see;
have regard for this vine,
    the stock that your right hand planted. (Ps. 80:7-9, 14-15)

Additional Readings

Jeremiah 2:14-22
The choice vine becomes degenerate

Colossians 2:16-23
Hold fast to Christ, the head

Hymn: Like the Murmur of the Dove's Song, ELW 403

O God, in baptism your seed of faith is planted deep in our hearts. May it take root, grow, and flourish as we feed it with your word and at your table.

Friday, October 3, 2014

Time after Pentecost

Philippians 2:14-18; 3:1-4a
Boast only in Jesus Christ

Do all things without murmuring and arguing, so that you may be blameless and innocent, children of God without blemish in the midst of a crooked and perverse generation, in which you shine like stars in the world. It is by your holding fast to the word of life that I can boast on the day of Christ that I did not run in vain or labor in vain. But even if I am being poured out as a libation over the sacrifice and the offering of your faith, I am glad and rejoice with all of you—and in the same way you also must be glad and rejoice with me. (Phil. 2:14-18)

Psalm
Psalm 80:7-15
Look down from heaven, O God

Additional Reading
Jeremiah 2:23-37
Israel shall be shamed

Hymn: O Savior, Precious Savior, ELW 820

When we quarrel and tear one another down, we destroy your church. Forgive us for times when we do not treat our brothers and sisters with the dignity, respect, and love they deserve.

Saturday, October 4, 2014

Time after Pentecost

Francis of Assisi, renewer of the church, died 1226
Theodor Fliedner, renewer of society, died 1864

Jeremiah 6:1-10
Gleaning a remnant from the vine

Thus says the LORD of hosts:
Glean thoroughly as a vine
    the remnant of Israel;
like a grape-gatherer, pass your hand again
    over its branches.

To whom shall I speak and give warning,
    that they may hear?
See, their ears are closed,
    they cannot listen.
The word of the LORD is to them an object of scorn;
    they take no pleasure in it. (Jer. 6:9-10)

Psalm
Psalm 80:7-15
Look down from heaven, O God

Additional Reading
John 7:40-52
Some accept, others reject Jesus Christ

Hymn: Dearest Jesus, at Your Word, ELW 520

When, O Lord, do we hear your call yet turn away? Prune away the hardened, self-reliant parts of our hearts so that we might be fertile soil where love and faithfulness grow.

Sunday, October 5, 2014

Time after Pentecost

Matthew 21:33-46
The parable of the vineyard owner's son

Jesus said to them, "Have you never read in the scriptures:
  'The stone that the builders rejected
    has become the cornerstone;
  this was the Lord's doing,
    and it is amazing in our eyes'?
Therefore I tell you, the kingdom of God will be taken away from you and given to a people that produces the fruits of the kingdom. The one who falls on this stone will be broken to pieces; and it will crush anyone on whom it falls."

When the chief priests and the Pharisees heard his parables, they realized that he was speaking about them. They wanted to arrest him, but they feared the crowds, because they regarded him as a prophet. (Matt. 21:42-46)

Psalm
Psalm 80:7-15
Look down from heaven, O God

Additional Readings
Isaiah 5:1-7
The song of the vineyard

Philippians 3:4b-14
Nothing surpasses knowing Christ

Hymn: Build Us Up, Lord, ELW 670

Beloved God, from you come all things that are good. Lead us by the inspiration of your Spirit to know those things that are right, and by your merciful guidance, help us to do them, through Jesus Christ, our Savior and Lord.

Monday, October 6, 2014

Time after Pentecost

William Tyndale, translator, martyr, died 1536

Psalm 144
Prayer for blessing

Blessed be the LORD, my rock,
  who trains my hands for war, and my fingers for battle;
my rock and my fortress,
  my stronghold and my deliverer,
my shield, in whom I take refuge,
  who subdues the peoples under me.

O LORD, what are human beings that you regard them,
  or mortals that you think of them?
They are like a breath;
  their days are like a passing shadow. (Ps. 144:1-4)

Additional Readings
Ezekiel 19:10-14
A lament for Israel the vine

1 Peter 2:4-10
Christ the cornerstone

Hymn: My Hope Is Built on Nothing Less, ELW 596/597

*How can it be, generous Lord, that you not only created human beings
but care so deeply for them—flaws, foibles, faithlessness, and all? Your
well of mercy must be never-ending. Thank you for pouring it out on us.*

Tuesday, October 7, 2014

Time after Pentecost

Henry Melchior Muhlenberg, pastor in North America, died 1787

2 Corinthians 5:17-21
God reconciles us through Christ

So if anyone is in Christ, there is a new creation: everything old has passed away; see, everything has become new! All this is from God, who reconciled us to himself through Christ, and has given us the ministry of reconciliation; that is, in Christ God was reconciling the world to himself, not counting their trespasses against them, and entrusting the message of reconciliation to us. So we are ambassadors for Christ, since God is making his appeal through us; we entreat you on behalf of Christ, be reconciled to God. For our sake he made him to be sin who knew no sin, so that in him we might become the righteousness of God. (2 Cor. 5:17-21)

Psalm	**Additional Reading**
Psalm 144	Isaiah 27:1-6
Prayer for blessing	*God will save Israel the vine*

Hymn: Rise, Shine, You People! ELW 665

You renew your people and your church as you build bridges, forgive sins, and use faithful believers to bring hope to the world. May their word of grace take root and bear the fruit of changed, grateful hearts.

Wednesday, October 8, 2014

Time after Pentecost

John 11:45-57

Critics plan to silence Jesus

Now the Passover of the Jews was near, and many went up from the country to Jerusalem before the Passover to purify themselves. They were looking for Jesus and were asking one another as they stood in the temple, "What do you think? Surely he will not come to the festival, will he?" Now the chief priests and the Pharisees had given orders that anyone who knew where Jesus was should let them know, so that they might arrest him. (John 11:55-57)

Psalm

Psalm 144

Prayer for blessing

Additional Reading

Song of Solomon 8:5-14

A love song for the vineyard

Hymn: Oh, Love, How Deep, ELW 322

You know betrayal, suspicion, and disappointment all too well, Lord. When we feel as though the world has turned against us, give us courage to stand firm and look to you as our guide.

Thursday, October 9, 2014

Psalm 23
You spread a table before me

The LORD is my shepherd, I shall not want.
　He makes me lie down in green pastures;
he leads me beside still waters;
　he restores my soul.
He leads me in right paths for his name's sake.

Even though I walk through the darkest valley,
　I fear no evil;
for you are with me;
　your rod and your staff—they comfort me.

You prepare a table before me
　in the presence of my enemies;
you anoint my head with oil;
　my cup overflows.
Surely goodness and mercy shall follow me all the days of my life,
and I shall dwell in the house of the LORD
　my whole life long. (Ps. 23:1-6)

Additional Readings

Isaiah 22:1-8a
A futile cry to the mountains for help

1 Peter 5:1-5, 12-14
Stand fast, the chief shepherd is coming

Hymn: Savior, like a Shepherd Lead Us, ELW 789

Watchful Shepherd, with care and compassion you give us what we need to live—daily food, meaningful work, fulfilling relationships, a rich and abundant planet, and assurance of your constant presence. Thank you.

Friday, October 10, 2014

Time after Pentecost

James 4:4-10
Humble yourselves before God

Submit yourselves therefore to God. Resist the devil, and he will flee from you. Draw near to God, and he will draw near to you. Cleanse your hands, you sinners, and purify your hearts, you double-minded. Lament and mourn and weep. Let your laughter be turned into mourning and your joy into dejection. Humble yourselves before the Lord, and he will exalt you. (James 4:7-10)

Psalm
Psalm 23
You spread a table before me

Additional Reading
Isaiah 22:8b-14
False joy instead of repentance

Hymn: Lord, Whose Love in Humble Service, ELW 712

Help us see humility not as weakness, but as strength—strength in the name of Jesus Christ. May we be single-minded in our devotion to you and open to whatever opportunities for service may arise today.

Saturday, October 11, 2014

Time after Pentecost

Isaiah 24:17-23

God judges the earth from Mount Zion

On that day the LORD will punish
   the host of heaven in heaven,
   and on earth the kings of the earth.
They will be gathered together
   like prisoners in a pit;
they will be shut up in a prison,
   and after many days they will be punished.
Then the moon will be abashed,
   and the sun ashamed;
for the LORD of hosts will reign
   on Mount Zion and in Jerusalem,
and before his elders he will manifest his glory. (Isa. 24:21-23)

Psalm
Psalm 23
You spread a table before me

Additional Reading
Mark 2:18-22
No fasting when the bridegroom is present

Hymn: Oh, Happy Day When We Shall Stand, ELW 441

Your justice, O Lord, can be sharp and swift. For the times when we have failed to care for the poor, follow your teachings, or live as your disciples, we ask for your forgiveness and pray for your mercy.

Sunday, October 12, 2014

Time after Pentecost

Matthew 22:1-14

The parable of the unwelcome guest

"But when the king came in to see the guests, he noticed a man there who was not wearing a wedding robe, and he said to him, 'Friend, how did you get in here without a wedding robe?' And he was speechless. Then the king said to the attendants, 'Bind him hand and foot, and throw him into the outer darkness, where there will be weeping and gnashing of teeth.' For many are called, but few are chosen." (Matt. 22:11-14)

Psalm

Psalm 23

You spread a table before me

Additional Readings

Isaiah 25:1-9

The feast of victory

Philippians 4:1-9

Rejoice in the Lord always

Hymn: All Who Hunger, Gather Gladly, ELW 461

Lord of the feast, you have prepared a table before all peoples and poured out your life with abundance. Call us again to your banquet. Strengthen us by what is honorable, just, and pure, and transform us into a people of righteousness and peace, through Jesus Christ, our Savior and Lord.

Monday, October 13, 2014

Day of Thanksgiving (Canada)

A Blessing of the Household for Thanksgiving Day is provided on page 366.

Psalm 34
Taste and see

O taste and see that the LORD is good;
   happy are those who take refuge in him.
O fear the LORD, you his holy ones,
   for those who fear him have no want.
The young lions suffer want and hunger,
   but those who seek the LORD lack no good thing. (Ps. 34:8-10)

Additional Readings
Exodus 19:7-20
God meets Moses on the mountain

Jude 17-25
Prepare for the Lord's coming

Hymn: Taste and See, ELW 493

We pray for hungry people everywhere, that they might be fed with food that nourishes their bodies and hope that fills their souls. To those of us who have enough, give us generous hearts to share what we have so that others may eat.

Tuesday, October 14, 2014

Time after Pentecost

Amos 9:5-15

Sweet wine from the mountains

The time is surely coming, says the LORD,
  when the one who plows shall overtake the one who reaps,
  and the treader of grapes the one who sows the seed;
the mountains shall drip sweet wine,
  and all the hills shall flow with it.
I will restore the fortunes of my people Israel,
  and they shall rebuild the ruined cities and inhabit them;
they shall plant vineyards and drink their wine,
  and they shall make gardens and eat their fruit.
I will plant them upon their land,
  and they shall never again be plucked up
  out of the land that I have given them,
                    says the LORD your God. (Amos 9:13-15)

Psalm
Psalm 34
Taste and see

Additional Reading
Philippians 3:13—4:1
Hold fast to Christ

Hymn: Sing to the Lord of Harvest, ELW 694

We pray for sojourners everywhere, that they might walk with you as they travel. As we encounter new places and new people, may we be gracious and hospitable as we offer your sense of welcome.

Wednesday, October 15, 2014

Time after Pentecost

Teresa of Avila, teacher, renewer of the church, died 1582

Song of Solomon 7:10—8:4

Love like rich fruit

I am my beloved's,
   and his desire is for me.
Come, my beloved,
   let us go forth into the fields,
   and lodge in the villages;
let us go out early to the vineyards,
   and see whether the vines have budded,
whether the grape blossoms have opened
   and the pomegranates are in bloom.
There I will give you my love.
The mandrakes give forth fragrance,
   and over our doors are all choice fruits,
new as well as old,
   which I have laid up for you, O my beloved. (Song of Sol. 7:10-13)

Psalm
Psalm 34
Taste and see

Additional Reading
John 6:25-35
God will feed the believer

Hymn: Come, Beloved of the Maker, ELW 306

We pray for families everywhere, that spouses care for each other with respect and devotion, parents affirm and encourage their children, children obey and cherish their parents, and Christ's love be shared in all relationships.

Thursday, October 16, 2014

Time after Pentecost

Psalm 96:1-9 [10-13]
God's glory among the nations

O sing to the LORD a new song;
   sing to the LORD, all the earth.
Sing to the LORD, bless his name;
   tell of his salvation from day to day.
Declare his glory among the nations,
   his marvelous works among all the peoples.
For great is the LORD, and greatly to be praised;
   he is to be revered above all gods. (Ps. 96:1-4)

Additional Readings
Judges 17:1-6   3 John 9-12
Before Israel had a king   *Imitate what is good*

Hymn: Earth and All Stars! ELW 731

We pray for believers everywhere, that as we worship we might find the strength to speak out for justice, stand up for truth, and give of ourselves freely and in love.

Friday, October 17, 2014

Time after Pentecost

Ignatius, Bishop of Antioch, martyr, died around 115

1 Peter 5:1-5

Exemplary leadership

Now as an elder myself and a witness of the sufferings of Christ, as well as one who shares in the glory to be revealed, I exhort the elders among you to tend the flock of God that is in your charge, exercising the oversight, not under compulsion but willingly, as God would have you do it—not for sordid gain but eagerly. Do not lord it over those in your charge, but be examples to the flock. And when the chief shepherd appears, you will win the crown of glory that never fades away. In the same way, you who are younger must accept the authority of the elders. And all of you must clothe yourselves with humility in your dealings with one another, for

"God opposes the proud,
     but gives grace to the humble." (1 Peter 5:1-5)

Psalm
Psalm 96:1-9 [10-13]
God's glory among the nations

Additional Reading
Deuteronomy 17:14-20
The limitations of royal authority

Hymn: We All Are One in Mission, ELW 576

We pray for church leaders everywhere, that they might be guided by your Spirit, preach the gospel faithfully, and lead a broken world into the ministry of reconciliation.

Saturday, October 18, 2014

Luke, Evangelist

Luke 1:1-4; 24:44-53
Luke witnesses to the ministry of Jesus

Since many have undertaken to set down an orderly account of the events that have been fulfilled among us, just as they were handed on to us by those who from the beginning were eyewitnesses and servants of the word, I too decided, after investigating everything carefully from the very first, to write an orderly account for you, most excellent Theophilus, so that you may know the truth concerning the things about which you have been instructed. (Luke 1:1-4)

Psalm
Psalm 124
Our help is in God

Additional Readings
Isaiah 43:8-13
You are my witness

2 Timothy 4:5-11
The good fight of faith

Hymn: I Love to Tell the Story, ELW 661

Almighty God, you inspired your servant Luke to reveal in his gospel the love and healing power of your Son. Give your church the same love and power to heal, and to proclaim your salvation among the nations to the glory of your name, through Jesus Christ, your Son, our healer, who lives and reigns with you and the Holy Spirit, one God, now and forever.

Sunday, October 19, 2014

Time after Pentecost

Matthew 22:15-22

A teaching about the emperor and God

But Jesus, aware of [the Pharisees'] malice, said, "Why are you putting me to the test, you hypocrites? Show me the coin used for the tax." And they brought him a denarius. Then he said to them, "Whose head is this, and whose title?" They answered, "The emperor's." Then he said to them, "Give therefore to the emperor the things that are the emperor's, and to God the things that are God's." When they heard this, they were amazed; and they left him and went away. (Matt. 22:18-22)

Psalm

Psalm 96:1-9 [10-13]

God's glory among the nations

Additional Readings

Isaiah 45:1-7

An earthly ruler works God's will

1 Thessalonians 1:1-10

Thanksgiving for the church at Thessalonica

Hymn: We Give Thee but Thine Own, ELW 686

Sovereign God, raise your throne in our hearts. Created by you, let us live in your image; created for you, let us act for your glory; redeemed by you, let us give you what is yours, through Jesus Christ, our Savior and Lord.

Monday, October 20, 2014

Time after Pentecost

Psalm 98
God reigns over the nations

O sing to the LORD a new song,
    for he has done marvelous things.
His right hand and his holy arm
    have gotten him victory.
The LORD has made known his victory;
    he has revealed his vindication in the sight of the nations.
He has remembered his steadfast love and faithfulness
    to the house of Israel.
All the ends of the earth have seen
    the victory of our God. (Ps. 98:1-3)

Additional Readings
Daniel 3:1-18
Three disobey Nebuchadnezzar

Revelation 18:1-10, 19-20
The fall of Babylon

Hymn: Oh, Sing to the Lord, ELW 822

When we look at what you have done for your people throughout the generations, Lord, how can we keep from singing your praise? May your steadfast love inspire us to be faithful in serving you.

Tuesday, October 21, 2014

Time after Pentecost

Daniel 3:19-30

God saves three men in the furnace

Nebuchadnezzar then approached the door of the furnace of blazing fire and said, "Shadrach, Meshach, and Abednego, servants of the Most High God, come out! Come here!" So Shadrach, Meshach, and Abednego came out from the fire. And the satraps, the prefects, the governors, and the king's counselors gathered together and saw that the fire had not had any power over the bodies of those men; the hair of their heads was not singed, their tunics were not harmed, and not even the smell of fire came from them. Nebuchadnezzar said, "Blessed be the God of Shadrach, Meshach, and Abednego, who has sent his angel and delivered his servants who trusted in him. They disobeyed the king's command and yielded up their bodies rather than serve and worship any god except their own God. Therefore I make a decree: Any people, nation, or language that utters blasphemy against the God of Shadrach, Meshach, and Abednego shall be torn limb from limb, and their houses laid in ruins; for there is no other god who is able to deliver in this way." (Dan. 3:26-29)

Psalm

Psalm 98
God reigns over the nations

Additional Reading

Revelation 18:21-24
Babylon will be found no more

Hymn: Evening and Morning, ELW 761

Mighty Lord, you have the power to do miraculous things. When we face hardship beyond belief, give us confidence that you are on our side. Save us from the time of trial and help us endure.

Wednesday, October 22, 2014

Time after Pentecost

Matthew 17:22-27

Jesus pays the temple tax

When they reached Capernaum, the collectors of the temple tax came to Peter and said, "Does your teacher not pay the temple tax?" He said, "Yes, he does." And when he came home, Jesus spoke of it first, asking, "What do you think, Simon? From whom do kings of the earth take toll or tribute? From their children or from others?" When Peter said, "From others," Jesus said to him, "Then the children are free. However, so that we do not give offense to them, go to the sea and cast a hook; take the first fish that comes up; and when you open its mouth, you will find a coin; take that and give it to them for you and me." (Matt. 17:24-27)

Psalm

Psalm 98

God reigns over the nations

Additional Reading

Daniel 6:1-28

Daniel disobeys King Darius

Hymn: Oh, Praise the Gracious Power, ELW 651

Where do we find our sense of worth? Where do we see value in the world? It all comes from your generous hand. Give us this perspective when we get caught up with worries about what is rightfully ours, because everything belongs to you.

Thursday, October 23, 2014

Time after Pentecost

James of Jerusalem, martyr, died around 62

Psalm 1
Their delight is in the law

Happy are those
   who do not follow the advice of the wicked,
or take the path that sinners tread,
   or sit in the seat of scoffers;
but their delight is in the law of the LORD,
   and on his law they meditate day and night.
They are like trees
   planted by streams of water,
which yield their fruit in its season,
   and their leaves do not wither.
In all that they do, they prosper. (Ps. 1:1-3)

Additional Readings
Numbers 5:5-10
Restitution for wronged neighbors

Titus 1:5-16
Troublemakers deny God

Hymn: Oh, That the Lord Would Guide My Ways, ELW 772

Your word, O Lord, is life. Nourish us, sustain us, and give us deep and abiding joy as we meditate on your law and your love.

Friday, October 24, 2014

Time after Pentecost

Titus 2:7-8, 11-15
A life devoted to good works

For the grace of God has appeared, bringing salvation to all, training us to renounce impiety and worldly passions, and in the present age to live lives that are self-controlled, upright, and godly, while we wait for the blessed hope and the manifestation of the glory of our great God and Savior, Jesus Christ. He it is who gave himself for us that he might redeem us from all iniquity and purify for himself a people of his own who are zealous for good deeds. (Titus 2:11-14)

Psalm
Psalm 1
Their delight is in the law

Additional Reading
Deuteronomy 9:25—10:5
The second set of commandments

Hymn: Salvation unto Us Has Come, ELW 590

Lord, your Son, Jesus, showed us how to walk alongside people of every station. Equip your people with zeal for justice, hearts of compassion, and hands that aren't afraid to get dirty as they reach out in your name.

Saturday, October 25, 2014

Time after Pentecost

John 5:39-47
Moses judges the disobedient

[Jesus said to the Jews:] "I have come in my Father's name, and you do not accept me; if another comes in his own name, you will accept him. How can you believe when you accept glory from one another and do not seek the glory that comes from the one who alone is God? Do not think that I will accuse you before the Father; your accuser is Moses, on whom you have set your hope. If you believed Moses, you would believe me, for he wrote about me. But if you do not believe what he wrote, how will you believe what I say?" (John 5:43-47)

Psalm
Psalm 1
Their delight is in the law

Additional Reading
Proverbs 24:23-34
Rise above retribution

Hymn: We All Believe in One True God, ELW 411

Do we truly know you, Lord? Can we possibly find the strength to believe? With humble hearts we bow before you and ask you to make your truth known to us.

Sunday, October 26, 2014

Time after Pentecost

Philipp Nicolai, died 1608; Johann Heermann, died 1647; Paul Gerhardt, died 1676; hymnwriters

Matthew 22:34-46
Loving God and neighbor

When the Pharisees heard that [Jesus] had silenced the Sadducees, they gathered together, and one of them, a lawyer, asked him a question to test him. "Teacher, which commandment in the law is the greatest?" He said to him, "'You shall love the Lord your God with all your heart, and with all your soul, and with all your mind.' This is the greatest and first commandment. And a second is like it: 'You shall love your neighbor as yourself.' On these two commandments hang all the law and the prophets." (Matt. 22:34-40)

Psalm
Psalm 1
Their delight is in the law

Additional Readings
Leviticus 19:1-2, 15-18
Acts of justice

1 Thessalonians 2:1-8
The apostle's concern

Hymn: Rise, O Church, like Christ Arisen, ELW 548

O Lord God, you are the holy lawgiver, you are the salvation of your people. By your Spirit renew us in your covenant of love, and train us to care tenderly for all our neighbors, through Jesus Christ, our Savior and Lord.

Monday, October 27, 2014

Time after Pentecost

Psalm 119:41-48
I will keep God's law

Let your steadfast love come to me, O LORD,
    your salvation according to your promise.
Then I shall have an answer for those who taunt me,
    for I trust in your word.
Do not take the word of truth utterly out of my mouth,
    for my hope is in your ordinances.
I will keep your law continually,
    forever and ever. (Ps. 119:41-44)

Additional Readings
Deuteronomy 6:1-9, 20-25   James 2:8-13
The great commandment   *Fulfilling the royal law*

Hymn: O Jesus, I Have Promised, ELW 810

As we feed our bodies with food, may we feed our hearts with your word. Help us see that you give us limits because you love us, and that when we turn to you, you will always show us the way to live.

Tuesday, October 28, 2014

Simon and Jude, Apostles

John 14:21-27

Those who love Jesus will keep his word

[Jesus said,] "They who have my commandments and keep them are those who love me; and those who love me will be loved by my Father, and I will love them and reveal myself to them." Judas (not Iscariot) said to him, "Lord, how is it that you will reveal yourself to us, and not to the world?" Jesus answered him, "Those who love me will keep my word, and my Father will love them, and we will come to them and make our home with them. Whoever does not love me does not keep my words; and the word that you hear is not mine, but is from the Father who sent me." (John 14:21-24)

Psalm

Psalm 11

Take refuge in God

Additional Readings

Jeremiah 26:[1-6]
7-16

Jeremiah promises the judgment of God

1 John 4:1-6

Do not believe every spirit of this world

Hymn: Here, O Lord, Your Servants Gather, ELW 530

O God, we thank you for the glorious company of the apostles, and especially on this day for Simon and Jude. We pray that, as they were faithful and zealous in your mission, so we may with ardent devotion make known the love and mercy of our Savior Jesus Christ, who lives and reigns with you and the Holy Spirit, one God, now and forever.

Wednesday, October 29, 2014

Time after Pentecost

Matthew 19:16-22

Keeping the commandments

Then someone came to him and said, "Teacher, what good deed must I do to have eternal life?" And he said to him, "Why do you ask me about what is good? There is only one who is good. If you wish to enter into life, keep the commandments." He said to him, "Which ones?" And Jesus said, "You shall not murder; You shall not commit adultery; You shall not steal; You shall not bear false witness; Honor your father and mother; also, You shall love your neighbor as yourself." The young man said to him, "I have kept all these; what do I still lack?" Jesus said to him, "If you wish to be perfect, go, sell your possessions, and give the money to the poor, and you will have treasure in heaven; then come, follow me." When the young man heard this word, he went away grieving, for he had many possessions. (Matt. 19:16-22)

Psalm
Psalm 119:41-48
I will keep God's law

Additional Reading
Proverbs 16:1-20
It is good to obey

Hymn: How Clear Is Our Vocation, Lord, ELW 580

Open our fists when we grasp too tightly at the things in our lives, and give us confidence that in the long run they cannot save us, protect us, comfort us, or encourage us like your Son, Jesus, does.

Thursday, October 30, 2014

Time after Pentecost

Psalm 43
Send out your light and truth

Vindicate me, O God, and defend my cause
    against an ungodly people;
from those who are deceitful and unjust
    deliver me!
For you are the God in whom I take refuge;
    why have you cast me off?
Why must I walk about mournfully
    because of the oppression of the enemy?

O send out your light and your truth;
    let them lead me;
let them bring me to your holy hill
    and to your dwelling.
Then I will go to the altar of God,
    to God my exceeding joy;
and I will praise you with the harp,
    O God, my God. (Ps. 43:1-4)

Additional Readings
1 Samuel 2:27-36
Hope for a better priesthood

Romans 2:17-29
Real circumcision a matter of the heart

Hymn: Christ, Be Our Light, ELW 715

Send your light and your truth into the darkest places of this world: places torn apart by war, relationships shattered by abuse, villages stricken by disease and poverty, and hearts heavy with grief and despair.

Friday, October 31, 2014

Reformation Day

John 8:31-36
The truth will set you free

Then Jesus said to the Jews who had believed in him, "If you continue in my word, you are truly my disciples; and you will know the truth, and the truth will make you free." They answered him, "We are descendants of Abraham and have never been slaves to anyone. What do you mean by saying, 'You will be made free'?"

Jesus answered them, "Very truly, I tell you, everyone who commits sin is a slave to sin. The slave does not have a permanent place in the household; the son has a place there forever. So if the Son makes you free, you will be free indeed." (John 8:31-36)

Psalm

Psalm 46

The God of Jacob is our stronghold

Additional Readings

Jeremiah 31:31-34

I will write my law in their hearts

Romans 3:19-28

Justified by God's grace as a gift

Hymn: Lord, Keep Us Steadfast in Your Word, ELW 517

Almighty God, gracious Lord, we thank you that your Holy Spirit renews the church in every age. Pour out your Holy Spirit on your faithful people. Keep them steadfast in your word, protect and comfort them in times of trial, defend them against all enemies of the gospel, and bestow on the church your saving peace, through Jesus Christ, our Savior and Lord, who lives and reigns with you and the Holy Spirit, one God, now and forever.

PRAYER LIST FOR NOVEMBER

_____

_____

_____

_____

_____

_____

_____

_____

_____

_____

Time after Pentecost

November

The month of November is unique in that it begins with All Saints Day (November 1) and ends with the feast of Christ the King (often the last Sunday of November). The Sunday and daily readings seem to extend the harvest, but in a new way: they speak of God's harvest of *human beings* into their heavenly home.

Perhaps it is no coincidence that November's scriptural emphasis on the consummation of all things in Christ is reflected in the landscape and the chilling temperatures. Yet in the midst of this turning of the seasons and the reminders of death's presence, Christians hold forth the central feast of the year: the death and resurrection of Christ present in baptism and the holy supper. In these last days of the church's year, Christians are invited to celebrate the reign of Christ, whose death on the cross has transformed our deaths into the gate of everlasting life.

Table Prayer for November

Stay with us, God of life,
as we share the bounty of this food and drink.
We give you thanks for those who have gone before us in faith.
Bring us, with them, to the harvest of everlasting life,
where all people will feast forever at your abundant table.
We ask this through Christ our Lord. Amen.

Remembering Those Who Have Died

Use this prayer in the home or at the grave.

O God, our help in ages past and our hope for years to come:
We give you thanks for all your faithful people
who have followed the light of your word throughout the centuries
into our time and place.

Here individual names may be spoken.

As we remember these people,
strengthen us to follow Christ through this world
until we are carried into the harvest of eternal life,
where suffering and death will be no more.
Hear our prayer in the name of the good and gracious shepherd,
Jesus Christ, our Savior and Lord. Amen.

or

With reverence and affection we remember before you,
O everlasting God,
all our departed friends and relatives.
Keep us in union with them here
through faith and love toward you,
that hereafter we may enter into your presence
and be numbered with those who serve you
and look upon your face in glory everlasting,
through your Son, Jesus Christ our Lord. Amen.

Saturday, November 1, 2014

All Saints Day

Matthew 5:1-12
Blessed are the poor in spirit

"Blessed are those who are persecuted for righteousness' sake, for theirs is the kingdom of heaven.

"Blessed are you when people revile you and persecute you and utter all kinds of evil against you falsely on my account. Rejoice and be glad, for your reward is great in heaven, for in the same way they persecuted the prophets who were before you." (Matt. 5:10-12)

Psalm
Psalm 34:1-10, 22
Fear the Lord, you saints

Additional Readings
Revelation 7:9-17
The multitudes of heaven worship the Lamb

1 John 3:1-3
We are God's children

Hymn: Blest Are They, ELW 728

Almighty God, you have knit your people together in one communion in the mystical body of your Son, Jesus Christ our Lord. Grant us grace to follow your blessed saints in lives of faith and commitment, and to know the inexpressible joys you have prepared for those who love you, through Jesus Christ, our Savior and Lord, who lives and reigns with you and the Holy Spirit, one God, now and forever.

Sunday, November 2, 2014

Time after Pentecost

Matthew 23:1-12
Humble yourselves

Then Jesus said to the crowds and to his disciples, "The scribes and the Pharisees sit on Moses' seat; therefore, do whatever they teach you and follow it; but do not do as they do, for they do not practice what they teach. They tie up heavy burdens, hard to bear, and lay them on the shoulders of others; but they themselves are unwilling to lift a finger to move them. They do all their deeds to be seen by others; for they make their phylacteries broad and their fringes long." (Matt. 23:1-5)

Psalm
Psalm 43
Send out your light and truth

Additional Readings
Micah 3:5-12
Judgment upon corrupt leaders

1 Thessalonians 2:9-13
The apostle's teaching

Hymn: Will You Let Me Be Your Servant, ELW 659

O God, generous and supreme, your loving Son lived among us, instructing us in the ways of humility and justice. Continue to ease our burdens, and lead us to serve alongside of him, Jesus Christ, our Savior and Lord.

Monday, November 3, 2014

Time after Pentecost

Martín de Porres, renewer of society, died 1639

Psalm 5
God blesses the righteous

Give ear to my words, O Lord;
 give heed to my sighing.
Listen to the sound of my cry,
 my King and my God,
 for to you I pray.
O Lord, in the morning you hear my voice;
 in the morning I plead my case to you, and watch. . . .

Lead me, O Lord, in your righteousness
 because of my enemies;
 make your way straight before me. (Ps. 5:1-3, 8)

Additional Readings

Jeremiah 5:18-31
Prophets and priests who mislead

1 Thessalonians 2:13-20
Words to the church

Hymn: Golden Breaks the Dawn, ELW 852

O God of every morning, hear our cry at the start of the day. We do not know what may come before the sun sets once more. Graces and troubles await, and much is beyond our control. But we know you hear our hearts and will open a way for us.

Tuesday, November 4, 2014

Time after Pentecost

Lamentations 2:13-17

When prophets see false visions

What can I say for you, to what compare you,
  O daughter Jerusalem?
To what can I liken you, that I may comfort you,
  O virgin daughter Zion?
For vast as the sea is your ruin;
  who can heal you?
Your prophets have seen for you
  false and deceptive visions;
they have not exposed your iniquity
  to restore your fortunes,
but have seen oracles for you
  that are false and misleading.
All who pass along the way
  clap their hands at you;
they hiss and wag their heads
  at daughter Jerusalem;
"Is this the city that was called
  the perfection of beauty,
  the joy of all the earth?" (Lam. 2:13-15)

Psalm
Psalm 5
God blesses the righteous

Additional Reading
Acts 13:1-12
Paul and Barnabas confront a false prophet

Hymn: Jerusalem, My Happy Home, ELW 628

Speak truth to our hearts, O Lord, that we may walk the way that leads to life. Your guidance and correction direct us that we may not fall to ruin. Thank you for a love that seeks our joy and protects us from wrong.

Wednesday, November 5, 2014

Time after Pentecost

Proverbs 16:21-33

The wise heart and persuasive lips

The wise of heart is called perceptive,
    and pleasant speech increases persuasiveness.
Wisdom is a fountain of life to one who has it,
    but folly is the punishment of fools.
The mind of the wise makes their speech judicious,
    and adds persuasiveness to their lips. (Prov. 16:21-23)

Psalm

Psalm 5

God blesses the righteous

Additional Reading

Matthew 15:1-9

Lips that misrepresent the heart

Hymn: Holy God, Holy and Glorious, ELW 637

You are the fountain of all wisdom, Holy One, and you love all creation, hating nothing you have made. So we will listen to your voice, gently caring for all that comes to us this day, seeking justice and blessing for all we see.

Thursday, November 6, 2014

Time after Pentecost

Psalm 70

You are my helper and deliverer

Be pleased, O God, to deliver me.
  O LORD, make haste to help me!
Let those be put to shame and confusion
  who seek my life.
Let those be turned back and brought to dishonor
  who desire to hurt me.
Let those who say, "Aha, Aha!"
  turn back because of their shame.

Let all who seek you
  rejoice and be glad in you.
Let those who love your salvation
  say evermore, "God is great!"
But I am poor and needy;
  hasten to me, O God!
You are my help and my deliverer;
  O LORD, do not delay! (Ps. 70:1-5)

Additional Readings

Amos 1:1—2:5
God judges Israel's neighbors

Revelation 8:6—9:12
The trumpet of God's judgment

Hymn: Immortal, Invisible, God Only Wise, ELW 834

Come quickly to our aid. Save us from the powers and pains that press on our hearts and drag us to the dust. Deliver us from all that oppresses body and spirit that our praise of your goodness may flow like a fountain.

Friday, November 7, 2014

Time after Pentecost

John Christian Frederick Heyer, died 1873; Bartholomaeus Ziegenbalg, died 1719; Ludwig Nommensen, died 1918; missionaries

Amos 3:1-12
Israel's guilt and punishment

Proclaim to the strongholds in Ashdod,
    and to the strongholds in the land of Egypt,
and say, "Assemble yourselves on Mount Samaria,
    and see what great tumults are within it,
    and what oppressions are in its midst."
They do not know how to do right, says the LORD,
    those who store up violence and robbery in their strongholds.
Therefore thus says the Lord GOD:
An adversary shall surround the land,
    and strip you of your defense;
    and your strongholds shall be plundered. (Amos 3:9-11)

Psalm
Psalm 70
You are my helper and deliverer

Additional Reading
Revelation 9:13-21
Unrepentant humankind persists in sin

Hymn: My Life Flows On in Endless Song, ELW 763

Open our eyes to injustice, and turn our hearts to seek the right. Stir us to lift our voices so the oppressed may taste the sweetness of your justice. Help us lead the wandering toward the goodness of your will.

Saturday, November 8, 2014

Time after Pentecost

Matthew 24:1-14

Jesus foretells the end

When [Jesus] was sitting on the Mount of Olives, the disciples came to him privately, saying, "Tell us, when will this be, and what will be the sign of your coming and of the end of the age?" Jesus answered them, "Beware that no one leads you astray. For many will come in my name, saying, 'I am the Messiah!' and they will lead many astray. And you will hear of wars and rumors of wars; see that you are not alarmed; for this must take place, but the end is not yet." (Matt. 24:3-6)

Psalm	**Additional Reading**
Psalm 70	Amos 4:6-13
You are my helper and deliverer	*Israel, prepare to meet your God*

Hymn: Lord Christ, When First You Came to Earth, ELW 727

Calm our hearts and quiet our minds when the restless world shakes our souls and stirs our fears. Grant assurance and peace amid the tumult of these times, for your unfailing love is our beginning and our end.

Sunday, November 9, 2014

Time after Pentecost

Matthew 25:1-13

Wise and foolish bridesmaids

"Then the kingdom of heaven will be like this. Ten bridesmaids took their lamps and went to meet the bridegroom. Five of them were foolish, and five were wise. When the foolish took their lamps, they took no oil with them; but the wise took flasks of oil with their lamps." (Matt. 25:1-4)

Psalm

Psalm 70

You are my helper and deliverer

Additional Readings

Amos 5:18-24

Let justice roll down like waters

1 Thessalonians 4:13-18

The promise of the resurrection

Hymn: Rejoice, Rejoice, Believers, ELW 244

O God of justice and love, you illumine our way through life with the words of your Son. Give us the light we need, and awaken us to the needs of others, through Jesus Christ, our Savior and Lord.

Monday, November 10, 2014

Time after Pentecost

Psalm 63
God is a rich feast

My soul is satisfied as with a rich feast,
    and my mouth praises you with joyful lips
when I think of you on my bed,
    and meditate on you in the watches of the night;
for you have been my help,
    and in the shadow of your wings I sing for joy.
My soul clings to you;
    your right hand upholds me. (Ps. 63:5-8)

Additional Readings
Amos 8:7-14
A famine of hearing God's word

1 Corinthians 14:20-25
They will not listen to me

Hymn: Thy Holy Wings, ELW 613

You are a rich feast of grace and joy beyond all speaking. Fill us with the pleasure of your presence that, tasting your love, we may savor your goodness and smile, knowing our heart's delight.

Tuesday, November 11, 2014

Time after Pentecost

Martin, Bishop of Tours, died 397
Søren Aabye Kierkegaard, teacher, died 1855

1 Thessalonians 3:6-13
Stand firm in the faith

Now may our God and Father himself and our Lord Jesus direct our
way to you. And may the Lord make you increase and abound in
love for one another and for all, just as we abound in love for you.
And may he so strengthen your hearts in holiness that you may be
blameless before our God and Father at the coming of our Lord Jesus
with all his saints. (1 Thess. 3:11-13)

Psalm
Psalm 63
God is a rich feast

Additional Reading
Joel 1:1-14
Call to repentance

Hymn: Blest Be the Tie That Binds, ELW 656

*You draw us into the community of Christ that we might share the
goodness of the love you are. Bear us into the arms of sisters and
brothers who know and love you that our hearts may be firm and true,
trusting you in all things.*

Wednesday, November 12, 2014

Time after Pentecost

Matthew 24:29-35

My words will not pass away

"From the fig tree learn its lesson: as soon as its branch becomes tender and puts forth its leaves, you know that summer is near. So also, when you see all these things, you know that he is near, at the very gates. Truly I tell you, this generation will not pass away until all these things have taken place. Heaven and earth will pass away, but my words will not pass away." (Matt. 24:32-35)

Psalm
Psalm 63
God is a rich feast

Additional Reading
Joel 3:9-21
Promise of a glorious future

Hymn: My Lord, What a Morning, ELW 438

Limbs once green now stand bare in autumn winds. Everything we see and touch fades and fails like our strength at the close of the day. But not you, Holy One. Your grace and promise stand firm, unshakable, that we may trust you amid a world of change.

Thursday, November 13, 2014

Time after Pentecost

Psalm 90:1-8 [9-11] 12
Number your days

Lord, you have been our dwelling place
    in all generations.
Before the mountains were brought forth,
    or ever you had formed the earth and the world,
    from everlasting to everlasting you are God.

You turn us back to dust,
    and say, "Turn back, you mortals."
For a thousand years in your sight
    are like yesterday when it is past,
    or like a watch in the night. (Ps. 90:1-4)

Additional Readings
Ezekiel 6:1-14
Judgment on idolatrous Israel

Revelation 16:1-7
God's judgments are true and just

Hymn: How Small Our Span of Life, ELW 636

You are our home from everlasting to everlasting. Ever waiting, ever welcoming, always present and steadfast, certain and sure when all else falls away. Welcome us this day into your arms that our wandering souls may come home to dwell in you.

Friday, November 14, 2014

Ezekiel 7:1-9
The end is upon us

The word of the LORD came to me: You, O mortal, thus says the Lord
GOD to the land of Israel:
An end! The end has come
upon the four corners of the land.
Now the end is upon you,
I will let loose my anger upon you;
I will judge you according to your ways,
I will punish you for all your abominations.
My eye will not spare you, I will have no pity.
I will punish you for your ways,
while your abominations are among you.
Then you shall know that I am the LORD. (Ezek. 7:1-4)

Psalm
Psalm 90:1-8 [9-11] 12
Number your days

Additional Reading
Revelation 16:8-21
The judged curse God

Hymn: My God, How Wonderful Thou Art, ELW 863

*Who can stand when you judge our sins and faults, O Lord? But your
compassion towers above the guilt and condemnation that weigh on us.
Your mercy is greater than all our wrongs. Lift us to newness above the
sorrow of our sins.*

Saturday, November 15, 2014

Time after Pentecost

Matthew 12:43-45
From bad to worse

"When the unclean spirit has gone out of a person, it wanders through waterless regions looking for a resting place, but it finds none. Then it says, 'I will return to my house from which I came.' When it comes, it finds it empty, swept, and put in order. Then it goes and brings along seven other spirits more evil than itself, and they enter and live there; and the last state of that person is worse than the first. So will it be also with this evil generation." (Matt. 12:43-45)

Psalm
Psalm 90:1-8 [9-11] 12
Number your days

Additional Reading
Ezekiel 7:10-27
You shall know that the Lord is God

Hymn: Goodness Is Stronger than Evil, ELW 721

Our hearts ache for the fullness of a love that will never leave us. Fill the empty and barren places in our souls with your presence that we may not fall prey to evils of heart and hand that come.

Sunday, November 16, 2014

Time after Pentecost

Matthew 25:14-30
Slaves entrusted with talents

"Then the [slave] who had received the one talent also came forward, saying, 'Master, I knew that you were a harsh man, reaping where you did not sow, and gathering where you did not scatter seed; so I was afraid, and I went and hid your talent in the ground. Here you have what is yours.' But his master replied, 'You wicked and lazy slave! You knew, did you, that I reap where I did not sow, and gather where I did not scatter? Then you ought to have invested my money with the bankers, and on my return I would have received what was my own with interest. So take the talent from him, and give it to the one with the ten talents.'" (Matt. 25:24-28)

Psalm
Psalm 90:1-8 [9-11] 12
Number your days

Additional Readings
Zephaniah 1:7, 12-18
The day of the Lord

1 Thessalonians 5:1-11
Be alert for the day of the Lord

Hymn: God, Whose Giving Knows No Ending, ELW 678

Righteous God, our merciful master, you own the earth and all its peoples, and you give us all that we have. Inspire us to serve you with justice and wisdom, and prepare us for the joy of the day of your coming, through Jesus Christ, our Savior and Lord.

Monday, November 17, 2014

Time after Pentecost

Elizabeth of Hungary, renewer of society, died 1231

Psalm 9:1-14
God's reward for the righteous

I will give thanks to the LORD with my whole heart;
  I will tell of all your wonderful deeds.
I will be glad and exult in you;
  I will sing praise to your name, O Most High.
When my enemies turned back,
  they stumbled and perished before you.
For you have maintained my just cause;
  you have sat on the throne giving righteous judgment. (Ps. 9:1-4)

Additional Readings
Zechariah 1:7-17
God's judgment and mercy

Romans 2:1-11
The righteous judgment of God

Hymn: Lord, I Lift Your Name on High, ELW 857

We lift our hands to you, O Lord, and pour out our praise. For you come to us in every time of trouble, lifting our souls that we may breathe the joy of deliverance. Uphold our cause that our hearts may sing.

Tuesday, November 18, 2014

Time after Pentecost

Zechariah 2:1-5; 5:1-4
Visions of mercy and judgment

I looked up and saw a man with a measuring line in his hand. Then I asked, "Where are you going?" He answered me, "To measure Jerusalem, to see what is its width and what is its length." Then the angel who talked with me came forward, and another angel came forward to meet him, and said to him, "Run, say to that young man: Jerusalem shall be inhabited like villages without walls, because of the multitude of people and animals in it. For I will be a wall of fire all around it, says the LORD, and I will be the glory within it." (Zech. 2:1-5)

Psalm
Psalm 9:1-14
God's reward for the righteous

Additional Reading
1 Thessalonians 5:12-18
The Christian life

Hymn: Rejoice, Ye Pure in Heart! ELW 873/874

Tear down the walls around our hearts and homes. Destroy the boundaries about our sanctuaries that all drawn by your grace may enter and bask in the warmth and glory of your presence.

Wednesday, November 19, 2014

Time after Pentecost

Matthew 24:45-51
Parable of the unfaithful slave

"Who then is the faithful and wise slave, whom his master has put in charge of his household, to give the other slaves their allowance of food at the proper time? Blessed is that slave whom his master will find at work when he arrives. Truly I tell you, he will put that one in charge of all his possessions." (Matt. 24:45-47)

Psalm
Psalm 9:1-14
God's reward for the righteous

Additional Reading
Job 16:1-21
A lament about unjust punishment

Hymn: Lord Jesus, You Shall Be My Song, ELW 808

You give the freshness of morning that we may have one more chance to know, love, and serve you. May our words and actions be faithful to you this day, for you are ever faithful to your promise to be with us always.

Thursday, November 20, 2014

Time after Pentecost

Psalm 95:1-7a
We are the people of God's pasture

O come, let us sing to the LORD;
> let us make a joyful noise to the rock of our salvation!
Let us come into his presence with thanksgiving;
> let us make a joyful noise to him with songs of praise!
For the LORD is a great God,
> and a great King above all gods.
In his hand are the depths of the earth;
> the heights of the mountains are his also.
The sea is his, for he made it,
> and the dry land, which his hands have formed. (Ps. 95:1-5)

Additional Readings
1 Kings 22:13-23   **Revelation 14:1-11**
Israel like sheep without a shepherd   *Fear God and give God glory*

Hymn: O Christ, What Can It Mean for Us, ELW 431

Open our eyes to the majesty of earth and sky, to the vastness of the sea, and to the depth of your saving love that our lips may pour out praise and joy. Lift us once more into your presence where our lives are complete.

Friday, November 21, 2014

Time after Pentecost

Revelation 22:1-9
Worship God alone

Then the angel showed me the river of the water of life, bright as crystal, flowing from the throne of God and of the Lamb through the middle of the street of the city. On either side of the river is the tree of life with its twelve kinds of fruit, producing its fruit each month; and the leaves of the tree are for the healing of the nations. Nothing accursed will be found there any more. But the throne of God and of the Lamb will be in it, and his servants will worship him; they will see his face, and his name will be on their foreheads. And there will be no more night; they need no light of lamp or sun, for the Lord God will be their light, and they will reign forever and ever. (Rev. 22:1-5)

Psalm
Psalm 95:1-7a
We are the people of God's pasture

Additional Reading
1 Chronicles 17:1-15
David, shepherd and king of Israel

Hymn: Crown Him with Many Crowns, ELW 855

A river of healing grace flows from your divine heart, O Lord, healing the ache of our souls for you. Let us drink from this stream of life that we may be made whole and bring your healing to all we meet and touch.

Saturday, November 22, 2014

Time after Pentecost

Matthew 12:46-50

The true kindred of Jesus

While [Jesus] was still speaking to the crowds, his mother and his brothers were standing outside, wanting to speak to him. Someone told him, "Look, your mother and your brothers are standing outside, wanting to speak to you." But to the one who had told him this, Jesus replied, "Who is my mother, and who are my brothers?" And pointing to his disciples, he said, "Here are my mother and my brothers! For whoever does the will of my Father in heaven is my brother and sister and mother." (Matt. 12:46-50)

Psalm

Psalm 95:1-7a

We are the people of God's pasture

Additional Reading

Isaiah 44:21-28

Cyrus, a shepherd for the Lord

Hymn: What God Ordains Is Good Indeed, ELW 776

You call us from our aloneness into holy communion with all who seek your love and love your will. Open our hearts and minds to receive the blessed oneness we share with all our sisters and brothers who belong to you.

Sunday, November 23, 2014

Christ the King

Clement, Bishop of Rome, died around 100
Miguel Agustín Pro, martyr, died 1927

Matthew 25:31-46
The separation of sheep and goats

"Then [the king] will say to those at his left hand, 'You that are accursed, depart from me into the eternal fire prepared for the devil and his angels; for I was hungry and you gave me no food, I was thirsty and you gave me nothing to drink, I was a stranger and you did not welcome me, naked and you did not give me clothing, sick and in prison and you did not visit me.' Then they also will answer, 'Lord, when was it that we saw you hungry or thirsty or a stranger or naked or sick or in prison, and did not take care of you?' Then he will answer them, 'Truly I tell you, just as you did not do it to one of the least of these, you did not do it to me.'" (Matt. 25:41-45)

Psalm
Psalm 95:1-7a
We are the people of God's pasture

Additional Readings
Ezekiel 34:11-16, 20-24
God will shepherd Israel

Ephesians 1:15-23
The reign of Christ

Hymn: Soon and Very Soon, ELW 439

O God of power and might, your Son shows us the way of service, and in him we inherit the riches of your grace. Give us the wisdom to know what is right and the strength to serve the world you have made, through Jesus Christ, our Savior and Lord, who lives and reigns with you and the Holy Spirit, one God, now and forever.

Monday, November 24, 2014

Time after Pentecost

Justus Falckner, died 1723; Jehu Jones, died 1852; William Passavant, died 1894; pastors in North America

Psalm 7
God the righteous judge

O let the evil of the wicked come to an end,
    but establish the righteous,
you who test the minds and hearts,
    O righteous God.
God is my shield,
    who saves the upright in heart.
God is a righteous judge,
    and a God who has indignation every day. (Ps. 7:9-11)

Additional Readings
Esther 2:1-18
Lowly Esther becomes queen

2 Timothy 2:8-13
Those who endure with Christ reign with him

Hymn: Jesus Shall Reign, ELW 434

Who can stand, Holy One, when you test human hearts? Our sins and mistakes haunt us in the night. Yet we dare come to you again because your heart is righteous and true to your promise to cleanse our souls and make us new.

Tuesday, November 25, 2014

Time after Pentecost

Isaac Watts, hymnwriter, died 1748

Esther 8:3-17

Queen Esther saves her people

Then Esther spoke again to the king; she fell at his feet, weeping and pleading with him to avert the evil design of Haman the Agagite and the plot that he had devised against the Jews. The king held out the golden scepter to Esther, and Esther rose and stood before the king. She said, "If it pleases the king, and if I have won his favor, and if the thing seems right before the king, and I have his approval, let an order be written to revoke the letters devised by Haman son of Hammedatha the Agagite, which he wrote giving orders to destroy the Jews who are in all the provinces of the king. For how can I bear to see the calamity that is coming on my people? Or how can I bear to see the destruction of my kindred?" (Esther 8:3-6)

Psalm

Psalm 7

God the righteous judge

Additional Reading

Revelation 19:1-9

Praise of God's judgments

Hymn: The Trumpets Sound, the Angels Sing, ELW 531

Deliver us from evil, O Lord, and awaken our hearts to the plight of those who bear the weight of oppression. Rouse our hearts from easy comfort and apathy that we may be true to your calling to do justice and mercy.

Wednesday, November 26, 2014

Time after Pentecost

John 5:19-40
The judgment of the Son

"Very truly, I tell you, the hour is coming, and is now here, when the dead will hear the voice of the Son of God, and those who hear will live. For just as the Father has life in himself, so he has granted the Son also to have life in himself; and he has given him authority to execute judgment, because he is the Son of Man. Do not be astonished at this; for the hour is coming when all who are in their graves will hear his voice and will come out—those who have done good, to the resurrection of life, and those who have done evil, to the resurrection of condemnation." (John 5:25-29)

Psalm
Psalm 7
God the righteous judge

Additional Reading
Ezekiel 33:7-20
The righteous will live

Hymn: You Are Mine, ELW 581

Blessed are you, God of the living and the dead, for even the dead are alive to you. You see where we fall and call us all home to share in the resurrection you have prepared for those who hunger for your kindness.

Blessing of the Household for Thanksgiving Day

We gather this day to give thanks to God for the gifts of this land and its people, for God has been generous to us. As we ask God's blessing upon this food we share, may we be mindful of the lonely and the hungry.

As we prepare to offer thanks to God,
let us listen to the words of scripture:

I give thanks to my God always for you because of the grace of God that has been given you in Christ Jesus, for in every way you have been enriched in him, in speech and knowledge of every kind—just as the testimony of Christ has been strengthened among you—so that you are not lacking in any spiritual gift as you wait for the revealing of our Lord Jesus Christ. He will also strengthen you to the end, so that you may be blameless on the day of our Lord Jesus Christ. (1 Cor. 1:4-8)

Let us pray.
God most provident,
we join all creation in offering you praise through Jesus Christ.
For generations the people of this land have sung of your bounty.
With them, we offer you thanksgiving
for the rich harvest we have received at your hands.
Bless us and this food that we share with grateful hearts.
Continue to make our land fruitful
and let our love for you be seen in our pursuit of justice and peace
and in our generous response to those in need.
We ask this through Christ our Lord. Amen.

May Christ, the living bread, bring us to the feast of eternal life.
Amen.

Thursday, November 27, 2014

Day of Thanksgiving (U.S.A.)

Psalm 80:1-7, 17-19
We shall be saved

Give ear, O Shepherd of Israel,
  you who lead Joseph like a flock!
You who are enthroned upon the cherubim, shine forth
  before Ephraim and Benjamin and Manasseh.
Stir up your might,
  and come to save us!

Restore us, O God;
  let your face shine, that we may be saved. (Ps. 80:1-3)

Additional Readings
Zechariah 13:1-9
The coming day of God brings cleansing

Revelation 14:6-13
Hold fast to the faith

Hymn: Praise the Lord, Rise Up Rejoicing, ELW 544

We live in the smile of your delight, Holy One, and we die when you seem to turn away. Shine the light of your pleasure on us that we may warm ourselves in that love that will never let us go.

Friday, November 28, 2014

Time after Pentecost

1 Thessalonians 4:1-18

A life pleasing God to the end

But we do not want you to be uninformed, brothers and sisters, about those who have died, so that you may not grieve as others do who have no hope. For since we believe that Jesus died and rose again, even so, through Jesus, God will bring with him those who have died. For this we declare to you by the word of the Lord, that we who are alive, who are left until the coming of the Lord, will by no means precede those who have died. For the Lord himself, with a cry of command, with the archangel's call and with the sound of God's trumpet, will descend from heaven, and the dead in Christ will rise first. Then we who are alive, who are left, will be caught up in the clouds together with them to meet the Lord in the air; and so we will be with the Lord forever. (1 Thess. 4:13-17)

Psalm
Psalm 80:1-7, 17-19
We shall be saved

Additional Reading
Zechariah 14:1-9
God will come to rule

Hymn: Lo! He Comes with Clouds Descending, ELW 435

We do not grieve as those who have no hope, O Lord, for we know you. You liberate our dreams because we know it is your pleasure to raise us from death and overwhelm our sorrows with the joy of everlasting life.

Saturday, November 29, 2014

Time after Pentecost

Micah 2:1-13
God will gather all

I will surely gather all of you, O Jacob,
 I will gather the survivors of Israel;
I will set them together
 like sheep in a fold,
like a flock in its pasture;
 it will resound with people.
The one who breaks out will go up before them;
 they will break through and pass the gate,
 going out by it.
Their king will pass on before them,
 the LORD at their head. (Micah 2:12-13)

Psalm
Psalm 80:1-7, 17-19
We shall be saved

Additional Reading
Matthew 24:15-31
Be ready for that day

Hymn: The King of Love My Shepherd Is, ELW 502

Holy and loving Shepherd, you lead us into pastures of your presence so we may feast on the fullness of love and life that our hearts desire. May we follow where you lead and live our days within the safety of your arms.

ADVENT

In the days of Advent, Christians prepare to celebrate the presence of God's Word among us in our own day. During these four weeks, we pray that the reign of God, which Jesus preached and lived, would come among us. We pray that God's justice would flourish in our land, that the people of the earth would live in peace, that the weak and the sick and the hungry would be strengthened, healed, and fed with God's merciful presence.

During the last days of Advent, Christians welcome Christ with names inspired by the prophets: wisdom, liberator of slaves, mighty power, radiant dawn and sun of justice, the keystone of the arch of humanity, and Emmanuel—God with us.

Table Prayer for Advent

Blessed are you, O Lord our God,
the one who is, who was, and who is to come.
At this table you fill us with good things.
May these gifts strengthen us
to share with the hungry and all those in need,
as we wait and watch for your coming among us
in Jesus Christ our Lord. Amen.

The Advent Wreath

One of the best known customs for the season is the Advent wreath. The wreath and winter candle-lighting in the midst of growing darkness strengthen some of the Advent images found in the Bible. The unbroken circle of greens is clearly an image of everlasting life, a victory wreath, the crown of Christ, or the wheel of time itself. Christians use the wreath as a sign that Christ reaches into our time to lead us to the light of everlasting life. The four candles mark the progress of the four weeks of Advent and the growth of light. Sometimes the wreath is embellished with natural dried flowers or fruit. Its evergreen branches lead the household and the congregation to the evergreen Christmas tree. In many homes, the family gathers for prayer around the wreath.

Lighting the Advent Wreath

Use this blessing when lighting the first candle.

Blessed are you, O Lord our God, ruler of the universe.
You call all nations to walk in your light
and to seek your ways of justice and peace,
for the night is past, and the dawn of your coming is near.
Bless us as we light the first candle of this wreath.
Rouse us from sleep,
that we may be ready to greet our Lord when he comes
and welcome him into our hearts and homes,
for he is our light and our salvation.
Blessed be God forever.

Sunday, November 30, 2014

First Sunday of Advent

Andrew, Apostle (transferred to December 1)

Mark 13:24-37

The coming of the Son of Man

"But about that day or hour no one knows, neither the angels in heaven, nor the Son, but only the Father. Beware, keep alert; for you do not know when the time will come. It is like a man going on a journey, when he leaves home and puts his slaves in charge, each with his work, and commands the doorkeeper to be on the watch. Therefore, keep awake—for you do not know when the master of the house will come, in the evening, or at midnight, or at cockcrow, or at dawn, or else he may find you asleep when he comes suddenly. And what I say to you I say to all: Keep awake." (Mark 13:32-37)

Psalm

Psalm 80:1-7, 17-19
We shall be saved

Additional Readings

Isaiah 64:1-9
God will come with power and compassion

1 Corinthians 1:3-9
Gifts of grace sustain us

Hymn: Wake, Awake, for Night Is Flying, ELW 436

Stir up your power, Lord Christ, and come. By your merciful protection awaken us to the threatening dangers of our sins, and keep us blameless until the coming of your new day, for you live and reign with the Father and the Holy Spirit, one God, now and forever.

_____

_____

_____

_____

_____

_____

_____

_____

_____

_____

Monday, December 1, 2014

Andrew, Apostle (*transferred*)

John 1:35-42
Jesus calls Andrew

One of the two who heard John speak and followed him was Andrew, Simon Peter's brother. He first found his brother Simon and said to him, "We have found the Messiah" (which is translated Anointed). He brought Simon to Jesus, who looked at him and said, "You are Simon son of John. You are to be called Cephas" (which is translated Peter). (John 1:40-42)

Psalm

Psalm 19:1-6

The heavens declare God's glory

Additional Readings

Ezekiel 3:16-21

A sentinel for the house of Israel

Romans 10:10-18

Faith comes from the word of Christ

Hymn: Jesus Calls Us; o'er the Tumult, ELW 696

Almighty God, you gave your apostle Andrew the grace to obey the call of your Son and to bring his brother to Jesus. Give us also, who are called by your holy word, grace to follow Jesus without delay and to bring into his presence those who are near to us, for he lives and reigns with you and the Holy Spirit, one God, now and forever.

Tuesday, December 2, 2014

Week of Advent I

Revelation 18:1-10

Judgment upon human pride

After this I saw another angel coming down from heaven, having great authority; and the earth was made bright with his splendor. He called out with a mighty voice,

"Fallen, fallen is Babylon the great!
　It has become a dwelling place of demons,
a haunt of every foul spirit,
　a haunt of every foul bird,
　a haunt of every foul and hateful beast.
For all the nations have drunk
　of the wine of the wrath of her fornication,
and the kings of the earth have committed fornication with her,
　and the merchants of the earth have grown rich
　　from the power of her luxury." (Rev. 18:1-3)

Psalm

Psalm 79

Prayer for deliverance

Additional Reading

Micah 4:6-13

A promise of restoration after exile

Hymn: Come, Thou Long-Expected Jesus, ELW 254

Redeemer God, how often we feel that we dwell with demons and other foul and hateful beasts. Remind us that our redemption is at hand and give us courage to turn away from the fallen Babylons of our time.

Wednesday, December 3, 2014

Week of Advent 1

Francis Xavier, missionary to Asia, died 1552

Micah 5:1-5a

A promise of a shepherd

But you, O Bethlehem of Ephrathah,
    who are one of the little clans of Judah,
from you shall come forth for me
    one who is to rule in Israel,
whose origin is from of old,
    from ancient days.
Therefore he shall give them up until the time
    when she who is in labor has brought forth;
then the rest of his kindred shall return
    to the people of Israel.
And he shall stand and feed his flock in the strength of the Lord,
    in the majesty of the name of the Lord his God.
And they shall live secure, for now he shall be great
    to the ends of the earth;
and he shall be the one of peace. (Micah 5:2-5a)

Psalm

Psalm 79
Prayer for deliverance

Additional Reading

Luke 21:34-38
Be alert for that day

Hymn: Come Now, O Prince of Peace, ELW 247

Shepherd God, we know that we can never wander too far away to be found. Gather your flock back to your safety. Bring us the security that only you can give and lead us to pastures of peace and plenty.

Thursday, December 4, 2014

Week of Advent 1

John of Damascus, theologian and hymnwriter, died around 749

Psalm 85:1-2, 8-13
Righteousness and peace

Let me hear what God the LORD will speak,
   for he will speak peace to his people,
   to his faithful, to those who turn to him in their hearts.
Surely his salvation is at hand for those who fear him,
   that his glory may dwell in our land.

Steadfast love and faithfulness will meet;
   righteousness and peace will kiss each other.
Faithfulness will spring up from the ground,
   and righteousness will look down from the sky.
The LORD will give what is good,
   and our land will yield its increase. (Ps. 85:8-12)

Additional Readings
Hosea 6:1-6
Return to the God of life and love

1 Thessalonians 1:2-10
Paul thanks God for the Thessalonians

Hymn: People, Look East, ELW 248

Fertile God, transform us into faith-supporting soil. Turn our stony hearts into soft spaces where seeds can sprout and good can increase. Let our hearts be a home where righteousness and peace can kiss each other.

Friday, December 5, 2014

Week of Advent 1

Jeremiah 1:4-10

God appoints a prophet

Now the word of the LORD came to me saying,
    "Before I formed you in the womb I knew you,
    and before you were born I consecrated you;
    I appointed you a prophet to the nations."
Then I said, "Ah, Lord GOD! Truly I do not know how to speak, for I
am only a boy." But the LORD said to me,
    "Do not say, 'I am only a boy';
    for you shall go to all to whom I send you.
    and you shall speak whatever I command you.
    Do not be afraid of them,
    for I am with you to deliver you,

                says the LORD." (Jer. 1:4-8)

Psalm
Psalm 85:1-2, 8-13
Righteousness and peace

Additional Reading
Acts 11:19-26
The new community called "Christian"

Hymn: Here I Am, Lord, ELW 574

*Creator God, who knew us from our earliest formation, remind us of
the potential that often only you can see in us. Reconsecrate us for our
truest purpose and deliver us from all that threatens us.*

Saturday, December 6, 2014

Week of Advent 1

Nicholas, Bishop of Myra, died around 342

Ezekiel 36:24-28

A new heart and a new spirit

I will take you from the nations, and gather you from all the countries, and bring you into your own land. I will sprinkle clean water upon you, and you shall be clean from all your uncleannesses, and from all your idols I will cleanse you. A new heart I will give you, and a new spirit I will put within you; and I will remove from your body the heart of stone and give you a heart of flesh. I will put my spirit within you, and make you follow my statutes and be careful to observe my ordinances. Then you shall live in the land that I gave to your ancestors; and you shall be my people, and I will be your God. (Ezek. 36:24-28)

Psalm
Psalm 85:1-2, 8-13
Righteousness and peace

Additional Reading
Mark 11:27-33
Jesus a prophet like John the Baptist

Hymn: God, My Lord, My Strength, ELW 795

O God, you know we long to trade our hearts of stone for hearts of flesh. Wash us with the water only you can give. Cleanse us and restore to us a right spirit, your spirit.

Lighting the Advent Wreath

Use this blessing when lighting the first two candles.

Blessed are you, O Lord our God, ruler of the universe.
John the Baptist calls all people to prepare the Lord's way,
for the kingdom of heaven is near.
Bless us as we light the candles on this wreath.
Baptize us with the fire of your Spirit,
that we may be a light shining in the darkness,
welcoming others as Christ has welcomed us,
for he is our light and our salvation.
Blessed be God forever.

Sunday, December 7, 2014

Second Sunday of Advent

Ambrose, Bishop of Milan, died 397

Mark 1:1-8

John appears from the wilderness

John the baptizer appeared in the wilderness, proclaiming a baptism of repentance for the forgiveness of sins. And people from the whole Judean countryside and all the people of Jerusalem were going out to him, and were baptized by him in the river Jordan, confessing their sins. Now John was clothed with camel's hair, with a leather belt around his waist, and he ate locusts and wild honey. He proclaimed, "The one who is more powerful than I is coming after me; I am not worthy to stoop down and untie the thong of his sandals. I have baptized you with water; but he will baptize you with the Holy Spirit." (Mark 1:4-8)

Psalm
Psalm 85:1-2, 8-13
Righteousness and peace

Additional Readings
Isaiah 40:1-11
God's coming to the exiles

2 Peter 3:8-15a
Waiting for the day of God

Hymn: Hark! A Thrilling Voice Is Sounding! ELW 246

Stir up our hearts, Lord God, to prepare the way of your only Son. By his coming strengthen us to serve you with purified lives; through Jesus Christ, our Savior and Lord, who lives and reigns with you and the Holy Spirit, one God, now and forever.

Monday, December 8, 2014

Week of Advent 2

Psalm 27
God's level path

Teach me your way, O LORD,
    and lead me on a level path
    because of my enemies.
Do not give me up to the will of my adversaries,
    for false witnesses have risen against me,
    and they are breathing out violence.

I believe that I shall see the goodness of the LORD
    in the land of the living.
Wait for the LORD;
    be strong, and let your heart take courage;
    wait for the LORD! (Ps. 27:11-14)

Additional Readings
Isaiah 26:7-15
The way of the righteous is level

Acts 2:37-42
Baptism in the name of Jesus

Hymn: Lead Me, Guide Me, ELW 768

Savior God, we have waited long nights in darkness. Give us courage as we keep our watch. Help our hearts be strong. Lead us always to the land of the living and away from those who breathe violence.

Tuesday, December 9, 2014

Week of Advent 2

Isaiah 4:2-6

God will wash Israel clean

On that day the branch of the LORD shall be beautiful and glorious, and the fruit of the land shall be the pride and glory of the survivors of Israel. Whoever is left in Zion and remains in Jerusalem will be called holy, everyone who has been recorded for life in Jerusalem, once the LORD has washed away the filth of the daughters of Zion and cleansed the bloodstains of Jerusalem from its midst by a spirit of judgment and by a spirit of burning. Then the LORD will create over the whole site of Mount Zion and over its places of assembly a cloud by day and smoke and the shining of a flaming fire by night. Indeed over all the glory there will be a canopy. It will serve as a pavilion, a shade by day from the heat, and a refuge and a shelter from the storm and rain. (Isa. 4:2-6)

Psalm
Psalm 27
God's level path

Additional Reading
Acts 11:1-18
John and Peter baptize

Hymn: Lost in the Night, ELW 243

Cleansing God, come to us in fire, water, smoke, and shade. Be our refuge and our shelter from all the storms that batter us. Let us shine in the darkness that surrounds us.

Wednesday, December 10, 2014

Week of Advent 2

Luke 1:5-17
The messenger in the temple

The angel said to [Zechariah], "Do not be afraid, Zechariah, for your prayer has been heard. Your wife Elizabeth will bear you a son, and you will name him John. You will have joy and gladness, and many will rejoice at his birth, for he will be great in the sight of the Lord. He must never drink wine or strong drink; even before his birth he will be filled with the Holy Spirit. He will turn many of the people of Israel to the Lord their God. With the spirit and power of Elijah he will go before him, to turn the hearts of parents to their children, and the disobedient to the wisdom of the righteous, to make ready a people prepared for the Lord." (Luke 1:13-17)

Psalm
Psalm 27
God's level path

Additional Reading
Malachi 2:10—3:1
The coming messenger

Hymn: Comfort, Comfort Now My People, ELW 256

God of miracles, who can bring fertility out of both barrenness and virginity, help us always to remember that you are not limited by our imaginations. Give us the courage to say yes to your dreams.

Thursday, December 11, 2014

Week of Advent 2

Psalm 126

God does great things for us

When the LORD restored the fortunes of Zion,
    we were like those who dream.
Then our mouth was filled with laughter,
    and our tongue with shouts of joy;
then it was said among the nations,
    "The LORD has done great things for them."
The LORD has done great things for us,
    and we rejoiced. (Ps. 126:1-3)

Additional Readings
Habakkuk 2:1-5
A vision concerning the end

Philippians 3:7-11
The righteousness that comes through faith

Hymn: Hark, the Glad Sound! ELW 239

God of visions, in this time when so many of us have forgotten how to dream, restore to us our imaginations. Let us rejoice to realize our redemption. Let us shout with joy as we share the good news.

Friday, December 12, 2014

Week of Advent 2

Philippians 3:12-16

The prize of God's call in Christ

Not that I have already obtained this or have already reached the goal; but I press on to make it my own, because Christ Jesus has made me his own. Beloved, I do not consider that I have made it my own; but this one thing I do: forgetting what lies behind and straining forward to what lies ahead, I press on toward the goal for the prize of the heavenly call of God in Christ Jesus. Let those of us then who are mature be of the same mind; and if you think differently about anything, this too God will reveal to you. Only let us hold fast to what we have attained. (Phil. 3:12-16)

Psalm

Psalm 126

God does great things for us

Additional Reading

Habakkuk 3:2-6

A prayer for God's glory and mercy

Hymn: My Faith Looks Up to Thee, ELW 759

Steadfast God, you know how easily distracted we can be. Help us to press on toward the prizes you have prepared. Help us to hold fast to the goals you have for us and lead us to your revelations.

Saturday, December 13, 2014

Week of Advent 2

Lucy, martyr, died 304

Habakkuk 3:13-19

God's devastation, God's deliverance

Though the fig tree does not blossom,
    and no fruit is on the vines;
though the produce of the olive fails
    and the fields yield no food;
though the flock is cut off from the fold
    and there is no herd in the stalls,
yet I will rejoice in the LORD;
    I will exult in the God of my salvation.
God, the LORD, is my strength;
    he makes my feet like the feet of a deer,
    and makes me tread upon the heights. (Hab. 3:17-19)

Psalm

Psalm 126

God does great things for us

Additional Reading

Matthew 21:28-32

Resistance to God in the present generation

Hymn: Fling Wide the Door, ELW 259

Gardener God, you come to us even in our parched and withered state. Remind us that you can restore us to lushness and give us the strength and agility to scale the heights before us.

Lighting the Advent Wreath

Use this blessing when lighting three candles.

Blessed are you, O Lord our God, ruler of the universe.
Your prophets spoke of a day when the desert would blossom
and waters would break forth in the wilderness.
Bless us as we light the candles on this wreath.
Strengthen our hearts
as we prepare for the coming of the Lord.
May he give water to all who thirst,
for he is our light and our salvation.
Blessed be God forever.

Sunday, December 14, 2014

Third Sunday of Advent

John of the Cross, renewer of the church, died 1591

John 1:6-8, 19-28
A witness to the light

This is the testimony given by John when the Jews sent priests and Levites from Jerusalem to ask him, "Who are you?" He confessed and did not deny it, but confessed, "I am not the Messiah." And they asked him, "What then? Are you Elijah?" He said, "I am not." "Are you the prophet?" He answered, "No." Then they said to him, "Who are you? Let us have an answer for those who sent us. What do you say about yourself?" He said,

"I am the voice of one crying out in the wilderness,
  'Make straight the way of the Lord,'"

as the prophet Isaiah said. (John 1:19-23)

Psalm
Psalm 126
God does great things for us

Additional Readings
Isaiah 61:1-4, 8-11
Righteousness and praise flourish like a garden

1 Thessalonians 5:16-24
Kept in faith until the coming of Christ

Hymn: There's a Voice in the Wilderness, ELW 255

Stir up the wills of your faithful people, Lord God, and open our ears to the words of your prophets, that, anointed by your Spirit, we may testify to your light; through Jesus Christ, our Savior and Lord, who lives and reigns with you and the Holy Spirit, one God, now and forever.

Monday, December 15, 2014

Week of Advent 3

Psalm 125

Prayer for blessing

Those who trust in the LORD are like Mount Zion,
  which cannot be moved, but abides forever.
As the mountains surround Jerusalem,
  so the LORD surrounds his people,
  from this time on and forevermore.
For the scepter of wickedness shall not rest
  on the land allotted to the righteous,
so that the righteous might not stretch out
  their hands to do wrong.
Do good, O LORD, to those who are good,
  and to those who are upright in their hearts.
But those who turn aside to their own crooked ways
  the LORD will lead away with evildoers.
  Peace be upon Israel! (Ps. 125:1-5)

Additional Readings

1 Kings 18:1-18   Ephesians 6:10-17
Elijah condemns King Ahab   *The armor of God against the powers*

Hymn: Light One Candle to Watch for Messiah, ELW 240

God of solidness, help us to be steadfast in our trust of you. Let the scepter of wickedness pass over us as we keep our arms by our sides. Transform us into mountains of Zion, upright and unmovable.

Tuesday, December 16, 2014

Week of Advent 3

Acts 3:17—4:4
Peter preaches about the prophets

While Peter and John were speaking to the people, the priests, the captain of the temple, and the Sadducees came to them, much annoyed because they were teaching the people and proclaiming that in Jesus there is the resurrection of the dead. So they arrested them and put them in custody until the next day, for it was already evening. But many of those who heard the word believed; and they numbered about five thousand. (Acts 4:1-4)

Psalm
Psalm 125
Prayer for blessing

Additional Reading
2 Kings 2:9-22
Elisha receives Elijah's spirit

Hymn: Gracious Spirit, Heed Our Pleading, ELW 401

Help us to be like Peter and John, unafraid. Let our witness convince those who hear us. In our Advent waiting, let us remember the Easter message, that death and darkness will not have the final word.

Wednesday, December 17, 2014

Week of Advent 3

O Wisdom, proceeding from the mouth of the Most High,
pervading and permeating all creation,
mightily ordering all things:
Come and teach us the way of prudence.

Mark 9:9-13

Questions about Elijah

As they were coming down the mountain, he ordered them to tell no one about what they had seen, until after the Son of Man had risen from the dead. So they kept the matter to themselves, questioning what this rising from the dead could mean. Then they asked him, "Why do the scribes say that Elijah must come first?" He said to them, "Elijah is indeed coming first to restore all things. How then is it written about the Son of Man, that he is to go through many sufferings and be treated with contempt? But I tell you that Elijah has come, and they did to him whatever they pleased, as it is written about him." (Mark 9:9-13)

Psalm

Psalm 125

Prayer for blessing

Additional Reading

Malachi 3:16—4:6

Elijah and the coming one

Hymn: Tree of Life and Awesome Mystery, ELW 334

You have sent us centuries of prophets, O God, and we have not always had ears to hear. Help us to stay alert for signs of your presence. Give us the courage of the earliest believers.

Thursday, December 18, 2014

Week of Advent 3

O Adonai and ruler of the house of Israel,
who appeared to Moses in the burning bush
and gave him the Law on Sinai:
Come with an outstretched arm and redeem us.

Psalm 89:1-4, 19-26
I sing of your love

I will sing of your steadfast love, O LORD, forever;
    with my mouth I will proclaim your faithfulness to all generations.
I declare that your steadfast love is established forever;
    your faithfulness is as firm as the heavens.

You said, "I have made a covenant with my chosen one,
    I have sworn to my servant David:
'I will establish your descendants forever,
    and build your throne for all generations.'" (Ps. 89:1-4)

Additional Readings
2 Samuel 6:1-11
The advent of the ark of the Lord

Hebrews 1:1-4
In the last days God speaks by a son

Hymn: Great Is Thy Faithfulness, ELW 733

Steadfast God, help us to trust in this covenant that you have sworn,
a faithfulness as firm as the heavens, a love that lasts forever. May we
always be inspired to sing of your love and faithfulness.

Friday, December 19, 2014

Week of Advent 3

O Root of Jesse, standing as an ensign before the peoples,
before whom all kings are mute,
to whom the nations will do homage:
Come quickly to deliver us.

Hebrews 1:5-14

The advent of one higher than angels

For to which of the angels did God ever say,

"You are my Son; today I have begotten you"?

Or again,

"I will be his Father, and he will be my Son"?

And again, when he brings the firstborn into the world, he says,

"Let all God's angels worship him."

Of the angels he says,

"He makes his angels winds,

and his servants flames of fire."

But of the Son he says,

"Your throne, O God, is forever and ever,

and the righteous scepter is the scepter of your kingdom.

You have loved righteousness and hated wickedness;

therefore God, your God, has anointed you

with the oil of gladness beyond your companions." (Heb. 1:5-9)

Psalm

Psalm 89:1-4, 19-26

I sing of your love

Additional Reading

2 Samuel 6:12-19

The ark of God enters Jerusalem

Hymn: As the Dark Awaits the Dawn, ELW 261

God of joy, we confess the ways that we waste this Advent season. Instead of anticipation, we sink into dread. Instead of watchful waiting, we waste our days in frenzy. Drench us with the oil of gladness.

Saturday, December 20, 2014

Week of Advent 3

Katharina von Bora Luther, renewer of the church, died 1552

O Key of David and scepter of the house of Israel,
you open and no one can close,
you close and no one can open:
Come and rescue the prisoners
who are in darkness and the shadow of death.

John 7:40-52
The Messiah, David, and Bethlehem

When they heard these words, some in the crowd said, "This is really the prophet." Others said, "This is the Messiah." But some asked, "Surely the Messiah does not come from Galilee, does he? Has not the scripture said that the Messiah is descended from David and comes from Bethlehem, the village where David lived?" So there was a division in the crowd because of him. Some of them wanted to arrest him, but no one laid hands on him. (John 7:40-44)

Psalm
Psalm 89:1-4, 19-26
I sing of your love

Additional Reading
Judges 13:2-24
The birth of Samson

Hymn: O Come, O Come, Emmanuel, ELW 257

O God, how often we fail to see you in the smallest corners and most ordinary places. Remind us to keep our candles lit so that we will see you even in the most unexpected circumstances.

Lighting the Advent Wreath

Use this blessing when lighting all four candles.

Blessed are you, O Lord our God, ruler of the universe.
In your Son, Emmanuel,
you have shown us your light
and saved us from the power of sin.
Bless us as we light the candles on this wreath.
Increase our longing for your presence,
that at the celebration of your Son's birth
his Spirit might dwell anew in our midst,
for he is our light and our salvation.
Blessed be God forever.

Sunday, December 21, 2014

Fourth Sunday of Advent

O Dayspring, splendor of light everlasting:
Come and enlighten those who sit in darkness
and in the shadow of death.

Luke 1:26-38
The angel appears to Mary

In the sixth month the angel Gabriel was sent by God to a town in Galilee called Nazareth, to a virgin engaged to a man whose name was Joseph, of the house of David. The virgin's name was Mary. And he came to her and said, "Greetings, favored one! The Lord is with you." But she was much perplexed by his words and pondered what sort of greeting this might be. The angel said to her, "Do not be afraid, Mary, for you have found favor with God. And now, you will conceive in your womb and bear a son, and you will name him Jesus." (Luke 1:26-31)

Psalm
Luke 1:46b-55
The Mighty One raises the lowly

Additional Readings
2 Samuel 7:1-11, 16
God's promise to David

Romans 16:25-27
The mystery revealed in Jesus Christ

Hymn: The Angel Gabriel from Heaven Came, ELW 265

Stir up your power, Lord Christ, and come. With your abundant grace and might, free us from the sin that would obstruct your mercy, that willingly we may bear your redeeming love to all the world, for you live and reign with the Father and the Holy Spirit, one God, now and forever.

Monday, December 22, 2014

Week of Advent 4

O King of the nations, the ruler they long for,
the cornerstone uniting all people:
Come and save us all, whom you formed out of clay.

Luke 1:46b-55

The Lord lifts up the lowly

"My soul magnifies the Lord,
   and my spirit rejoices in God my Savior,
for he has looked with favor on the lowliness of his servant.
   Surely, from now on all generations will call me blessed;
for the Mighty One has done great things for me,
   and holy is his name.
His mercy is for those who fear him
   from generation to generation." (Luke 1:46b-50)

Additional Readings

1 Samuel 1:1-18   Hebrews 9:1-14
Hannah is promised a child   *Christ comes as high priest*

Hymn: Canticle of the Turning, ELW 723

Creator God, who finds fertility in the most unlikely places, we long to be blessed like Mary. Find favor with us, even in our lowliness, and raise us up to rejoicing. May we always magnify you.

Tuesday, December 23, 2014

Week of Advent 4

O Emmanuel, our king and our lawgiver,
the anointed of the nations and their Savior:
Come and save us, Lord our God.

Hebrews 8:1-13

The mediator replaces the sanctuary

For every high priest is appointed to offer gifts and sacrifices; hence it is necessary for this priest also to have something to offer. Now if he were on earth, he would not be a priest at all, since there are priests who offer gifts according to the law. They offer worship in a sanctuary that is a sketch and shadow of the heavenly one; for Moses, when he was about to erect the tent, was warned, "See that you make everything according to the pattern that was shown you on the mountain." But Jesus has now obtained a more excellent ministry, and to that degree he is the mediator of a better covenant, which has been enacted through better promises. (Heb. 8:3-6)

Additional Readings

1 Samuel 1:19-28
Hannah presents Samuel to God

Luke 1:46b-55
The Lord lifts up the lowly

Hymn: Savior of the Nations, Come, ELW 263

O God, who gives us so many gifts, remind us of all we have to offer. Lead us to be stronger ministers and help us to discover all that you have promised.

Christmas

Over the centuries, various customs have developed that focus the household on welcoming the light of Christ: the daily or weekly lighting of the Advent wreath, the blessing of the lighted Christmas tree, the candle-lit procession of Las Posadas, the flickering lights of the luminaria, the Christ candle at Christmas.

The Christian household not only welcomes the light of Christ at Christmas, but celebrates the presence of that light throughout the Twelve Days, from Christmas until the Epiphany, January 6. In the Christmas season, Christians welcome the light of Christ that is already with us through faith. In word and gesture, prayer and song, in the many customs of diverse cultures, Christians celebrate this life-giving Word and ask that it dwell more deeply in the rhythm of daily life.

Table Prayer for the Twelve Days of Christmas

With joy and gladness we feast upon your love, O God.
You have come among us in Jesus, your Son,
and your presence now graces this table.
May Christ dwell in us that we might bear his love to all the world,
for he is Lord forever and ever. Amen.

Blessing of the Christmas Tree

Let the heavens rejoice, and let the earth be glad;
let the sea thunder and all that is in it;
let the field be joyful and all that is therein.
Then shall all the trees of the wood shout for joy
at your coming, O LORD,
for you come to judge the earth.
You will judge the world with righteousness
and the peoples with your truth. (Ps. 96:11-13)

Be praised, O God, for the blessings around us that point to you.
Be praised, O God, for the signs of this holy season
that awaken in us wonder.
Praise for the steadfast green of this tree,
like your love, enduring all seasons.
Praise for the light that illumines our darkness,
like Christ, who brings light to the world.
Join our voices with those of the tree and of all creation,
who sing at your coming:
Glory to God in the highest, and peace to God's people on earth.
Amen.

Blessing of the Nativity Scene

This blessing may be used when figures are added to the nativity scene throughout the days of Christmas.

Bless us, O God, bless us who gather around this stable.
As we celebrate Christ's birth into the world,
may we receive the Christ child into our hearts
with gratitude and song. Amen.

Wednesday, December 24, 2014

Nativity of Our Lord
Christmas Eve

Luke 2:1-14 [15-20]
God with us

In that region there were shepherds living in the fields, keeping watch over their flock by night. Then an angel of the Lord stood before them, and the glory of the Lord shone around them, and they were terrified. But the angel said to them, "Do not be afraid; for see—I am bringing you good news of great joy for all the people: to you is born this day in the city of David a Savior, who is the Messiah, the Lord. This will be a sign for you: you will find a child wrapped in bands of cloth and lying in a manger." (Luke 2:8-12)

Psalm
Psalm 96
Let the earth be glad

Additional Readings
Isaiah 9:2-7
A child is born for us

Titus 2:11-14
The grace of God has appeared

Hymn: Angels We Have Heard on High, ELW 289

Almighty God, you made this holy night shine with the brightness of the true Light. Grant that here on earth we may walk in the light of Jesus' presence and in the last day wake to the brightness of his glory; through your Son, Jesus Christ our Lord, who lives and reigns with you and the Holy Spirit, one God, now and forever.

Thursday, December 25, 2014

Nativity of Our Lord
Christmas Day

John 1:1-14
The Word became flesh

In the beginning was the Word, and the Word was with God, and the Word was God. He was in the beginning with God. All things came into being through him, and without him not one thing came into being. What has come into being in him was life, and the life was the light of all people. The light shines in the darkness, and the darkness did not overcome it. (John 1:1-5)

Psalm
Psalm 98
The victory of our God

Additional Readings
Isaiah 52:7-10
Heralds announce God's salvation

Hebrews 1:1-4 [5-12]
God has spoken by a son

Hymn: O Come, All Ye Faithful, ELW 283

Almighty God, you gave us your only Son to take on our human nature and to illumine the world with your light. By your grace adopt us as your children and enlighten us with your Spirit, through Jesus Christ, our Redeemer and Lord, who lives and reigns with you and the Holy Spirit, one God, now and forever.

Friday, December 26, 2014

Stephen, Deacon and Martyr

Acts 6:8—7:2a, 51-60

Stephen is stoned to death

Now during those days, when the disciples were increasing in number, the Hellenists complained against the Hebrews because their widows were being neglected in the daily distribution of food. And the twelve called together the whole community of the disciples and said, "It is not right that we should neglect the word of God in order to wait on tables. Therefore, friends, select from among yourselves seven men of good standing, full of the Spirit and of wisdom, whom we may appoint to this task, while we, for our part, will devote ourselves to prayer and to serving the word." What they said pleased the whole community, and they chose Stephen, a man full of faith and the Holy Spirit, together with Philip, Prochorus, Nicanor, Timon, Parmenas, and Nicolaus, a proselyte of Antioch. (Acts 6:1-5)

Psalm

Psalm 17:1-9, 15

I call upon you, O God

Additional Readings

2 Chronicles 24:17-22

Zechariah is stoned to death

Matthew 23:34-39

Jesus laments that Jerusalem kills her prophets

Hymn: What Child Is This, ELW 296

We give you thanks, O Lord of glory, for the example of Stephen the first martyr, who looked to heaven and prayed for his persecutors. Grant that we also may pray for our enemies and seek forgiveness for those who hurt us, through Jesus Christ, our Savior and Lord, who lives and reigns with you and the Holy Spirit, one God, now and forever.

Saturday, December 27, 2014

John, Apostle and Evangelist

John 21:20-25

The beloved disciple remains with Jesus

Peter turned and saw the disciple whom Jesus loved following them; he was the one who had reclined next to Jesus at the supper and had said, "Lord, who is it that is going to betray you?" When Peter saw him, he said to Jesus, "Lord, what about him?" Jesus said to him, "If it is my will that he remain until I come, what is that to you? Follow me!" So the rumor spread in the community that this disciple would not die. Yet Jesus did not say to him that he would not die, but, "If it is my will that he remain until I come, what is that to you?"

This is the disciple who is testifying to these things and has written them, and we know that his testimony is true. But there are also many other things that Jesus did; if every one of them were written down, I suppose that the world itself could not contain the books that would be written. (John 21:20-25)

Psalm

Psalm 116:12-19
The death of faithful servants

Additional Readings

Genesis 1:1-5, 26-31
Humankind is created by God

1 John 1:1—2:2
Jesus, the word of life

Hymn: The Bells of Christmas, ELW 298

Merciful God, through John the apostle and evangelist you have revealed the mysteries of your Word made flesh. Let the brightness of your light shine on your church, so that all your people, instructed in the holy gospel, may walk in the light of your truth and attain eternal life, through Jesus Christ, our Savior and Lord, who lives and reigns with you and the Holy Spirit, one God, now and forever.

Sunday, December 28, 2014

First Sunday of Christmas

The Holy Innocents, Martyrs (transferred to December 29)

Luke 2:22-40

The presentation of the child

Now there was a man in Jerusalem whose name was Simeon; this man was righteous and devout, looking forward to the consolation of Israel, and the Holy Spirit rested on him. It had been revealed to him by the Holy Spirit that he would not see death before he had seen the Lord's Messiah. Guided by the Spirit, Simeon came into the temple; and when the parents brought in the child Jesus, to do for him what was customary under the law, Simeon took him in his arms and praised God. (Luke 2:25-28a)

Psalm

Psalm 148

God's splendor is over earth and heaven

Additional Readings

Isaiah 61:10—62:3

Clothed in garments of salvation

Galatians 4:4-7

Children and heirs of God

Hymn: O Lord, Now Let Your Servant, ELW 313

Almighty God, you wonderfully created the dignity of human nature and yet more wonderfully restored it. In your mercy, let us share the divine life of the one who came to share our humanity, Jesus Christ, your Son, our Lord, who lives and reigns with you and the Holy Spirit, one God, now and forever.

Monday, December 29, 2014

The Holy Innocents, Martyrs (*transferred*)

Matthew 2:13-18
Herod kills innocent children

Now after [the wise men] had left, an angel of the Lord appeared to Joseph in a dream and said, "Get up, take the child and his mother, and flee to Egypt, and remain there until I tell you; for Herod is about to search for the child, to destroy him." Then Joseph got up, took the child and his mother by night, and went to Egypt, and remained there until the death of Herod. This was to fulfill what had been spoken by the Lord through the prophet, "Out of Egypt I have called my son."

When Herod saw that he had been tricked by the wise men, he was infuriated, and he sent and killed all the children in and around Bethlehem who were two years old or under, according to the time that he had learned from the wise men. (Matt. 2:13-16)

Psalm
Psalm 124
We have escaped like a bird

Additional Readings
Jeremiah 31:15-17
Rachel weeps for her children

1 Peter 4:12-19
Continue to do good while suffering

Hymn: How Long, O God, ELW 698

We remember today, O God, the slaughter of the innocent children of Bethlehem by order of King Herod. Receive into the arms of your mercy all innocent victims. By your great might frustrate the designs of evil tyrants and establish your rule of justice, love, and peace, through Jesus Christ, our Savior and Lord, who lives and reigns with you and the Holy Spirit, one God, now and forever.

Tuesday, December 30, 2014

Week of Christmas 1

Psalm 148
God's splendor is over earth and heaven

Praise the LORD!
  Praise the LORD from the heavens;
  praise him in the heights!
Praise him, all his angels;
  praise him, all his host!

Praise him, sun and moon;
  praise him, all you shining stars!
Praise him, you highest heavens,
  and you waters above the heavens!

Let them praise the name of the LORD,
  for he commanded and they were created. (Ps. 148:1-5)

Additional Readings
Proverbs 9:1-12   2 Peter 3:8-13
Your days will be multiplied   *A thousand years as one day*

Hymn: When Long before Time, ELW 861

Awe-inspiring God, as we approach the end of another year, help us to remember the lessons of the past months, the possibilities that you offer, the visions that you share, and the praise that we can give.

Wednesday, December 31, 2014

Week of Christmas 1

John 8:12-19
I am the light

Again Jesus spoke to them, saying, "I am the light of the world. Whoever follows me will never walk in darkness but will have the light of life." Then the Pharisees said to him, "You are testifying on your own behalf; your testimony is not valid." Jesus answered, "Even if I testify on my own behalf, my testimony is valid because I know where I have come from and where I am going, but you do not know where I come from or where I am going. You judge by human standards; I judge no one. Yet even if I do judge, my judgment is valid; for it is not I alone who judge, but I and the Father who sent me." (John 8:12-16)

Psalm
Psalm 148
God's splendor is over earth and heaven

Additional Reading
1 Kings 3:5-14
God grants a discerning mind

Hymn: Love Has Come, ELW 292

O God, who is the light of the world, trim our wicks and fill our lamps with oil. Help us to shine with the light of your grace and illuminate the paths that you call us to travel.

Lesser Festivals and Commemorations

January 1 – Name of Jesus Every Jewish boy was circumcised and formally named on the eighth day of his life. Already in his infancy, Jesus bore the mark of a covenant that he made new through the shedding of his blood on the cross.

January 2 – Johann Konrad Wilhelm Loehe Wilhelm Loehe was a pastor in nineteenth-century Germany. From the small town of Neuendettelsau he sent pastors to North America, Australia, New Guinea, Brazil, and the Ukraine.

January 15 – Martin Luther King Jr. Martin Luther King Jr. is remembered as an American prophet of justice among races and nations. Many churches hold commemorations near Dr. King's birth date of January 15, in conjunction with the American civil holiday honoring him.

January 17 – Antony of Egypt Antony was one of the earliest Egyptian desert fathers. He became the head of a group of monks that lived in a cluster of huts and devoted themselves to communal prayer, worship, and manual labor.

January 17 – Pachomius Another of the desert fathers, Pachomius was born in Egypt about 290. He organized hermits into a religious community in which the members prayed together and held their goods in common.

January 18 – Confession of Peter; Beginning of the Week of Prayer for Christian Unity The Week of Prayer for Christian Unity is framed by two commemorations, the Confession of Peter and the Conversion of Paul. On this day the church remembers that Peter was led by God's grace to acknowledge Jesus as "the Christ, the Son of the living God" (Matt. 16:16).

January 19 – Henry When Erik, king of Sweden, determined to invade Finland for the purpose of converting the people there to Christianity, Henry went with him. Henry is recognized as the patron saint of Finland.

January 21 – Agnes Agnes was a girl of about thirteen living in Rome, who had chosen a life of service to Christ as a virgin, despite the Roman emperor Diocletian's ruling that had outlawed all Christian activity. She gave witness to her faith and was put to death as a result.

January 25 – Conversion of Paul; End of the Week of Prayer for Christian Unity As the Week of Prayer for Christian Unity comes to an end, the church remembers how a man of Tarsus named Saul, a former persecutor of the early Christian church, was led to become one of its chief preachers.

January 26 – Timothy, Titus, Silas On the two days following the celebration of the Conversion of Paul, his companions are remembered. Timothy, Titus, and Silas were missionary coworkers with Paul.

January 27 – Lydia, Dorcas, Phoebe On this day the church remembers three women who were companions in Paul's ministry.

January 28 – Thomas Aquinas Thomas Aquinas was a brilliant and creative theologian who immersed himself in the thought of Aristotle and worked to explain Christian beliefs in the philosophical culture of the day.

February 2 – Presentation of Our Lord Forty days after the birth of Christ, the church marks the day Mary and Joseph presented him in the temple in accordance with Jewish law. Simeon greeted Mary and Joseph, responding with the canticle that begins "Now, Lord, you let your servant go in peace."

February 3 – Ansgar Ansgar was a monk who led a mission to Denmark and later to Sweden. His work ran into difficulties with the rulers of the day, and he was forced to withdraw into Germany, where he served as a bishop in Hamburg.

February 5 – The Martyrs of Japan In the sixteenth century, Jesuit missionaries, followed by Franciscans, introduced the Christian faith in Japan. By 1630, Christianity was driven underground. This day commemorates the first martyrs of Japan, twenty-six missionaries and converts, who were killed by crucifixion.

February 14 – Cyril, Methodius These brothers from a noble family in Thessalonika in northeastern Greece were priests who are regarded as the founders of Slavic literature. Their work in preaching and worshiping in the language of the people is honored by Christians in both East and West.

February 18 – Martin Luther On this day Luther died at the age of sixty-two. For a time, he was an Augustinian monk, but it is primarily for his work as a biblical scholar, translator of the Bible, reformer of the liturgy, theologian, educator, and father of German vernacular literature that he is remembered.

February 23 – Polycarp Polycarp was bishop of Smyrna and a link between the apostolic age and the church at the end of the second century. At the age of eighty-six he was martyred for his faith.

February 25 – Elizabeth Fedde Fedde was born in Norway and trained as a deaconess. Among her notable achievements is the establishment of the Deaconess House in Brooklyn and the Deaconess House and Hospital of the Lutheran Free Church in Minneapolis.

March 1 – George Herbert Herbert was ordained a priest in 1630 and served the little parish of St. Andrew Bremerton until his death. He is best remembered, however, as a writer of poems and hymns such as "Come, My Way, My Truth, My Life" and "The King of Love My Shepherd Is."

March 2 – John Wesley, Charles Wesley The Wesleys were leaders of a revival in the Church of England. Their spiritual methods of frequent communion, fasting, and advocacy for the poor earned them the name "Methodists."

March 7 – Perpetua, Felicity In the year 202 the emperor Septimius Severus forbade conversions to Christianity. Perpetua, a noblewoman; Felicity, a slave; and other companions were all catechumens at Carthage

in North Africa, where they were imprisoned and sentenced to death.

March 10 – Harriet Tubman, Sojourner Truth Harriet Tubman helped about three hundred slaves to escape via the Underground Railroad until slavery was abolished in the United States. After slavery was abolished in New York in 1827, Sojourner Truth became deeply involved in Christianity, and in later life she was a popular speaker against slavery and for women's rights.

March 12 – Gregory the Great Gregory held political office and at another time lived as a monk, all before he was elected to the papacy. He also established a school to train church musicians; thus Gregorian chant is named in his honor.

March 17 – Patrick Patrick went to Ireland from Britain to serve as a bishop and missionary. He made his base in the north of Ireland and from there made many missionary journeys, with much success.

March 19 – Joseph The Gospel of Luke shows Joseph acting in accordance with both civil and religious law by returning to Bethlehem for the census and by presenting the child Jesus in the temple on the fortieth day after his birth.

March 21 – Thomas Cranmer Cranmer's lasting achievement is contributing to and overseeing the creation of the Book of Common Prayer, which remains (in revised form) the worship book of the Anglican Communion. He was burned at the stake under Queen Mary for his support of the Protestant Reformation.

March 22 – Jonathan Edwards Edwards was a minister in Connecticut and has been described as the greatest of the New England Puritan preachers. Edwards carried out mission work among the Housatonic Indians of Massachusetts and became president of the College of New Jersey, later to be known as Princeton University.

March 24 – Oscar Arnulfo Romero Romero is remembered for his advocacy on behalf of the poor in El Salvador, though it was not a characteristic of his early priesthood. After several years of threats to his life, Romero was assassinated while presiding at the eucharist.

March 25 – Annunciation of Our Lord Nine months before Christmas the church celebrates the annunciation. In Luke the angel

Gabriel announces to Mary that she will give birth to the Son of God, and she responds, "Here am I, the servant of the Lord."

March 29 – Hans Nielsen Hauge Hans Nielsen Hauge was a layperson who began preaching in Norway and Denmark after a mystical experience that he believed called him to share the assurance of salvation with others. At the time, itinerant preaching and religious gatherings held without the supervision of a pastor were illegal, and Hauge was arrested several times.

March 31 – John Donne This priest of the Church of England is commemorated for his poetry and spiritual writing. Most of his poetry was written before his ordination and is sacred and secular, intellectual and sensuous.

April 4 – Benedict the African Although Benedict was illiterate, his fame as a confessor brought many visitors to him, and he was eventually named superior of a Franciscan community. A patron saint of African Americans, Benedict is remembered for his patience and understanding when confronted with racial prejudice and taunts.

April 6 – Albrecht Dürer, Matthias Grünewald, Lucas Cranach These great artists revealed through their work the mystery of salvation and the wonder of creation. Though Dürer remained a Roman Catholic, at his death Martin Luther wrote to a friend, "Affection bids us mourn for one who was the best." Several religious works are included in Grünwald's small surviving corpus, the most famous being the Isenheim Altarpiece. Lucas Cranach was widely known for his woodcuts, some of which illustrated the first German printing of the New Testament.

April 9 – Dietrich Bonhoeffer In 1933, and with Hitler's rise to power, Bonhoeffer became a leading spokesman for the Confessing Church, a resistance movement against the Nazis. After leading a worship service on April 8, 1945, at Schönberg prison, he was taken away to be hanged the next day.

April 10 – Mikael Agricola Agricola began a reform of the Finnish church along Lutheran lines. He translated the New Testament, the prayer book, hymns, and the mass into Finnish and through this work set the rules of orthography that are the basis of modern Finnish spelling.

April 19 – Olavus Petri, Laurentius Petri These two brothers are commemorated for their introduction of the Lutheran movement to the Church of Sweden after studying at the University of Wittenberg. Together the brothers published a complete Bible in Swedish and a revised liturgy in 1541.

April 21 – Anselm This eleventh-century Benedictine monk stands out as one of the greatest theologians between Augustine and Thomas Aquinas. He is perhaps best known for his "satisfaction" theory of atonement, where God takes on human nature in Jesus Christ in order to make the perfect payment for sin.

April 23 – Toyohiko Kagawa Toyohiko Kagawa's vocation to help the poor led him to live among them. He was arrested for his efforts to reconcile Japan and China after the Japanese attack of 1940.

April 25 – Mark Though Mark himself was not an apostle, it is likely that he was a member of one of the early Christian communities. The Gospel attributed to him is brief and direct and is considered by many to be the earliest Gospel.

April 29 – Catherine of Siena Catherine of Siena was a member of the Order of Preachers (Dominicans), and among Roman Catholics she was the first woman to receive the title Doctor of the Church. She also advised popes and any uncertain persons who told her their problems.

May 1 – Philip, James Philip and James are commemorated together because the remains of these two saints were placed in the Church of the Apostles in Rome on this day in 561.

May 2 – Athanasius At the Council of Nicea in 325 and when he himself served as bishop of Alexandria, Athanasius defended the full divinity of Christ against the Arian position held by emperors, magistrates, and theologians.

May 4 – Monica Almost everything known about Monica comes from Augustine's *Confessions*, his autobiography. Her dying wish was that her son remember her at the altar of the Lord, wherever he was.

May 8 – Julian of Norwich Julian was most likely a Benedictine nun living in an isolated cell attached to the Carrow Priory in Norwich, England. When she was about thirty years old, she reported visions that she later compiled into a book, *Sixteen Revelations of Divine Love*, which is a classic of medieval mysticism.

May 9 – Nicolaus Ludwig von Zinzendorf Drawn from an overly intellectual Lutheran faith to Pietism, at the age of twenty-two Count Zinzendorf permitted a group of Moravians to live on his lands. Zinzendorf participated in worldwide missions emanating from this community and is also remembered for writing hymns characteristic of his Pietistic faith.

May 14 – Matthias After Christ's ascension, the apostles met in Jerusalem to choose a replacement for Judas. Though little is known about him, Matthias had traveled among the disciples from the time of Jesus' baptism until his ascension.

May 18 – Erik Erik, long considered the patron saint of Sweden, ruled there from 1150 to 1160. He is honored for efforts to bring peace to the nearby pagan kingdoms and for his crusades to spread the Christian faith in Scandinavia.

May 21 – Helena Helena was the mother of Constantine, a man who later became the Roman emperor. Helena is remembered for traveling through Palestine and building churches on the sites she believed to be where Jesus was born, where he was buried, and from which he ascended.

May 24 – Nicolaus Copernicus, Leonhard Euler Copernicus formally studied astronomy, mathematics, Greek, Plato, medicine, and canon law and is chiefly remembered for his work as an astronomer and his idea that the sun, not the earth, is the center of the solar system. Euler is regarded as one of the founders of the science of pure mathematics and made important contributions to mechanics, hydrodynamics, astronomy, optics, and acoustics.

May 27 – John Calvin Having embraced the views of the Reformation by his mid-twenties, John Calvin was a preacher in Geneva, was banished once, and later returned to reform the city with a rigid, theocratic discipline. Calvin is considered the father of the Reformed churches.

May 29 – Jiří Tranovský Jiří Tranovský is considered the "Luther of the Slavs" and the father of Slovak hymnody. He produced a translation of the Augsburg Confession and published his hymn collection *Cithara Sanctorum* (Lyre of the Saints), also known as the Tranoscius, which is the foundation of Slovak Lutheran hymnody.

May 31 – Visit of Mary to Elizabeth Sometime after the annunciation, Mary visited her cousin Elizabeth, who greeted Mary with the words, "Blessed are you among women," and Mary responded with her famous song, the Magnificat.

June 1 – Justin Justin was a teacher of philosophy and engaged in debates about the truth of Christian faith. Having been arrested and jailed for practicing an unauthorized religion, he refused to renounce his faith and he and six of his students were beheaded.

June 3 – The Martyrs of Uganda King Mwanga of Uganda was angered by Christian members of the court whose first allegiance was not to him but to Christ. On this date in 1886, thirty-two young men were burned to death for refusing to renounce Christianity. Their persecution led to a much stronger Christian presence in the country.

June 3 – John XXIII Despite the expectation upon his election that the seventy-seven-year old John XXIII would be a transitional pope, he had great energy and spirit. He convened the Second Vatican Council in order to open the windows of the church. The council brought about great changes in Roman Catholic worship and ecumenical relationships.

June 5 – Boniface Boniface led large numbers of Benedictine monks and nuns in establishing churches, schools, and seminaries. Boniface was preparing a group for confirmation on the eve of Pentecost when he and others were killed by a band of pagans.

June 7 – Seattle The city of Seattle was named after Noah Seattle against his wishes. After Chief Seattle became a Roman Catholic, he began the practice of morning and evening prayer in the tribe, a practice that continued after his death.

June 9 – Columba, Aidan, Bede These three monks from the British Isles were pillars among those who kept alive the light of learning and devotion during the Middle Ages. Columba founded three monasteries, including one on the island of Iona, off the coast of Scotland. Aidan, who helped bring Christianity to the Northumbria area of England, was known for his pastoral style and ability to stir people to charity and good works. Bede was a Bible translator and scripture scholar who wrote a history of the English church and was the first historian to date events *anno Domini* (A.D.), the "year of our Lord."

June 11 – Barnabas Though he was not among the Twelve mentioned in the Gospels, the book of Acts gives Barnabas the title of apostle. When Paul came to Jerusalem after his conversion, Barnabas took him in over the fears of the other apostles who doubted Paul's discipleship.

June 14 – Basil the Great, Gregory of Nyssa, Gregory of Nazianzus, Macrina The three men in this group are known as the Cappadocian fathers; all three explored the mystery of the Holy Trinity. Basil's Longer Rule and Shorter Rule for monastic life are the basis for Eastern monasticism to this day, and express a preference for communal monastic life over that of hermits. Gregory of Nazianzus defended Orthodox trinitarian and christological doctrine, and his preaching won over the city of Constantinople. Gregory of Nyssa is remembered as a writer on spiritual life and the contemplation of God in worship and sacraments. Macrina was the older sister of Basil and Gregory of Nyssa, and her teaching was influential within the early church.

June 21 – Onesimos Nesib Onesimos, an Ethiopian, was captured by slave traders and taken from his homeland to Eritrea, where he was bought, freed, and educated by Swedish missionaries. He translated the Bible into Oromo and returned to his homeland to preach the gospel there.

June 24 – John the Baptist The birth of John the Baptist is celebrated exactly six months before Christmas Eve. For Christians in the Northern Hemisphere, these two dates are deeply symbolic, since John said that he must decrease as Jesus increased. John was born as the days are longest and then steadily decrease, while Jesus was born as the days are shortest and then steadily increase.

June 25 – Presentation of the Augsburg Confession On this day in 1530 the German and Latin editions of the Augsburg Confession were presented to Emperor Charles of the Holy Roman Empire. The Augsburg Confession was written by Philipp Melanchthon and endorsed by Martin Luther and consists of a brief summary of points in which the reformers saw their teaching as either agreeing with or differing from that of the Roman Catholic Church of the time.

June 25 – Philipp Melanchthon Though he died on April 19, Philipp Melanchthon is commemorated today because of his connection with the Augsburg Confession.

Colleague and co-reformer with Martin Luther, Melanchthon was a brilliant scholar, known as "the teacher of Germany."

June 27 – Cyril Remembered as an outstanding theologian, Cyril defended the orthodox teachings about the person of Christ against Nestorius, who was at that time bishop of Constantinople. Eventually it was decided that Cyril's interpretation, that Christ's person included both divine and human natures, was correct.

June 28 – Irenaeus Irenaeus believed that only Matthew, Mark, Luke, and John were trustworthy Gospels. As a result of his battles with the Gnostics, he was one of the first to speak of the church as "catholic," meaning that congregations did not exist by themselves, but were linked to one another throughout the whole church.

June 29 – Peter, Paul One of the things that unites Peter and Paul is the tradition that says they were martyred together on this date in A.D. 67 or 68. What unites them even more closely is their common confession of Jesus Christ.

July 1 – Catherine Winkworth, John Mason Neale Many of the most beloved hymns in the English language are the work of these gifted poets. Catherine Winkworth devoted herself to the translation of German hymns into English, while John Mason Neale specialized in translating many ancient Latin and Greek hymns.

July 3 – Thomas Alongside the doubt for which Thomas is famous, the Gospel according to John shows Thomas moving from doubt to deep faith. Thomas makes one of the strongest confessions of faith in the New Testament, "My Lord and my God!" (John 20:28).

July 6 – Jan Hus Jan Hus was a Bohemian priest who spoke against abuses in the church of his day in many of the same ways Luther would a century later. The followers of Jan Hus became known as the Czech Brethren and later became the Moravian Church.

July 11 – Benedict of Nursia Benedict is known as the father of Western monasticism. Benedict encourages a generous spirit of hospitality. Visitors to Benedictine communities are to be welcomed as Christ himself.

July 12 – Nathan Söderblom In 1930 this Swedish theologian, ecumenist, and social activist received the Nobel Prize for peace.

Söderblom organized the Universal Christian Council on Life and Work, which was one of the organizations that in 1948 came together to form the World Council of Churches.

July 17 – Bartolomé de Las Casas Bartolomé de Las Casas was a Spanish priest and a missionary in the Western Hemisphere. Throughout the Caribbean and Central America, he worked to stop the enslavement of native people, to halt the brutal treatment of women by military forces, and to promote laws that humanized the process of colonization.

July 22 – Mary Magdalene The Gospels report Mary Magdalene was one of the women of Galilee who followed Jesus. As the first person to whom the risen Lord appeared, she returned to the disciples with the news and has been called "the apostle to the apostles" for her proclamation of the resurrection.

July 23 – Birgitta of Sweden Birgitta's devotional commitments led her to give to the poor and needy all that she owned while she began to live a more ascetic life. She founded an order of monks and nuns, the Order of the Holy Savior (Birgittines), whose superior was a woman.

July 25 – James James was one of the sons of Zebedee and is counted as one of the twelve disciples. James was the first of the Twelve to suffer martyrdom and is the only apostle whose martyrdom is recorded in scripture.

July 28 – Johann Sebastian Bach, Heinrich Schütz, George Frederick Handel These three composers did much to enrich the worship life of the church. Johann Sebastian Bach drew on the Lutheran tradition of hymnody and wrote about two hundred cantatas, including at least two for each Sunday and festival day in the Lutheran calendar of his day. George Frederick Handel was not primarily a church musician, but his great work *Messiah* is a musical proclamation of the scriptures. Heinrich Schütz wrote choral settings of biblical texts and paid special attention to ways his composition would underscore the meaning of the words.

July 29 – Mary, Martha, Lazarus of Bethany Mary and Martha are remembered for the hospitality and refreshment they offered Jesus in their home. Following the characterization drawn by Luke, Martha represents the active life, and Mary, the contemplative.

July 29 – Olaf Olaf is considered the patron saint of Norway. While at war in the Baltic and in Normandy, he became a Christian; then he returned to Norway and declared himself king, and from then on Christianity was the dominant religion of the realm.

August 8 – Dominic Dominic believed that a stumbling block to restoring heretics to the church was the wealth of clergy, so he formed an itinerant religious order, the Order of Preachers (Dominicans), who lived in poverty, studied philosophy and theology, and preached against heresy.

August 10 – Lawrence Lawrence was one of seven deacons of the congregation at Rome and, like the deacons appointed in Acts, was responsible for financial matters in the church and for the care of the poor.

August 11 – Clare At age eighteen, Clare of Assisi heard Francis preach a sermon. With Francis's help she and a growing number of companions established a women's Franciscan community called the Order of Poor Ladies, or Poor Clares.

August 13 – Florence Nightingale, Clara Maass Nightingale led a group of thirty-eight nurses to serve in the Crimean War, where they worked in appalling conditions. She returned to London as a hero and there resumed her work for hospital reform. Clara Maass was born in New Jersey and served as a nurse in the Spanish-American War, where she encountered the horrors of yellow fever. Later responding to a call for subjects in research on yellow fever, Maass contracted the disease and died.

August 14 – Maximilian Kolbe, Kaj Munk Confined in Auschwitz, Father Kolbe was a Franciscan priest who gave generously of his meager resources and finally volunteered to be starved to death in place of another man who was a husband and father. Kaj Munk, a Danish Lutheran pastor and playwright, was an outspoken critic of the Nazis. His plays frequently highlighted the eventual victory of the Christian faith despite the church's weak and ineffective witness.

August 15 – Mary, Mother of Our Lord The honor paid to Mary as mother of our Lord goes back to biblical times, when Mary herself sang "From now on all generations will call me blessed" (Luke 1:48). Mary's song speaks of reversals in the reign of God: the mighty are cast down, the lowly are lifted up, the hungry are fed, and the rich are sent away empty-handed.

August 20 – Bernard of Clairvaux Bernard was a Cistercian monk who became an abbot of great spiritual depth. Through translation his several devotional writings and hymns are still read and sung today.

August 24 – Bartholomew Bartholomew is mentioned as one of Jesus' disciples in Matthew, Mark, and Luke. Except for his name on these lists of the Twelve, little is known.

August 28 – Augustine As an adult Augustine came to see Christianity as a religion appropriate for a philosopher. Augustine was baptized by Ambrose at the Easter Vigil in 387, was made bishop of Hippo in 396, and was one of the greatest theologians of the Western church.

August 28 – Moses the Black A man of great strength and rough character, Moses the Black was converted to Christian faith toward the close of the fourth century. The change in his heart and life had a profound impact on his native Ethiopia.

September 2 – Nikolai Frederik Severin Grundtvig Grundtvig was a prominent Danish theologian of the nineteenth century. From his university days he was convinced that poetry spoke to the human spirit better than prose, and he wrote more than a thousand hymns.

September 9 – Peter Claver Peter Claver was born into Spanish nobility and was persuaded to become a Jesuit missionary. He served in Cartagena (in what is now Colombia) by teaching and caring for the slaves.

September 13 – John Chrysostom John was a priest in Antioch and an outstanding preacher. His eloquence earned him the nickname "Chrysostom" ("golden mouth"), but he also preached against corruption among the royal court, whereupon the empress sent him into exile.

September 14 – Holy Cross Day The celebration of Holy Cross Day commemorates the dedication of the Church of the Resurrection in 335 on the location believed to have been where Christ was buried.

September 16 – Cyprian During Cyprian's time as bishop, many people had denied the faith under duress. In contrast to some who held the belief that the church should not receive these people back, Cyprian believed they ought to be welcomed into full communion after a period of penance.

September 17 – Hildegard of Bingen Hildegard lived virtually her entire life in convents yet was widely influential. She advised and reproved kings and popes, wrote poems and hymns, and produced treatises in medicine, theology, and natural history.

September 18 – Dag Hammarskjöld Dag Hammarskjöld was a Swedish diplomat and humanitarian who served as secretary general of the United Nations. The depth of Hammarskjöld's Christian faith was unknown until his private journal, *Markings*, was published following his death.

September 21 – Matthew Matthew was a tax collector, an occupation that was distrusted, since tax collectors were frequently dishonest and worked as agents for the Roman occupying government; yet it was these outcasts to whom Jesus showed his love. Since the second century, tradition has attributed the First Gospel to him.

September 29 – Michael and All Angels The scriptures speak of angels who worship God in heaven, and in both testaments angels are God's messengers on earth. Michael is an angel whose name appears in Daniel as the heavenly being who leads the faithful dead to God's throne on the day of resurrection, while in the book of Revelation, Michael fights in a cosmic battle against Satan.

September 30 – Jerome Jerome translated the scriptures into the Latin that was spoken and written by the majority of people in his day. His translation is known as the Vulgate, which comes from the Latin word for "common."

October 4 – Francis of Assisi Francis renounced wealth and future inheritance and devoted himself to serving the poor. Since Francis had a spirit of gratitude for all of God's creation, this commemoration has been a traditional time to bless pets and animals, creatures Francis called his brothers and sisters.

October 4 – Theodor Fliedner Fliedner's work was instrumental in the revival of the ministry of deaconesses among Lutherans. Fliedner's deaconess motherhouse in Kaiserswerth, Germany, inspired Lutherans all over the world to commission deaconesses to serve in parishes, schools, prisons, and hospitals.

October 6 – William Tyndale Tyndale's plan to translate the scriptures into English met opposition from Henry VIII. Though Tyndale completed work on the New Testament in 1525 and worked on a portion of the Old Testament, he was tried for heresy and burned at the stake.

October 7 – Henry Melchior Muhlenberg Muhlenberg was prominent in setting the course for Lutheranism in the United States by helping Lutheran churches make the transition from the state churches of Europe to independent churches of America. Among other things, he established the first Lutheran synod in America and developed an American Lutheran liturgy.

October 15 – Teresa of Ávila Teresa of Ávila (also known as Teresa de Jesús) chose the life of a Carmelite nun after reading the letters of Jerome. Teresa's writings on devotional life are widely read by members of various denominations.

October 17 – Ignatius Ignatius was the second bishop of Antioch in Syria. When his own martyrdom approached, he wrote in one of his letters, "I prefer death in Christ Jesus to power over the farthest limits of the earth. . . . Do not stand in the way of my birth to real life."

October 18 – Luke Luke, as author of both Luke and Acts, was careful to place the events of Jesus' life in both their social and religious contexts. Some of the most loved parables and canticles are found only in this Gospel.

October 23 – James of Jerusalem James is described in the New Testament as the brother of Jesus, and the secular historian Josephus called James the brother of Jesus, "the so-called Christ." Little is known about James, but Josephus reported that the Pharisees respected James for his piety and observance of the law.

October 26 – Philipp Nicolai, Johann Heermann, Paul Gerhardt These three outstanding hymnwriters all worked in Germany in the seventeenth century during times of war and plague. Philipp Nicolai's hymns "Wake, Awake, for Night Is Flying" and "O Morning Star, How Fair and Bright!" were included in a series of meditations he wrote to comfort his parishioners during the plague. The style of Johann Heermann's hymns (including "Ah, Holy Jesus") moved away from the more objective style of Reformation hymnody toward expressing the emotions of faith. Paul Gerhardt, whom some have called the greatest of Lutheran hymnwriters, lost a preaching position at St. Nicholas's Church in Berlin because he refused to sign a document stating he would not make theological arguments in his sermons.

October 28 – Simon, Jude Little is known about Simon and Jude. In New Testament lists of the apostles, Simon the "zealot" or Cananaean is mentioned, but he is never mentioned apart from these lists. Jude, sometimes called Thaddeus, is also mentioned in lists of the Twelve.

October 31 – Reformation Day By the end of the seventeenth century, many Lutheran churches celebrated a festival commemorating Martin Luther's posting of the Ninety-Five Theses, a summary of abuses in the church of his time. At the heart of the reform movement was the gospel, the good news that it is by grace through faith that we are justified and set free.

November 1 – All Saints Day The custom of commemorating all of the saints of the church on a single day goes back at least to the third century. All Saints Day celebrates the baptized people of God, living and dead, who make up the body of Christ.

November 3 – Martín de Porres Martín was a lay brother in the Order of Preachers (Dominicans) and engaged in many charitable works. He is recognized as an advocate for Christian charity and interracial justice.

November 7 – John Christian Frederick Heyer, Bartholomaeus Ziegenbalg, Ludwig Nommensen Heyer was the first missionary sent out by American Lutherans, and he became a missionary in the Andhra region of India. Ziegenbalg was a missionary to the Tamils of Tranquebar on the southeast coast of India. Nommensen worked among the Batak people, who had previously not seen Christian missionaries.

November 11 – Martin of Tours In 371 Martin was elected bishop of Tours. As bishop he developed a reputation for intervening on behalf of prisoners and heretics who had been sentenced to death.

November 11 – Søren Aabye Kierkegaard Kierkegaard, a nineteenth-century Danish theologian whose writings reflect his Lutheran heritage, was the founder of modern existentialism. Kierkegaard's work attacked the established church of his day—its complacency, its tendency to intellectualize faith, and its desire to be accepted by polite society.

November 17 – Elizabeth of Hungary This Hungarian princess gave away large sums of money, including her dowry, for relief of the poor and sick. She founded hospitals, cared for

392 orphans, and used the royal food supplies to feed the hungry.

November 23 – Clement Clement is best remembered for a letter he wrote to the Corinthian congregation still having difficulty with divisions in spite of Paul's canonical letters. Clement's letter is also a witness to early understandings of church government and the way each office in the church works for the good of the whole.

November 23 – Miguel Agustín Pro Miguel Agustín Pro grew up among oppression in Mexico and worked on behalf of the poor and homeless. Miguel and his two brothers were arrested, falsely accused of throwing a bomb at the car of a government official, and executed by a firing squad.

November 24 – Justus Falckner, Jehu Jones, William Passavant Not only was Falckner the first Lutheran pastor to be ordained in North America, but he published a catechism that was the first Lutheran book published on the continent. Jones was the Lutheran Church's first African American pastor and carried out missionary work in Philadelphia, which led to the formation there of the first African American Lutheran congregation (St. Paul's). William Passavant helped to establish hospitals and orphanages in a number of cities and was the first to introduce deaconesses to the work of hospitals in the United States.

November 25 – Isaac Watts Watts wrote about six hundred hymns, many of them in a two-year period beginning when he was twenty years old. When criticized for writing hymns not taken from scripture, he responded that if we can pray prayers that are not from scripture but written by us, then surely we can sing hymns that we have made up ourselves.

November 30 – Andrew Andrew was the first of the Twelve. As a part of his calling, he brought other people, including Simon Peter, to meet Jesus.

December 3 – Francis Xavier Francis Xavier became a missionary to India, Southeast Asia, Japan, and the Philippines. Together with Ignatius Loyola and five others, Francis formed the Society of Jesus (Jesuits).

December 4 – John of Damascus John left a career in finance and government to become a monk in an abbey near Jerusalem. He wrote many hymns as well as theological works, including *The Fount of Wisdom*, a work that touches on philosophy, heresy, and the orthodox faith.

December 6 – Nicholas Nicholas was a bishop in what is now Turkey. Legends that surround Nicholas tell of his love for God and neighbor, especially the poor.

December 7 – Ambrose Ambrose was baptized, ordained, and consecrated a bishop all on the same day. While bishop he gave away his wealth and lived in simplicity.

December 13 – Lucy Lucy was a young Christian of Sicily who was martyred during the persecutions under Emperor Diocletian. Her celebration became particularly important in Sweden and Norway, perhaps because the feast of Lucia (whose name means "light") originally fell on the shortest day of the year.

December 14 – John of the Cross John was a monk of the Carmelite religious order who met Teresa of Ávila when she was working to reform the Carmelite Order and return it to a stricter observance of its rules. His writings, like Teresa's, reflect a deep interest in mystical thought and meditation.

December 20 – Katharina von Bora Luther Katharina took vows as a nun, but around age twenty-four she and several other nuns who were influenced by the writings of Martin Luther left the convent. When she later became Luther's wife, she proved herself a gifted household manager and became a trusted partner.

December 26 – Stephen Stephen, a deacon and the first martyr of the church, was one of those seven upon whom the apostles laid hands after they had been chosen to serve widows and others in need. Later, Stephen's preaching angered the temple authorities, and they ordered him to be put to death by stoning.

December 27 – John John, the son of Zebedee, was a fisherman and one of the Twelve. Tradition has attributed authorship of the Gospel and the three epistles bearing his name to the apostle John.

December 28 – The Holy Innocents The infant martyrs commemorated on this day were the children of Bethlehem, two years old and younger, who were killed by Herod, who worried that his reign was threatened by the birth of a new king named Jesus.

Anniversary of Baptism (abbreviated)

This order is intended for use in the home. It may be adapted for use in another context, such as a Christian education setting. When used in the home, a parent or sponsor may be the leader. A more expanded version of this order appears in Evangelical Lutheran Worship Pastoral Care (pp. 128–135).

A bowl of water may be placed in the midst of those who are present.

GATHERING

A baptismal hymn or acclamation (see Evangelical Lutheran Worship #209–217, 442–459) may be sung.

The sign of the cross may be made by all in remembrance of their baptism as the leader begins.

In the name of the Father, and of the + Son, and of the Holy Spirit.
Amen.

The candle received at baptism or another candle may be used. As it is lighted, the leader may say:

Jesus said, I am the light of the world.
Whoever follows me will have the light of life.

READING

One or more scripture readings follow. Those present may share in reading.

A reading from Mark: People were bringing little children to Jesus in order that he might touch them; and the disciples spoke sternly to them. But when Jesus saw this, he was indignant and said, "Let the little children come to me; do not stop them; for it is to such as these that the kingdom of God belongs." And he took them up in his arms, laid his hands on them, and blessed them. *(Mark 10:13-14, 16)*

A reading from Second Corinthians: If anyone is in Christ, there is a new creation: everything old has passed away; see, everything has become new! *(2 Corinthians 5:17)*

A reading from First John: Beloved, let us love one another, because love is from God; everyone who loves is born of God and knows God. *(1 John 4:7)*

Those present may share experiences related to baptism and their lives as baptized children of God. A portion of the Small Catechism (Evangelical Lutheran Worship, pp. 1160–1167) may be read as part of this conversation.

A baptismal hymn or acclamation may be sung.

BAPTISMAL REMEMBRANCE

A parent or sponsor may trace a cross on the forehead of the person celebrating a baptismal anniversary. Water from a bowl placed in the midst of those present may be used. These or similar words may be said.

Name, when you were baptized, you were marked with the cross of Christ forever.
Remember your baptism with thanksgiving and joy.

PRAYERS

Prayers may include the following or other appropriate prayers. Others who are present may place a hand on the head or shoulder of the one who is celebrating the anniversary.

Let us pray.
Gracious God, we thank you for the new life you give us through holy baptism. Especially, we ask you to bless *name* on the anniversary of *her/his* baptism. Continue to strengthen *name* with the Holy Spirit, and increase in *her/him* your gifts of grace: the spirit of wisdom and understanding, the spirit of counsel and might, the spirit of knowledge and the fear of the Lord, the spirit of joy in your presence; through Jesus Christ, our Savior and Lord.
Amen.

The prayers may conclude with the Lord's Prayer.

Our Father in heaven,
hallowed be your name, your kingdom come,
your will be done, on earth as in heaven.
Give us today our daily bread.
Forgive us our sins
as we forgive those who sin against us.
Save us from the time of trial and deliver us from evil.
For the kingdom, the power, and the glory are yours,
now and forever. Amen.

BLESSING
The order may conclude with this or another suitable blessing.

Almighty God, who gives us a new birth by water and the Holy Spirit and forgives us all our sins, strengthen us in all goodness and by the power of the Holy Spirit keep us in eternal life through Jesus Christ our Lord.
Amen.

The greeting of peace may be shared by all.

Other suggested readings for this service:
John 3:1-8: *Born again from above*
Romans 6:3-11: *Raised with Christ in baptism*
Galatians 3:26-28: *All are one in Christ*
Ephesians 4:1-6: *There is one body and one Spirit*
Colossians 1:11-13: *Claimed by Christ, heirs of light*
1 Peter 2:2-3: *Long for spiritual food*
1 Peter 2:9: *Chosen in baptism to tell about God*
Revelation 22:1-2: *The river of the water of life*

Prayers during Sickness and for Other Occasions

One who is sick or injured

O God of power and love, be present with *name*, that *her/his* weakness may
be overcome and *her/his* strength restored; and that, *her/his* health being
renewed, *she/he* may bless your holy name; through Jesus Christ, our Savior
and Lord.

This prayer may be recited by a child, repeating brief phrases after the caregiver.
Gentle Jesus, stay beside me through this day [night]. Take away my pain.
Keep me safe. Help me when I'm afraid. Make my body strong again and my
heart glad. Thank you for your love that surrounds me.

Before a medical procedure or surgery

Almighty God, our heavenly Father, graciously protect *name* in *her/his*
surgery. Fill *her/his* heart with confidence that, though *she/he* may be
anxious, *she/he* may put *her/his* trust in you; through Jesus Christ our Lord.

After a medical procedure or surgery

Almighty and gracious God, we give you thanks that you have protected
name during surgery. Enable *her/him* to trust in your goodness, to find
comfort in your abiding presence, and to praise your holy name; through
Jesus Christ our Lord.

Difficult choices regarding treatment

Lord Jesus, in the night before your suffering and death, you struggled with
all you were about to encounter. Be with *name* [and *her/his* family] in this
anxious moment as they face difficult choices about medical treatment,
especially those that may involve suffering and pain. Through it all, Lord
Jesus, be a strong companion and guide along the way, for your love's sake.

Grieving loss

God of all grace, we give you thanks because by his death our Savior, Jesus Christ, destroyed the power of death and by his resurrection he opened the kingdom of heaven to all believers. Make us certain that because he lives we shall live also, and that neither death nor life, nor things present nor things to come, will be able to separate us from your love in Christ Jesus our Lord, who lives and reigns with you and the Holy Spirit, one God, now and forever.

Mental illness

Mighty God, in Jesus Christ you deal with forces that trouble our minds and set us against ourselves. Give peace to those who are cast down, beset by anxiety, or torn by inner conflict. By your great might, drive from us the powers that shake confidence and shatter love. Bring us into the light of your truth, and give us your strong assurance that we are your beloved children in Jesus Christ our Lord.

Addiction, recovery

O Lord, mercifully regard your servant *name*, who is bound with the chains of addiction. Give *her/him* strength, that *she/he* may be freed from fear and guilt and be restored in you to the liberty of the children of God, now and forever.

Caregivers and others who support the sick

God, our refuge and strength, our present help in time of trouble, care for those who tend the needs of *name*. Strengthen them in body and spirit. Refresh them when weary; console them when anxious; comfort them in grief; and hearten them in discouragement. Be with us all, and give us peace at all times and in every way; through Christ our peace.

Restoration of health

O Lord, your compassions never fail and your mercies are new every morning. We give you thanks for giving our *sister/brother [name]* both relief from pain and hope of health renewed. Continue in *her/him* the good work you have begun; that *she/he*, daily increasing in bodily strength and rejoicing in your goodness, may so order *her/his* life and conduct that *she/he* may always think and do those things that please you; through Jesus Christ our Lord.

From *Evangelical Lutheran Worship Pastoral Care*, pp. 169–197

Waking Prayers

We give thanks to you, heavenly Father,
through Jesus Christ your dear Son,
that you have protected us through the night
from all harm and danger.
We ask that you would also protect us today
from sin and all evil,
so that our life and actions may please you.
Into your hands we commend ourselves:
our bodies, our souls, and all that is ours.
Let your holy angels be with us,
so that the wicked foe may have no power over us.
Amen.

Luther's morning prayer

Jesus, bright morning star,
show us your mercy.
(*See Revelation 22:16*)

Upon waking, one may make the sign of the cross and say:
In the name of the Father,
and of the Son,
and of the Holy Spirit. Amen.

or

The Sacred Three be over me,
the blessing of the Trinity.

A Simplified Form for Morning Prayer

OPENING

O Lord, open my lips,
and my mouth shall proclaim your praise.
Glory to the Father, and to the Son,
and to the Holy Spirit:
as it was in the beginning, is now,
and will be forever. Amen.

The alleluia is omitted during Lent.
[Alleluia.]

PSALMODY

The psalmody may begin with Psalm 63, Psalm 67, Psalm 95, Psalm 100, or another psalm appropriate for morning. Psalms provided in this book for each week may be used instead of or in addition to the psalms mentioned.

A time of silence follows.

A hymn may follow (see the suggested hymn for each day).

READINGS

One or more readings for each day may be selected from those provided in this book. The reading of scripture may be followed by silence for reflection.

The reflection may conclude with these or similar words.
Long ago God spoke to our ancestors
in many and various ways by the prophets,
but in these last days God has spoken to us by the Son.

GOSPEL CANTICLE

The song of Zechariah may be sung or said.

Blessed are you, Lord, the God of Israel,
you have come to your people and set them free.
You have raised up for us a mighty Savior,
born of the house of your servant David.
Through your holy prophets, you promised of old
to save us from our enemies,
from the hands of all who hate us,
to show mercy to our forebears,
and to remember your holy covenant.
This was the oath you swore to our father Abraham:
to set us free from the hands of our enemies,
free to worship you without fear,
holy and righteous before you, all the days of our life.
And you, child, shall be called the prophet of the Most High,
for you will go before the Lord to prepare the way,
to give God's people knowledge of salvation
by the forgiveness of their sins.
In the tender compassion of our God
the dawn from on high shall break upon us,
to shine on those who dwell in darkness and the shadow of death,
and to guide our feet into the way of peace.

PRAYERS

Various intercessions may be spoken at this time. The prayer provided in this book for each day may also be used.

The following prayer is especially appropriate for morning.
Almighty and everlasting God,
you have brought us in safety to this new day.
Preserve us with your mighty power,
that we may not fall into sin
nor be overcome in adversity.

In all we do, direct us to the fulfilling of your purpose;
through Jesus Christ our Lord.
Amen.

THE LORD'S PRAYER

Our Father in heaven,
  hallowed be your name,
  your kingdom come,
  your will be done, on earth as in heaven.
Give us today our daily bread.
Forgive us our sins
  as we forgive those who sin against us.
Save us from the time of trial
  and deliver us from evil.
For the kingdom, the power, and the glory are yours,
  now and forever. Amen.

BLESSING

Let us bless the Lord.
Thanks be to God.

Almighty God,
the Father, + the Son, and the Holy Spirit,
bless and preserve us.
Amen.

Additional materials for daily prayer are available in Evangelical Lutheran
Worship *(pp. 295–331) and may supplement this simple order.*

A Simplified Form for Evening Prayer

OPENING

Jesus Christ is the light of the world,
the light no darkness can overcome.
Stay with us, Lord, for it is evening,
and the day is almost over.
Let your light scatter the darkness
and illumine your church.

PSALMODY

*The psalmody may begin with Psalm 141, Psalm 121, or another psalm
appropriate for evening. Psalms provided in this book for each week may be
used instead of or in addition to the psalms mentioned.*

A time of silence follows.

A hymn may follow (see the suggested hymn for each day).

READINGS

*One or more readings for each day may be selected from those provided in this
book. The reading of scripture may be followed by silence for reflection.*

The reflection may conclude with these or similar words.
Jesus said, I am the light of the world.
Whoever follows me will never walk in darkness.

GOSPEL CANTICLE

My soul proclaims the greatness of the Lord,
my spirit rejoices in God my Savior,
for you, Lord, have looked with favor on your lowly servant.
From this day all generations will call me blessed:
you, the Almighty, have done great things for me,
and holy is your name.
You have mercy on those who fear you,
from generation to generation.
You have shown strength with your arm
and scattered the proud in their conceit,
casting down the mighty from their thrones
and lifting up the lowly.
You have filled the hungry with good things
and sent the rich away empty.
You have come to the aid of your servant Israel,
to remember the promise of mercy,
the promise made to our forebears,
to Abraham and his children forever.

PRAYERS

Various intercessions may be spoken at this time. The prayer provided in this book for each day may also be used.

The following prayer is especially appropriate for evening.

We give thanks to you, heavenly Father,
through Jesus Christ your dear Son,
that you have graciously protected us today.
We ask you to forgive us all our sins, where we have done wrong,
and graciously to protect us tonight.
For into your hands we commend ourselves:
our bodies, our souls, and all that is ours.

Let your holy angels be with us,
so that the wicked foe may have no power over us.
Amen.

THE LORD'S PRAYER

Our Father in heaven,
  hallowed be your name,
  your kingdom come,
  your will be done, on earth as in heaven.
Give us today our daily bread.
Forgive us our sins
  as we forgive those who sin against us.
Save us from the time of trial
  and deliver us from evil.
For the kingdom, the power, and the glory are yours,
  now and forever. Amen.

BLESSING

Let us bless the Lord.
Thanks be to God.

The peace of God,
which surpasses all understanding,
keep our hearts and our minds in Christ Jesus.
Amen.

Additional materials for daily prayer are available in Evangelical Lutheran
Worship *(pp. 295–331) and may supplement this simple order.*

At Bedtime

Gracious God, we give you thanks for the day, especially for the good we were permitted to give and to receive; the day is now past and we commit it to you. We entrust to you the night; we rest securely, for you are our help, and you neither slumber nor sleep; through Jesus Christ our Lord. Amen.

Night Prayers with Children

Now I lay me down to sleep,
I pray the Lord my soul to keep.
God's love stay with me through the night
and keep me safe till morning light.

Lord, keep us safe this night,
secure from all our fears.
May angels guard us while we sleep,
till morning light appears.

A parent or caregiver may trace the cross on the child's forehead or heart and say one of these blessings:
God the Father, Son, and Holy Spirit watch over you.

May God protect you through the night.

May the Lord Jesus keep you in his love.

Suggestions for Daily Reflection

God's word for me this day is:

God's word will shape my day by:

I will share God's word with others through:

My prayers today will include:

- The church universal, its ministry, and the mission of the gospel
- The well-being of creation
- Peace and justice in the world, the nations and those in authority, the community
- The poor, oppressed, sick, bereaved, lonely
- All who suffer in body, mind, or spirit
- Special concerns